ENDANGERED

WILDLIFE ON THE BRINK OF EXTINCTION

ENDANGERED

WILDLIFE ON THE BRINK OF EXTINCTION

GEORGE C. McGAVIN

FIREFLY BOOKS

A FIREFLY BOOK

Published by Firefly Books Ltd. 2006

First printing

Publisher Cataloging-in-Publication Data (U.S.)

McGavin, George.
    Endangered : wildlife on the brink of extinction / George McGavin.
[192] p. : col. photos. ; cm.
Includes index.
Summary: Details plant and animal species that are endangered or severely threatened and the opportunities humanity has to save them.

ISBN-13: 978-1-55407-183-8
ISBN-10: 1-55407-183-6
                    1. Endangered species. I.Title.
                    591.68 dc22
                    QL83.M34 2006

Library and Archives Canada Cataloguing in Publication

McGavin, George
Endangered : wildlife on the brink of extinction / George McGavin.
Includes index.
ISBN-13: 978-1-55407-183-8
ISBN-10: 1-55407-183-6
1. Endangered species. 2. Rare animals. 3. Rare plants. I. Title.
QH75.M383 2006   578.68   C2006-903371-4

Published in the United States by Firefly Books (U.S.) Inc.
P.O. Box 1338, Ellicott Station
Buffalo, New York 14205

Published in Canada by
Firefly Books Ltd.
66 Leek Crescent
Richmond Hill, Ontario L4B 1H1

Published in Great Britain by Cassell Illustrated, a division of Octopus Publishing Group Ltd.
2-4 Heron Quays
Canary Wharf, London E14 4JP

Printed in China

Contents

Introduction

There was a time, long ago, when the effect humans had on their environment was minimal and localized. The capacity of animals and plants to regenerate was more than adequate to make up for the harvesting and hunting. But the exponential growth of the human population has changed the equation to the extent that ecosystems may not be able to recover. But why should we care about biodiversity? Is it really that important?

PESTS AND PARASITES

"What use are wasps?" A friend of mine who was visiting the Oxford University Museum of Natural History once posed this question to me. "What sort of wasps do you mean?" I replied, for the common name "wasp" refers to any one of tens of thousands of living species. Wasps range in size from minute creatures called fairyflies with feathery wings spanning a mere quarter of a millimeter to giant spider-hunting wasps such as the tarantula hawk with a body length of around 3 inches (7 cm). The wasps in question were, as I suspected, common, or social, wasps in the family Vespidae that make papery nests in which to rear their young. Many species are known as yellow jackets from their characteristic coloring and some of the large species are called hornets. In all, there are about 4,000 described species of social wasp and they all do more or less the same thing: sterile worker wasps catch insect prey, butcher it, taking only the best parts back to their nest, where they chew it up and feed it to the developing larvae of the colony's reproductive queen. When those larvae reach adulthood they too become hunters and nest builders – to what purpose? To make more wasps, of course! I gave the standard explanation to my interrogator that wasps do a very useful job ridding our gardens and orchards of pests. Wasn't the occasional sting from workers at the end of their lives, competing with us for sweet drinks and other sugary foods, a small price to pay? My friend was not a keen gardener and I could see that he was unconvinced. However, I knew that he was a big cricket fan, so I changed tactics. Did he know that wasps, too, are supporters of the game of cricket? In 1934, the number of wasps in England declined drastically due to extreme weather conditions and a concerted effort by humans to exterminate the "pests." Owing to the shortage of wasps, crane flies (which are preyed upon by wasps) greatly increased in number. As a result, the number of crane-fly grubs, known as leather jackets, also greatly multiplied in the soil – including the hallowed turf of Lord's Cricket Ground. The leather jackets feed upon the the roots of grass and the turf was severely damaged. The 1935 cricket season was "considerably spoiled." My friend left the Museum a staunch supporter of the wasp's right to exist.

FOOD CHAINS

Nevertheless, our conversation made me wonder if our planet really needed all 4,000 wasp species to function properly. What would happen if we were to lose some? You

VANISHING WILDERNESS Gentoo and chinstrap penguins are two of several species of penguin that survive in the hostile Antarctic environment. Even here, in the wilderness of ice, they are at risk from human impact. It is thought that over 5,000 square miles (13,000 sq km) of sea ice in the Antarctic Peninsula has been lost over the last 50 years.

might argue that as all wasps control the numbers of other insects they are all worth keeping. So are there any insects that the world would be better off without? Mosquitoes perhaps? The blood-feeding females of many species carry a number of diseases such as yellow fever, filariasis, encephalitis and, the biggest killer of all, malaria, which is responsible for one human death every 12 seconds or so. But mosquitoes and their larvae are a fundamental part of the food chains that feed countless birds, fish and other species and their removal would have far-reaching effects.

WORLDWIDE WEB

The simple truth is that the web of life is incredibly complex and we can only speculate as to the consequences of the disappearance of any particular species. One species will become extinct and there will be no apparent effects on its habitat or on other species; another species becomes extinct and an entire ecosystem collapses like a house of cards. The disappearance of the passenger pigeon, which once flocked in such vast numbers that it "darkened the skies" over the United States, must surely have had wide-ranging consequences for natural predators, but since its wider ecology was not studied we may never know. It was considered to be a crop pest and was hunted into oblivion by 1914. More recently, the local extinction of the sea otter in California had disastrous effects on the sea-kelp-forest ecosystem in which it lives. Among other things, sea otters eat sea urchins. When the number of otters declines, the number of sea urchins increases and they destroy the kelp forests. The death of the kelp forest removes the habitat for numerous other species. The sea otter is therefore considered to be a "keystone" species, critical to the survival of the sea-kelp community.

NEED AND GREED

We have benefited enormously from using the products of nature and we harvest or farm countless species for food and medicines. But there are countless species we have not yet cataloged and some we have exploited for centuries as a food source that we are now discovering possess many other uses. In losing species, we will certainly impoverish the store of medicinal and other compounds that might serve us well in the future. For example, scientists are only just beginning to realize the enormous medical bounty offered by various species of shark in the treatment of ailments as diverse as acne, arthritis and cancer. But many sharks are currently being driven toward extinction, largely because of their exploitation for soup. Utilitarian arguments should appeal, but it seems that short-term gain invariably wins out over conservation.

LIVE AND LET LIVE

Many people believe that biodiversity should be preserved not just because it is valuable to us, but simply because it exists. Such people believe that each species should be respected because it is the product of millions of years of evolution. They argue that we should be "stewards of the Earth" for future generations. But such people are very much in the minority, and many people who genuinely lament the loss of diversity simply don't have the time to give it more than a passing thought or are unaware of what the threats to diversity really are. How many of us, for example, own teak garden furniture? Teak is a very durable hardwood and ideal for outdoor use. But where does it come from?

It comes from tropical forests.

If an item of furniture purchased today is teak, it is unlikely to have come from a sustainable source, and forest clearance in the tropics is one of the biggest single causes of species extinctions. There are alternative materials and we do have a choice, but many of us are not aware of the implications of our purchase and many more do not care. Crucially, the vast majority of people on Earth do not have the luxury to care. For most people, just feeding themselves and their families is a daily struggle.

Beyond the commercial value of the trees themselves there are other lucrative markets. Land is required to supply the demand for soybeans and other cash crops. For example, the current world demand for palm oil, which finds its way into almost one-tenth of all supermarket products, is driving the conversion of tropical forests to plantation and bringing about the extirpation of countless species. And all the time the human population is continuing to grow.

CHECKING GROWTH

Ultimately, it is human population growth and increasing consumption that drives every aspect of environmental degradation. The need for more and more agricultural and urban land leads to the loss of biological diversity and the overexploitation of natural resources. We have already been responsible for the untimely end of a great many species and it is certain that many more will follow them as we continue to increase in numbers. Modern humans appeared only a few hundred thousand years ago and have since risen to dominate the planet. In this short space of time our species

has spread and multiplied by being able to transform the environment to our own advantage. We have also begun to describe and understand our home, its genesis and that of the universe of which it forms a part. We understand the origin of species and their importance to our survival. We know that the balance of nature is delicate and can see the often disastrous consequences of our tampering, whether accidental or otherwise. The accidental introduction of the common wasp (friend to gardeners and cricket fans in England) into Australia and New Zealand, where the species has no natural predators, has caused untold damage to fruit harvests and native species.

Does it matter if we lose a single wasp species, or a parrot or a panda? Perhaps not. But along with innumerable other scientists – five of whom have joined me to produce this book – I am convinced that as many as 25 percent or even 50 percent of all species may be lost in the next 100 years if things continue as they are. Losses of this magnitude will be a disaster in itself with far-reaching and unpredictable effects and may have serious consequences for humanity.

When I was born there were less than three billion people alive. As I write these lines there are more than double that number and around 200,000 join the human race every day. The human race is capable of remarkable things, but it remains to be seen if we can control our numbers sufficiently to preserve the biological diversity that sustains us.

DISAPPEARING FOREST During the last two decades of the 20th century, it is estimated that more than 1 million square miles (3 million sq km) of tropical forests – an area larger than the size of India – has been cleared for plantations, agriculture, mining or urban development.

CHIEF CONSULTANT AND CONTRIBUTING AUTHORITIES

DAVID BURNIE

David Burnie studied zoology at university and is a Fellow of the Zoological Society of London. After graduating, he worked as a nature reserve ranger and biologist, before starting a career as a writer and consultant, specializing in wildlife, plants and the environment. He has written or contributed to over a hundred books and multimedia titles, including a major wildlife encyclopedia. Several of his books have won awards; one of his environmental titles was shortlisted for the Aventis Prize in 2005. He lives and works in France, and is particularly interested in European butterflies and orchids – two groups of organisms currently undergoing a steep decline.

"It's often said that you can't miss what you've never had. But in the near future, the species that are disappearing today will be sorely missed indeed. From deep-sea fish to amphibians and pollinating bees, thousands of different animals look set to vanish, leaving gaping holes in natural ecosystems. Concern about this isn't a sign of misplaced sentiment, or a naive desire to turn back the clock. Instead, it's a rational reaction to one of the biggest threats facing the human race."

ANDY GOSLER

A University Research Lecturer in the Oxford University Department of Zoology, Dr. Andrew G. Gosler lectures in evolution, ecology and conservation biology. Based in the Edward Grey Institute of Field Ornithology, he has a lifelong passion for birds and conservation that has taken him to five continents. He has published more than 50 scientific papers and has written and edited many books. His consultancy work for the BBC has included *The Natural World: The World in a Wood*, the David Attenborough film *Song of the Earth* and *Springwatch*. He is a former Editor of *Ibis*, the scientific journal of the British Ornithologists' Union, and was admitted as a Fellow of the Linnean Society in 1998. He was awarded the Bernard Tucker Medal of the BTO in 1999.

MARK O'SHEA

Mark is Consultant Curator of Reptiles at West Midland Safari Park in Worcestershire, England. He has conducted fieldwork in more than 30 countries on six continents. His work with reptiles involves television, radio, lecturing, photography, writing and consultancies. Mark has appeared on many talk shows and children's programs and presented four series of adventure natural history documentaries, *O'Shea's Big Adventure*. He is a Fellow of the Explorers Club of New York, the Royal Geographical Society and the Zoological Society of London and an affiliate of the National Museum of Papua New Guinea. He received one of eight Millenium Awards from the Explorers' Club of New York in 2000 and an honorary Doctor of Sciences degree from the University of Wolverhampton in 2001. He lives in Shropshire, England.

STEVE PARKER

An author, editor and consultant, Steve Parker holds a First Class Honours BSc in zoology and is a Scientific Fellow of the Zoological Society of London. He has written or contributed to more than 200 books. He writes on a range of subjects including natural history, biology and general sciences. Before becoming a full-time author, Steve worked as an exhibition scientist at London's Natural History Museum. He also visits schools and libraries to give talks and workshops about educational aspects of nature and how we can learn to understand, respect and protect wildlife. Recently, Steve has taken up scuba diving to appreciate the fantastic watery world of shores and reefs.

KIM DENNIS-BRYAN

Kim Dennis-Bryan studied life sciences at university and went on to do research at the Natural History Museum in London, where she obtained a PhD in paleontology. Her specialist field is Devonian fossil fish, but she has long been interested in animal conservation and domestication. As well as continuing with her research work, Kim now works as a freelance writer and consultant of natural history and earth science books. She is an Associate Lecturer for the Open University in London, where she lectures on evolution, mammals and introductory science. She also teaches domestic animal anatomy and behavior for an MSc course in animal manipulation. She has been a Scientific Fellow of the Zoological Society for many years and is a Life Member of the Rare Breeds Survival Trust.

"...extinction and natural selection go hand in hand."
– Charles Darwin, *The Origin of Species*, 1859

"Life is a copiously branching bush, continually pruned by the grim reaper of extinction, not a ladder of predictable progress."
– Stephen Jay Gould, *Wonderful Life*, 1989

THE NATURE OF EXTINCTION

The fossil record is like a time machine that allows us to look at life in the distant past. It shows what individual species looked like, what lived alongside them, and when they first evolved. It also reveals the decline of species as they struggle for survival, until they finally die out and become extinct. Today, extinction is a scientifically established fact, but as little as 300 years ago, the very idea was unthinkable. At that time, it was almost universally accepted that each species was separately and divinely created, and that each one was a permanent part of life on Earth. But in the 18th century – with the help of fossils and other evidence –

naturalists such as Linnaeus, Lamarck and Darwin began to uncover the truth about evolution and extinction. It was Charles Darwin who finally convinced the scientific establishment that species evolve through a process he called natural selection. Darwin was convinced that evolution and extinction worked slowly but steadily – an idea that fossil sequences bear out well. But the fossil record also shows another and much darker side to this process. At rare intervals, Earth's biodiversity is decimated during mass extinctions. After each of these catastrophic events, life can take millions of years to fully recover.

The Quick and the Dead

To many people "extinction" is an entirely negative word. But extinction is a natural process, and it has been occurring ever since life began. Paradoxically, it has helped to create the rich diversity of species alive today. Charles Darwin was the first person to explain how the evolution and extinction of species are inextricably linked.

IN THE BEGINNING

For thousands of years humans have wondered about their origins and that of other organisms. Around the world, creation stories, typically based around supernatural beings, have developed as a way of explaining the rich variety of life on Earth. Not surprisingly, these stories reflect different environments and cultures, but they share a central theme: living things are "designed" for particular habitats and ways of life, and because of this, there is no need for them to change.

ENLIGHTENMENT

It was not until the 18th century, during a time now known as the Enlightenment, that people began to realize that species might change over time. Fossil records provided some of the most important evidence – particularly when they showed the gradual development of key features such as jaws and limbs. By the mid-19th century the theory of evolution, now the central concept of modern biology, was finally formulated.

The theory of evolution is actually two separate proposals that are closely linked. The first is that species can and do change – an idea put forward by the eminent French naturalist Jean-Baptiste Chevalier de Lamarck (1744–1829) in his *Philosophie Zoologique* of 1809. The mechanism that Lamarck suggested

COMPETING THEORIES Lamarck argued that if an animal constantly used a part of its anatomy this would lead to a change in its structure. He proposed, for example, that giraffes developed their long necks by stretching to reach higher foliage. Darwin argued that the giraffe's extraordinary neck was the result of natural selection.

SURVIVORS For emperor penguins, the struggle for survival is particularly intense. They breed in some of the coldest conditions on Earth, huddling together for protection during Antarctica's ferocious winter storms.

During his celebrated voyage as naturalist on the HMS *Beagle*, Darwin gathered the evidence that he would later use to support his theory of evolution. In his seminal work, *The Origin of Species,* he states, "The theory of natural selection is grounded in the belief that each new variety, and ultimately each new species, is produced and maintained by having some advantage over those with which it comes into competition; and the consequent extinction of less favoured forms inevitably follows."

was incorrect, but his work was a milestone of its time. It was also highly controversial because, in the early 1800s, most Europeans still believed in the literal truth of biblical creation.

The second proposal concerns the driving force that makes change take place. Known as natural selection, it was discovered independently by two British naturalists, Charles Darwin (1809–82) and Alfred Russel Wallace (1823–1913). Both men had read *An Essay on the Principle of Population*, which was written in 1798 by the economist Thomas Malthus (1766–1834). Although Malthus was concerned primarily with the human population, Darwin and Wallace realized its implications for the world of nature as a whole.

SURVIVAL OF THE FITTEST
In his essay, Malthus argued that all species can reproduce fast enough to outstrip the resources they need. As their numbers increase, resources are used up, creating a competition between individuals for survival.

NATURAL SELECTION Giraffe weevils show how environmental pressures can "select," or favor, certain features; very different species, such as this beetle and the giraffe itself, may evolve similar characteristics.

Darwin and Wallace could see this happening in the natural world, and they reasoned that if the Earth was continually changing, then species much change, too. This change comes about because individuals vary, and because inherited adaptations are passed on when parents reproduce. Useful adaptations help individuals to breed successfully, so these are the ones that are more likely to become widespread. Unsuccessful variations are "weeded out" by natural selection, in the daily struggle for survival. As a result, the balance of variation gradually shifts, making each species change.

Darwin and Wallace reasoned that biological diversity results from natural selection acting over immense periods of time. Those species that cannot survive in the face of change eventually die out – in other words, they become extinct.

END TO END
Evolution and extinction are two sides of the same coin, and both processes have been at work on Earth since life began, over 3.8 billion years ago. The ancient archaebacteria – microscopic organisms that were among the very earliest life forms to evolve – gave way to cyanobacteria about 2.5 billion years ago. Unlike their predecessors, cyanobacteria released oxygen into the air. This oxygen paved the way for animal life, because animals use oxygen to release the energy that they need. Much more recently, the world was dominated by the dinosaurs – the largest creatures ever to have walked the Earth. When they became extinct,

mammals evolved and diversified in their place. With mammals came the first self-aware life form – humankind. So in a very real sense, we exist only because so many earlier species have been swept away by extinction.

SEEING IS BELIEVING
In 1859, when Charles Darwin first published *The Origin of Species*, he presented a great mass of evidence to support the fact of evolution. Since then, further evidence has come from countless branches of science, from geology and paleontology to virology and genetics. But, as in Darwin's time, the fossil evidence remains the most striking proof of change – a record, written in stone, that is there for all of us to see.

Written in Stone

The study of geology in the 18th and 19th centuries revealed a clear sequence of fossil types in successively younger rock strata. This fossil record proved that the age of the Earth was far greater than people had thought. It also proved that seas once covered vast areas that are now deserts, and that evolution and extinction are the twin forces that "create" diversity.

DECODING THE EVIDENCE This fossil, discovered in Germany, was clearly not the remains of any creature alive today. In fact, it is a pterosaur from the Jurassic Period (over 140 million years ago). Such discoveries provided scientists with incontrovertible evidence for extinction.

LAYERS OF LIFE

The word "fossil" (Latin *fossilis*: "dug up") is generally used to refer to the preserved remains of life forms greater than 10,000 years old. Typically, they are much older and are preserved in sedimentary rocks formed from the buildup of sand, silt or mud. People have found fossils for thousands of years and many outlandish theories were formed to explain how the organisms became entombed in rock.

In the 17th century, one of the people who recognized the true origin of fossils was the pioneering Danish geologist Niels Stensen (1638–86), although, in keeping with prevailing thought, he believed that the creatures had been buried during biblical floods. Stensen is especially renowned for his contribution to stratigraphy – the study of rock strata. He stated that sediments are originally laid down horizontally and that, in an undisturbed sequence of sedimentary rock, the oldest strata are found at the bottom and the youngest at the top. These simple ideas are the basis for the relative dating of fossils today. Other geologists noted that rocks with the same composition of fossils must be the same age. Relative techniques like this allowed the construction of a rough chronology, which has now been dated accurately with the use of absolute methods such as radiometric dating. Records reveal that the Earth is 4.6 billion years old.

THE FOSSIL RECORD

Sadly, the fossil record is very patchy because the chances of any particular . creature becoming fossilized are very low and the vast majority of organisms will die and decay or be eaten by scavengers. It is thought that as few as 2 percent of all species that have ever

FROZEN IN TIME Fossilized fish from the Eocene Period (50 million years old) were discovered in Wyoming. Fossil records provide evidence of dramatic climate change – deserts now exist in areas that were once seas.

lived are present as fossils. But despite the gaps, there is enough evidence to see the broad sweep of evolutionary history.

Early studies of fossils showed that some organisms disappeared completely, leaving no descendents, again calling biblical stories of creation into question and showing that life was not fixed. In the late 18th century, the French zoologist George Cuvier (1769–1832) demonstrated that mammoth bones are different from those of the modern elephant – the inescapable conclusion being that mammoth species no longer existed. Since then, of course, fossils have been identified that cannot possibly be confused with any living creature. Perhaps the most spectacular fossil finds are those of the gigantic dinosaurs, but more exciting still, from a biologist's point of view, is the fossil evidence from the Cambrian Explosion, half a billion years ago, when all modern phyla (major groups of living things) arose in a relatively brief period of time. As well as the 30 or so animal phyla that form the modern biological world, there is fossil evidence of more than 50 other phyla that are "like something out of science fiction."

GRAND CANYON One of the natural wonders of the world, the Grand Canyon in Arizona was cut by vertical river erosion through the multicolored strata. The layers of rock defining geological eras are clearly visible.

Fossil evidence points to the evolution of millions of species during the 500 million years since the Cambrian era, and charts many major innovations. For example, the key difference between the creatures that existed before the Cambrian Explosion and those that follow is the appearance of skeletons, shells and other innovations that resulted from the need for protection from predators. Species had developed the ability to incorporate minerals in their bodies – an innovation known as biomineralization. Other major adaptations, such as flight, are also traceable in the fossil record.

So the next big questions are, when and how do species become extinct? Surprisingly, the study of extinction has been neglected by biologists until very recently. Today, with the spiraling incidences of extinctions happening around us, it is the subject of serious and increasingly urgent scientific study. We cannot help but witness in the world around us that the routes to oblivion are many and diverse.

VIRTUAL FOSSILS

A new technique where the rock containing a fossil is ground down a few microns at a time has revealed the three-dimensional shape of some very delicate fossils. As each section is ground off, a high-quality digital image is taken. When the grinding is finished a computer reassembles the separate pictures to allow the complete image of the fossil to be rotated and viewed from any angle. The photograph below shows the virtual fossil of a 425-million-year-old sea spider found in Silurian rocks in Herefordshire, England. The disadvantage of this remarkable new technique is that the original specimen is lost forever.

Routes to Oblivion

The fossil record provided the evidence to support Darwin's theory, but the cycle of evolution and extinction is not always the gradual process he supposed. Extinctions occur at very different rates. They can also occur on a variety of scales – local, regional and global – and the extent of a species' range has a significant effect on its chances of survival.

TYPES OF EXTINCTION

A species may extend over a large area of habitat that is suitable for its survival. Sometimes a species dies out locally, often at the edges of its range, where conditions for it may not be optimal. The extinction of the large copper butterfly in the United Kingdom is one such example. This species, which occurs all over Europe and temperate parts of Asia, favors the margins of marshland, where its caterpillars feed on water dock leaves. Before the mid-19th century, this species was common in the fenlands and marshes of eastern England, but drainage of the land for agricultural use decimated its numbers. As the species increased in rarity, its value among collectors increased and large numbers were caught to be sold.

This striking butterfly, which only attracted the attention of English entomologists in 1795, barely lasted another 50 years.

Of course, when a species becomes extinct locally, it is one step on the way to becoming extinct regionally, and if its range is confined to just a few regions then the threat of global extinction increases accordingly.

A species is said to be globally extinct when no surviving individuals of that species remain anywhere in the world. When species occur over a very small range, for example when they are endemic to an island, local and global extinction amounts to the same thing. Having a broader range increases a species' chances of survival but does not guarantee it. The tiger's range, for example, extends across much of Asia, yet three of the eight subspecies are now extinct, and the remaining five are endangered. The Javan tiger, unique to the Indonesian island, was hunted to extinction by 1972. The Caspian tiger, which had a much broader range – extending across Afghanistan, Iran, Mongolia and Russia – became extinct in the 1950s. Once again, hunting was the major factor, but habitat destruction also played its part.

A REPRIEVE?

Of course it is impossible to prove a negative, and the fact that there have been no sightings or traces of a species does not verify conclusively that it is extinct. However, it would be very surprising indeed if a mammoth or moa were discovered alive – the larger a species is and the longer ago it lived, the more likely it is to be truly extinct.

LIVING FOSSIL The coelacanth, often called a "living fossil" or "missing link," was one of the greatest zoological finds of the 20th century. It provides a direct link to ancient ocean fish alive in the time of the dinosaurs.

LOCAL EXTINCTION The continental subspecies of the large copper butterfly has been introduced into Britain to suitably restored habitats. These efforts have not always been successful and, in any case, whatever was unique to the British subspecies has gone forever.

The coelacanth is a member of a group called lobe-fin fishes, which date back to the Devonian Period, over 350 million years ago. The most recent coelacanth fossils date from around 65 million years ago, after which there is no record. So it was a remarkable discovery when a live coelacanth was caught off the coast of South Africa in 1938. It survives in deep parts of the Indian Ocean, especially around the Comoro Islands, where it has been sheltered from environmental changes for millennia.

PSEUDOEXTINCTION
Sometimes when geologists examine the fossil record it appears as if a species has gone extinct but, in reality, it has simply evolved to the extent that its descendants are recognized as being a different species. This process is known as pseudoextinction. For example, it is sometimes claimed that the dinohippus

BACK FROM THE DEAD Przewalski's horse was discovered in Mongolia in 1879 and was soon hunted to extinction in the wild. However, it was bred in captivity and has now been released back into its former home.

(a horse-like species that thrived in North America about 12 million years ago) is pseudoextinct, rather than extinct, and that it simply evolved into the horses – including zebras and wild asses – that we are familiar with today. Pseudoextinction can be applied to groups as well as individual species.

By far the most famous of all the pseudoextinctions is that of certain theropods, a group of small bipedal dinosaurs that included the velociraptor. They were once thought to have become extinct, but it seems increasingly likely that they evolved into modern-day birds.

EXTINCTION RATES
Until relatively recently, it was thought that evolution took place at a slow and steady rate, and that close examination of successive fossil strata would reveal a gradual, progressive change with organisms clearly transforming from one form to another. Likewise, it was thought that the extinction rate would be correspondingly slow and steady. Darwin himself steadfastly refused to accept the views of "catastrophists" who argued that extinct species were wiped out in cataclysms of biblical proportions.

The rate at which organisms have been disappearing from the fossil record over geological time – known as the background extinction rate – is, indeed, relatively low and constant. Background extinctions have been variously estimated at between 0.1 and 1 species per million years. This rather low rate, however, has indeed been punctuated by periodic crises where the extinction rate soars dramatically over a short period of time. These global catastrophes – mass-extinction events – have had far-reaching effects on the planet's ecosystems.

THE LIVING DEAD The kakapo is probably the world's only flightless parrot, and it is critically endangered. It is one of many species that scientists pessimistically term "the living dead."

Mass-extinction Events

Stand on a hilltop and look around you at the countryside below. What do you see? Fields, rivers, buildings and tracks? The chances are that the view has not changed much, in your memory at least, and it may well look the same for years to come. It is easy to think of the Earth as a fairly stable and relatively benign place, but nothing could be further from the truth.

PLATE TECTONICS

Immense forces beneath our feet are constantly rearranging the Earth's surface. Nearly half of the radius of the planet is made up of a very dense core at temperatures of up to 11,000°F (6,000°C). Surrounding the core and making up most of the rest of the planet's mass is the mantle – a layer of dense, partly molten rock. The solid outer crust on which all life has evolved, and on which we depend, is like the slowly solidifying skin floating on a bowl of hot custard and as thin as a postage stamp stuck to a football. It is made up of the continental crust, which is about 25 miles (40 km) thick, and the oceanic crust some 4½ miles (6 km) thick. The crust is made up of 10 large fragments, or plates, which move slowly about on the surface of the mantle, propelled by convection currents below. Where two plates collide, mountain ranges may be formed, with dramatic consequences for the

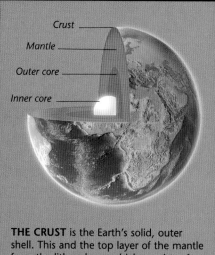

THE CRUST is the Earth's solid, outer shell. This and the top layer of the mantle form the lithosphere, which consists of semirigid plates that move.

Earth's climate. Earthquakes and volcanoes usually occur when one plate slides beneath the other – as in the San Andreas fault in California – to be remelted in the Earth's molten interior.

ACTIVE VOLCANO There are thought to be over 3,000 active or potentially active volcanoes concentrated around the plate margins. On average, 50 volcanoes erupt each year. The most recent major eruption of the Arenal Volcano in Costa Rica (shown here) was in 1968, when 78 people were killed. Some volcanoes are far more devastating – 36,000 people lost their lives following the eruption at Krakatoa in 1883.

As one area of crust disappears, a new crust is formed by a process called seafloor spreading. In certain places on the ocean floor, notably the mid-Atlantic, molten rock wells up from the mantle below, creating new crust, which then slowly spreads and pushes the plates on either side apart. Seafloor spreading happens at the rate of between 1 inch (2.5 cm) and 6 inches (15 cm) per year – about the same speed at which human fingernails grow. The Earth's plates move continuously and it is estimated that in about 50 million years Africa will have collided with Europe and the Mediterranean Sea will be a mountain range.

CATASTROPHIC EXTINCTION

The enormous forces that have shaped the Earth for millions of years have had a huge impact on the life that has evolved here. If we look at the past history of the Earth we see that, most of the time, the rate of extinction (or the loss of species) is at least matched by the rate of speciation (the appearance of new species). Overall, diversity is seen to increase, but, every so often, there have been huge dips in the record of biodiversity where very large numbers of species, or even whole groups of species, have become extinct in a relatively short time. These mass extinctions are caused by massive volcanism, with eruptions of vast quantities of magma lowering levels of sunlight and oxygen and increasing atmospheric carbon-dioxide levels; earthquake "storms" that cause massive devastation by themselves and trigger tsunamis and volcanic eruptions; glaciation and desertification causing falling and rising sea levels; and the impact of giant asteroids resulting in tsunamis, fire storms and unimaginable climatic upheaval. We now know of several mass-extinction events that were very large indeed, characterized by the loss of half the species present at that time. These are known to palaeontologists as the Big Five.

A MATTER OF TIME: LIFE IN ONE YEAR

It is difficult to comprehend the changes that have taken place on Earth and the huge timescale involved. Our species arose a mere 100,000 years or so ago, and our earliest records, such as cave paintings, date from only about 35,000–45,000 years ago. The most long-lived humans might reach an age of 100 years or so. The timeframe of the Earth and the physical phenomena that shape it are very different indeed. If you imagine that the whole of the Earth's 4.6-billion-year history is represented by a single year, you will see that the first signs of life appear in March, dinosaurs arrive in mid-December and are extinct 12 days later, while *Homo sapiens* join the party just before midnight on New Year's Eve.

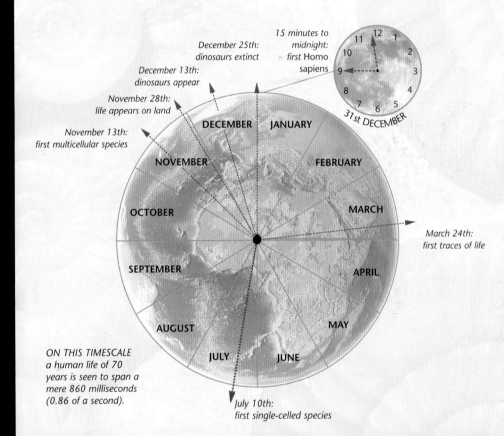

December 25th:
dinosaurs extinct

15 minutes to
midnight:
first Homo
sapiens

December 13th:
dinosaurs appear

November 28th:
life appears on land

November 13th:
first multicellular species

31st DECEMBER

March 24th:
first traces of life

ON THIS TIMESCALE
a human life of 70
years is seen to span a
mere 860 milliseconds
(0.86 of a second).

July 10th:
first single-celled species

LATE DEVELOPERS Mammals did not appear in the picture until very late in the day – mid-December in the time scheme above. The earliest mammals may have looked like this elephant shrew. The extinction of the dinosaurs 65 million years ago paved the way for the rise and radiation of mammals into the rich diversity that is seen today.

The Big Five

The Paleozoic Era began 542 million years ago with the relatively sudden appearance, in the oceans, of a multitude of organisms: the so-called Cambrian Explosion. It ended some 200 million years later with the loss of nearly all life on Earth during the most devastating mass-extinction event in the history of the Earth – a time known as the "Great Dying."

THE ORDOVICIAN EVENT

The first of the Big Five occurred near the end of the Ordovician Period. The climate was getting colder, leading to the formation of vast ice sheets. As glaciation continued, the sea level fell by as much as 330 feet (100 m), which had a huge impact on marine life as shallow seas covered vast areas of the land. The loss of marine habitats affected groups such as graptolites, cephalopods, conodont animals (primitive, eel-like vertebrates) and trilobites that had been common but which now lost more than half of their diversity.

THE DEVONIAN EVENT

By the middle of the Silurian Period, the climate was warmer and the seas were again home to a rich diversity of species. By the end of the Silurian, the invasion of the land had begun.

Toward the end of the Devonian Period there was a large loss of diversity, but the causes and timescales involved are not agreed upon. This second mass event may actually have been several separate extinctions, spanning several million years. Again, it was probably brought about by a period of global cooling that lowered the temperature of surface waters. The event had its greatest effects on shallow and low-latitude marine communities. More than 20 percent of all marine families disappeared and groups such as the brachiopods lost around 85 percent of all species. While it is estimated that about 70 percent of all species were lost, land communities were least affected.

During the Carboniferous Period biodiversity recovered and increased. The levels of oxygen in the atmosphere were steadily rising, perhaps due to the very large amounts of plant material becoming peat and not decaying to produce carbon dioxide. This abundance of oxygen would have enabled the development of early lungs and may have contributed to the large size of insects at this time – the dragonfly *Meganeura*, for example, had a wingspan of more than 2 feet (70 cm). The levels of carbon dioxide fell below 0.1 percent and the Earth's climate became cooler and drier.

THE GREAT DYING

The Permian Period was also a time of increasing biodiversity, but its close was marked by an event so colossal that it has been called the "Great Dying." In the seas, 80 percent of all genera and more than 50 percent of all families were lost. In all, it is thought that a staggering 96 percent of marine species became extinct. The effects were also felt on land with the loss of around 70 percent of all genera of terrestrial vertebrates. Even eight orders of insects became extinct. Plants were also hard hit, with the loss of many species, including extensive forests of the seed fern *Glossopteris*.

Many factors acting together or in succession over a short time caused this extinction. Multiple major glaciations in the southern hemisphere caused sea levels to fall, exposing all but 10 to 13 percent of the continental shelf and bringing about the death of all coral reefs and their rich communities. There

FOSSIL EVIDENCE Mesosaur fossils found on both sides of the Atlantic show that Africa and America were joined during the Permian Period.

were also periods of volcanism as continents collided to form the single "supercontinent," Pangea. In one episode, up to 960,000 cubic miles (4 million cu km) of molten rock spread over the surface of the Earth. This would have lowered levels of oxygen and sunlight and increased atmospheric carbon-dioxide concentrations. The flora and fauna would have been alternately exposed to hot and cold conditions and recent studies suggest that the huge volumes of volcanic gas produced would have damaged the Earth's ozone layer and made the land and seas acidic.

FIRE AND ICE The Permian Period was a time of extreme climatic contrast, with vast ice sheets forming over much of the southern hemisphere and desert conditions in northern land masses.

END OF THE LINE The last of the trilobites, which had thrived in great abundance and diversity since early Cambrian times, surviving two mass extinctions, finally succumbed to extinction during the Permian "Great Dying."

550
MYA

500
MYA

450
MYA

400
MYA

350
MYA

300
MYA

252
MYA

250
MYA

PALAEOZOIC ERA – ANCIENT LIFE

THE PALEOZOIC ERA 545–252 MYA

This timeline (continued on pages 22–23) represents the first two of the three eras that make up the past 545 million years of Earth's history. The first era, the Paleozoic (ancient life), began with the Cambrian Explosion and terminated in the Great Dying. The shaded area on the right-hand side represents the relatively low background extinction rate, interrupted by catastrophic extinction events.

The Cambrian (545–495 mya)

Known popularly as biology's "Big Bang," the Cambrian Period saw the appearance in the fossil record of an incredible assemblage of multicellular animals. Trilobites, other types of primitive arthropods, molluscs, sponges and worms were abundant. The one fundamental difference between the creatures that existed before the Cambrian and those that came after is the appearance of skeletons and other hard body parts. Although many of the creatures left no descendants, it is certain that some of them were the ancestors of all today's species.

The Ordovician (495–443 mya)

The seas in the Ordovician Period teemed with life, which had become more and more diverse, probably due to the relatively stable conditions that prevailed. By the middle of the period there was an abundance of marine invertebrates such as graptolites (small colonial filter feeders) and brachiopods (lampshells), echinoderms, types of reef-building coral and arthropods, as well as seaweeds and some very primitive fish. There is evidence that a few plant species had begun to colonize the land.

Ordovician
Event

The Silurian (443–417 mya)

The Silurian Period was one of the hottest in the Earth's history and massive coral reefs with a rich biodiversity formed in the waters of tropical regions. Trilobites, crinoids (sea lilies) and molluscs were abundant, as were eurypterids (sea scorpions). More species of primitive fish appeared, including some species with jaws. Toward the end of the period the invasion of the land had begun in earnest, perhaps via piles of shoreline debris. Primitive vascular land plants and the first terrestrial animal communities featuring arthropods such as springtails, mites, millipedes and centipedes became established.

The Devonian (417–354 mya)

During the Devonian Period there was a marked increase in the diversity and size of marine vertebrates, with the appearance of sharks, lobe-finned fish and bony fish. Some lobe-finned fish, the ancestors of amphibians, reptiles and all other four-limbed animals, developed strong limb-like fins and were the very first vertebrates to walk on land. Arthropods continued to colonize the land and there was a proliferation of plant life including many large fern-like and spore-bearing species, clubmosses, horsetails and the first trees.

Devonian
Event

The Carboniferous (354–295 mya)

During the Carboniferous Period dense forests developed, providing a huge increase in the number of ecological niches. Some plants, such as the giant clubmoss *Lepidodendron*, were 130 feet (40 m) tall and giant horsetails and tree ferns thrived in the hot and humid conditions of tropical regions. The first coniferous plant species appeared toward the end of the period. Fish were abundant and there were over 200 species of shark. The first reptiles became amphibious and terrestrial, preying on the rich insect fauna that dominated the swampy forests.

The Permian (295–248 mya)

Sea lilies, ammonites, corals and fish were abundant in the oceans, and amphibians and reptiles continued to diversify on land. Some reptiles became large; others evolved mammal-like features. Many new insects appeared, including those whose development included a pupal stage (complete metamorphosis). Toward the end of the Permian life on land was fully established.

Permian
Event

THE TRIASSIC EXTINCTION

Recovery from the devastating event that marked the end of the Paleozoic Era was relatively slow. The Triassic Period that followed was generally hot and quite dry. Reptiles were replacing invertebrates as the dominant life form and the first dinosaurs and large marine reptiles appeared. Other reptiles were becoming more mammal-like.

At the end of the Triassic Period there was a mass extinction event in which a little more than 50 percent of all genera of marine invertebrates, such as sponges, ammonites and brachiopods, became extinct. On land, too, there were significant changes in the flora with the loss of 85–90 percent of plant species. Nineteen families of tetrapod vertebrates disappeared, including the large amphibians. The extinction of many more primitive reptiles heralded the rise of the dinosaurs.

The causes of this mass extinction are still unknown, but, again, rapid climate change and drastically falling sea levels are probably the most important factors.

THE CRETACEOUS EVENT

Recovery from the extinction event that marked the end of the Triassic Period was relatively rapid. Throughout the Jurassic Period the climate was warm and cycads and conifers continued to flourish. Throughout the period, the supercontinent Pangea was breaking up, a process that would continue into the Cretaceous Period to produce an arrangement of land masses more similar to that of today. By the end of the Jurassic Period, the flora and fauna of the Earth was more diverse than it had ever been.

There was a very marked reduction in sea levels and associated climate change with much colder winters and hotter, drier summers toward the end of the Cretaceous Period. There is evidence that groups such as dinosaurs and some marine molluscs had been in decline for some time before the end of the Cretaceous, so perhaps a number of

DINOSAUR SURVIVOR It is now believed that certain theropod dinosaurs – a group of bipedal carnivores that included the famous velociraptor and the tyrannosaurus rex – are pseudoextinct and evolved into modern birds.

factors, such as climate change and volcanism, were once again responsible for getting the fifth great extinction underway. However, it was almost certainly an asteroid impact that delivered the coup de grace. The end of the Cretaceous Period (and of the Mesozoic Era) happened very abruptly 65 million years ago and caused the disappearance of an estimated 70–85 percent of all species on Earth. The last of the Big Five, it is the most recent and best documented of all the mass-extinction events. On land, dinosaurs and pterosaurs (flying reptiles), which had become very diverse, went extinct while the seas lost 15 percent of all marine families, including the marine reptiles. Ammonites, some of which had survived previous mass extinctions, finally perished, as did belemnites and many other invertebrate groups.

The impact of the large asteroid or comet would have resulted immediately in huge tidal waves and firestorms. The colossal quantities of ash, dust and aerosols generated would have darkened the sky for months, causing tremendous atmospheric changes and climatic upheaval. What is the evidence of this impact? The so-called "smoking gun" – an impact crater 65 million years old, which was made by an asteroid or comet 6–7 miles (10–12 km) across and now buried by thick marine sediment –

has been located off the Yucatan Peninsula and is named after the nearby village of Chicxulub. The devastating effects of an impactor of this size, which would have made a crater 90 miles (150 km) wide by 9 miles (15 km) deep, can only be imagined. It is certain that major food chains in the oceans would have been calamitously disrupted by the loss of phytoplankton through prolonged lack of sunlight and acidification and, on land, the demise of many plants would have had serious consequences for herbivores and the carnivores that preyed on them.

FUTURE EVENTS

The processes that have shaped the Earth and its biosphere for millennia will continue. Another climatic disaster, be it a meteor impact or a huge volcanic eruption, will eventually occur and may be just around the corner. The mantle hot spot now under Yellowstone Park, for instance, is overdue to erupt, and when it does it will certainly cause a global disaster. Not *if* but *when* the next great extinction occurs is just a matter of time and, once again, there will be a few lucky winners and many losers.

However, extinction is not always about bad luck. In the boom-and-bust scenario, a species is effectively a victim of its own success.

WORLDS COLLIDE The Barringer meteorite crater in the Arizona desert (shown here) was created approximately 50,000 years ago. The meteorite was 150 feet (45 m) across. The explosion created by its impact was 150 times the force of the atomic bomb that destroyed Hiroshima. The Chicxulub crater was caused by a meteorite over 6 miles (10 km) across!

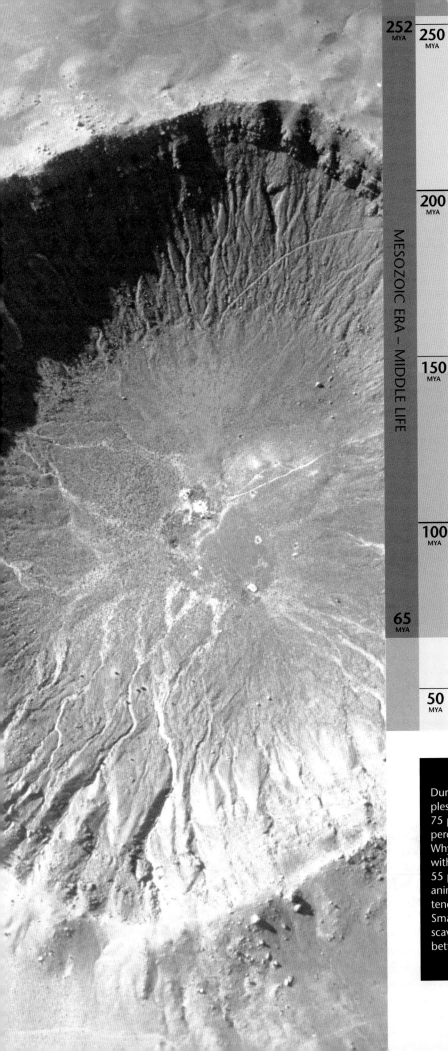

200 MYA

150 MYA

100 MYA

65 MYA

50 MYA

MESOZOIC ERA – MIDDLE LIFE

THE MESOZOIC ERA 252–65 MYA

The Mesozoic Era (middle life) that followed on from the Permian Extinction is sometimes called the "age of the dinosaurs"; certainly it was dominated by reptiles. The era came to a close 65 million years ago with a very large mass-extinction event, the most familiar casualties of which were the dinosaurs.

The Triassic (248–205 mya)

By the middle of the Triassic, seed ferns and clubmosses were common but conifers became more and more widespread. Lobsters and other complicated arthropods appeared in the seas, as did more modern coral species, bony fish and cephalopods with coiled shells – the first ammonites. Many types of marine reptiles evolved and, on land, reptiles became dominant. One group, the archosaurs, ancestral to the dinosaurs, pterosaurs and crocodilians, appeared, as did the first true amphibians. Late in the Triassic, the first mammals appeared, but these small, shrew-like creatures – our ancestors – remained of little consequence for the next 150 million years or so.

Triassic Event

The Jurassic (205–144 mya)

The seas were quite high and home to a rich invertebrate fauna, including molluscs, sea lilies and cephalopods such as ammonites and belemnites. The sea was also home to a large vertebrate fauna of fish, marine crocodiles and other large reptiles such as pliosaurs, plesiosaurs and ichthyosaurs. On land, dinosaurs and other large reptiles were the dominant herbivores and predators. Insects continued to diversify, and small, nocturnal, insectivorous mammals became more diverse. Insects and pterosaurs flew through the air and, toward the end of the Jurassic, the first bird and descendant of the dinosaurs, archaeopteryx, appeared.

The Cretaceous (144–65 mya)

The shallow seas had a diverse invertebrate fauna of sponges, sea urchins, ammonites and bivalve molluscs. The chalk cliffs around the south coast of the British Isles, composed of the compressed calcite remains of phytoplankton and skeletal residue of other minute invertebrates, are testament to the scale of productivity in Cretaceous marine habitats. Countless billions of these small creatures supported rich and complex food webs with sharks and marine reptiles such as plesiosaurs, mosasaurs, ichthyosaurs and crocodiles as the top predators. On land the flowering plants (Angiospermae) made an appearance, and while they diversified rapidly they remained less abundant than conifers. By the late Cretaceous, angiosperm trees had evolved a deciduous habit, allowing them to survive cold or dry periods more easily. The first snakes and several distinct groups of true (beaked) birds appeared.

Cretaceous Event

SIZE MATTERS

During the mass extinction at the end of the Cretaceous, dinosaurs, plesiosaurs and pterosaurs disappeared completely, while birds lost 75 percent of species, turtles only 25 percent and fish less than 20 percent. Snakes and amphibians, too, suffered relatively few losses. Why is this so? One clue is that no species with a mass of more than about 55 pounds (25 kg) survived. Larger animals need more food and tend to breed more slowly. Small, generalist species and scavengers are able to fare better when food is scarce.

Boom and Bust

Not all extinctions are the result of disastrous external influences. Extinctions big and small, local and global – natural cycles of proliferation and obliteration, "boom and bust" – happen all the time and on every imaginable scale. The extinction of St. Matthew Island's reindeer is a classic example – a population that exploded and collapsed in less than three decades.

ST. MATTHEW ISLAND

In 1944, 24 female and 5 male reindeer were taken to St. Matthew Island, in the middle of the Bering Sea, and were released by members of the United States Coast Guard for recreational hunting. Not long afterward, however, the coast guard station on the island was shut down and the reindeer were left to their own devices. Since there were no predators on the island, and the feeding was good and plentiful, the reindeer birth rate was correspondingly high and the death rate low. The reindeer's small population grew rapidly until, in 1963, just 19 years after those first 29 animals were first introduced to the island, it reached a peak of 6,000. However, a year later there were just 42 surviving animals, and, by 1966, the reindeer were officially declared extinct on St. Matthew Island.

MOVING ON Reindeer, or caribou, thrive in the tundra of Europe and North America. They feed mainly on lichens (reindeer moss) but they also eat dwarf willow and other shrubs. Small groups gather into larger herds for winter migrations.

RISE AND DEMISE

Ecologists who studied the "rise and fall" of the herd showed that the deer had been declining in condition and losing weight as the food became more scarce year after year. Lichen is a favorite food of reindeer and it also forms a very important part of their winter diet when nothing else is available. Ungrazed mats of lichen can reach 4–5 inches (10–12 cm) in depth but they are very slow growing. Under heavy grazing pressure and trampling, they cannot survive. The St. Matthew Island herd faced its last winter underfed and ill-prepared. The winter of 1963–64 proved to be exceptionally cold and the reindeer died of starvation.

Another piece of bad luck played a part in the ultimate extinction of the herd as 41 of the 42 survivors were females and the only male to make it was not yet reproductively active.

UNCHECKED GROWTH

The original 29 reindeer were transported to St. Matthew Island from the larger Nunivak Island, which is approximately 30 miles (50 km) off the coast of Alaska. Nunivak Island is populated by humans and the reindeer herds survive there because their numbers are controlled by hunting and culling. Once the human population abandoned St. Matthew Island, the reindeer population had no natural predator to keep it in check. The only carnivorous animal native to St. Matthew Island is the diminutive Arctic fox, which is far too small to tackle reindeer.

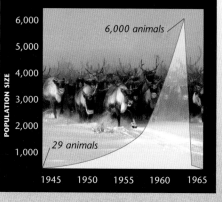

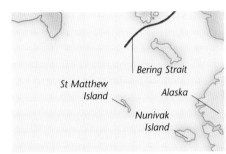

ST. MATTHEW ISLAND Less than 130 square miles (340 sq km) in area, St. Matthew Island lies in the Bering Sea between Alaska and Asia. The flora of this elongate, wind-swept island is composed mainly of grasses, lichens and low-growing willows.

CARRYING CAPACITY

The fate of the St. Matthew Island reindeer is a classic example of what happens when the ability of a habitat to support a species – the "carrying capacity" – is exceeded. This type of extinction can occur on a grand scale, as was the case on St. Matthew Island, but it is extremely simple to replicate on a microscopic scale.

Take a Petri dish containing a suitable growth medium for bacteria. Place a single bacterium in the Petri dish and very soon (in 20 minutes or so) there will be two bacteria. By a process of binary fission, the colony will grow ever larger (a colony of many billions will form in a matter of hours) until it is limited by some factor or other – typically the lack of nutrients and the buildup of their own metabolic waste products, which are toxic. As was the case with the doomed reindeer herd on St. Matthew Island, emigration is impossible and extinction inevitable.

Bacteria are usually cultured in Petri dishes filled with a jelly-like substance called agar gel, which is derived from certain species of seaweed. The gel has various nutrients added to it to support the growth of microorganisms. Of course, the time taken for the colony to exceed its carrying capacity depends on the size of the Petri dish and the quantity of nutrients made available in the first place, but the end result is still the same.

EXPONENTIAL GROWTH

It is easy to see how uncontrolled reproduction can produce large numbers – just how large and how fast depends on the number of offspring produced per individual and the generation time. A pair of small bean weevils, for example, can produce about 80 offspring with equal numbers of male and females every 21 days or so. Theoretically, the progeny of the second generation would number 3,200. The third generation would number 128,000 beetles. It is simple to calculate that by the 18th generation, a mere 432 days later, the beetles would number 1.4×10^{29} individuals and occupy a volume equal to that of the Earth! Of course this would never happen in reality as there would not be sufficient food, but it illustrates the potential for increase.

CHECKING GROWTH

Take a simpler arithmetic progression. Place one grain of rice on the first square of a chessboard. Place two grains on the next square, four on the third square, and so on until you reach the 64th and final square. How much rice do you imagine that you would need to place on the last square? The answer is an astonishing 9.2 million million million grains! The total number of grains on the chessboard would be 18.4 million million million – this much rice represents 570 times more rice than was grown in the entire world in 2000 and is probably more rice than has ever been farmed.

The boom-and-bust scenario is very real and its victims are not limited to reindeer and weevils. Ultimately, it could be a factor in the decline of the human population, which is currently still "exploding."

Population Explosion

The number of human beings on Earth has increased exponentially in recent times and has now reached a population of a little over six billion. The increase has been largely due to revolutions in agriculture, industrial production, and medicine allowing the feeding and survival of more and more individuals. In the past half century the human population has doubled.

SIX BILLION PEOPLE

Compare the population graph below with that of the St. Matthew Island reindeer population (see p. 24); there is at least one significant difference and some very disturbing similarities. The lag phase in the human-population-growth chart has spanned thousands of years during which predators and plagues, ice ages and rapid climate change has kept the numbers of humans in check. About 6000 BC it is thought that there were about 200 million people and in the following 7,000 years there was an increase of just over 100 million. However, with the advent of the Agricultural Revolution in the 18th century the population began to increase rapidly. And in the 1800s, during the Industrial Revolution, the world population first entered its exponential growth phase. In the past 50 years the population has more than doubled to over six billion!

URBAN GROWTH

The human population is very unevenly spread over the surface of the Earth. Large areas of wilderness, usually where it is either very cold or excessively hot and dry, are relatively unpopulated, while in some urban environments humans may live at densities of many hundreds per square mile (*see* box at far right). The most densely populated regions are in India, China and Europe, where the average density is 40–80 per square mile (100–200 per sq km), although there are pockets of extremely high density elsewhere. China, particularly, is rapidly approaching its carrying capacity and the effect on its

CROWDED PLANET Until recently, there has been little increase in the human population, which lagged below 300 million for thousands of years. However, the human population has exploded during the last 200 years and could reach a massive 10 billion by the year 2050.

7

6

5

4

WORLD POPULATION (BILLIONS)

3

2

1

0

FEEDING THE MULTITUDE Modern agriculture can be seen simply as the conversion of Earth's resources into more and more human bodies.

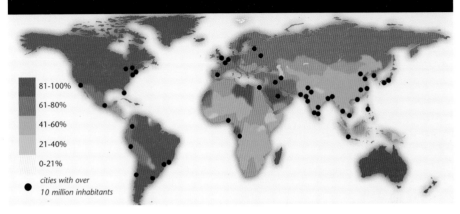

THE GROWTH OF CITIES

The first cities rose over 5,000 years ago, but it is only in the last 200 years – with the rise of industrialization – that resource-hungry urban areas have increased significantly in size and number. The map shows the percentage of the total population living in urban areas in 2000 and the most populous cities. Asia is the new hotbed of urban growth, especially China and India. Tokyo is still the most populous city with over 35 million inhabitants.

81-100%
61-80%
41-60%
21-40%
0-21%

● cities with over 10 million inhabitants

wildlife and forests has been devastating as more and more land is given over to food production or urbanization.

SLOWING DOWN

The rate of population growth peaked in the 1960s with an overall global increase of around 2 percent per year. Although recent studies indicate that the human population will not necessarily double again (the growth rate has slowed and has now fallen to about 1.6 percent increase per year), this still roughly translates to an additional 80 million individuals joining the human race every year. The slowing and decline of the growth rate has been largely brought about by a shift from high to low reproductive rates. This demographic transition, as it is known, has already taken place in all developed countries across the globe, but regions such as sub-Saharan Africa have yet to cross this threshold.

LIMITED RESOURCES

Although we have a constant supply of energy from the Sun, some of our basic resources, such as water and soil, are either finite or renewed at a very slow rate. If we use resources faster than they can be replaced, the result is predictable. Today, nearly one billion humans are undernourished and do not have ready access to regular supplies of drinkable water or health care. Earth's finite resources are unequally shared between six billion

people, increasing by three people every single second. Although one-sixth of these people are now undernourished, this proportion is likely to increase in the future. The vast majority of these would live in developing countries facing crippling shortages of land, food and water.

A NEW MASS EXTINCTION

The exponential growth of the human population coincides with a massive increase in the rate of extinctions. Contemporary species extinction rates are estimated to be 1,000 to 10,000 times higher than background rates. A

greater number of species have become extinct in the past 200 years than became extinct in more than 2,000 years before the start of the Industrial Revolution. And the figures are going to get a lot worse. There will be difficult times ahead for our own species as the population is likely to reach 10 billion by the year 2050, but the impact for the species that share our planet will be nothing short of devastating.

AGING POPULATION Diseases and ailments that once killed us after we had successfully reproduced are taking a dwindling toll. By the end of the 21st century one-third of all living humans may be over the age of 60.

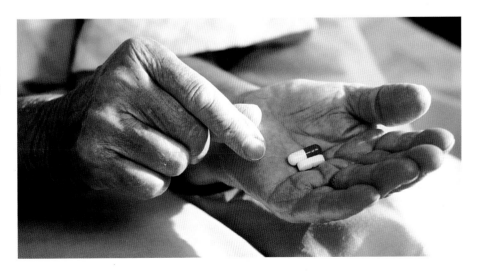

"Homo sapiens *has become the most dominant species on Earth. Unfortunately, our impact is devastating, and if we continue to destroy the environment as we do today, half the world's species will become extinct early in the next century.*"

– Richard Leakey & Roger Lewin, *The Sixth Extinction*, 1995

THE SIXTH
EVENT

Some people think of the problems of habitat loss and overhunting as modern phenomena that have come about as a result of the rapid rise in human populations during the last 200 years, but in reality these processes have been taking place ever since human beings appeared on the planet. As our numbers grew and our technological abilities improved, we changed the environment more and more to suit our own needs. These changes have enabled us to increase in numbers so dramatically that we

have spread to every corner of our world, even maintaining a small presence in Antarctica and in space. But all of this progress has come at a cost and along the way there have been very many casualties, large and small. Some now say that we are on the verge of a sixth mass extinction – one that will rival those seen in the Earth's past history – but they are wrong. We are right in the middle of it, and unlike the five mass extinction events that went before, the sixth event is entirely human-made.

The Rise of Humankind

The origin of our species is one of the most hotly debated topics in modern science. Genetic evidence shows that humans and chimpanzees share a common ancestor that lived about six million years ago. But while chimps remained on all fours, the human line produced creatures that walked upright – a small change that had a colossal impact on the rest of the living world.

MISSING LINKS

The study of human origins is hampered by the great lack of fossil material – indeed all the material ever collected ancestral to *Homo sapiens* and *Homo*

FIRST STEPS The human's closest living relative is the chimpanzee. By walking upright our ancestors traveled more efficiently across the larger distances between food sources following the appearance of grasslands. It is also easier to stay cool because a smaller area of the body is exposed when standing upright compared to when standing on all fours.

neanderthalensis would fit comfortably into a small number of domestic garbage cans. Nevertheless, it is still possible to piece together a fairly clear picture of the evolutionary history of our species. There are arguments over some of the details, but as more fossil material is collected and studied, the picture will become clearer.

THE FIRST HOMINIDS

The ancestors of the Hominoidea (gibbons and great apes) lived in the forests of East Africa, where around 24 million years ago there were several species in a group known as the proconsulids. These apes, such as those in the genus *Proconsul*, lived mainly in trees where they ate fruits but probably also ran along the ground on all fours.

The family Hominidae includes the orangutans, gorillas, chimpanzees and humans. The orangs diverged from the rest of the great apes about 14 million years ago, the remainder diverging around 7 million years ago to give rise to the gorilla lineage, which led to chimpanzees and humans. Molecular analysis shows that no less than 98.4 percent of our DNA is the same as that of chimpanzees. The DNA of a gorilla is 97.7 percent similar to the DNA of a chimpanzee. So, in short, chimpanzees are more closely related to humans than they are to gorillas.

THE HOMININS

In 2002, the incomplete skull of what may be the oldest hominin (a species belonging to the group that includes modern humans and related fossil species) was found in Chad, in Africa. Dating from six to seven million years ago, this species, which is called *Sahelanthropus tchadensis*, had a chimpanzee-sized brain but with smaller canines and a pronounced brow ridge. At this time the effect of the formation of the Rift Valley on local climate was dramatic. The eastern rift shoulder prevented moist air from the Indian Ocean from passing over East Africa, causing the region to dry out. Also, the topography of East Africa completely changed from a flat region covered by rainforest to a landscape with mountains, plateaus and valleys. Forests shrank as the climate became cooler and drier, favoring more open, savanna-like conditions.

BIPEDAL APES

The early hominins that ventured into these new habitats would have faced very different problems to those posed by life in the forest. The major adaptation was a move toward an upright, bipedal gait that would give better awareness of predators, minimize dehydration by reducing the area of the body exposed to the sun and allow more efficient movement over open terrain. In turn, it would have freed the arms and hands for carrying objects and using tools. Later hominins, the australopithecines, evolved into two types: robust species

THINKING MAN *Homo erectus* had a larger brain than earlier *Homo* species, and made a range of sharpened stone tools such as teardrop-shaped axes.

(*Paranthropus*) with massive nut-cracking jaws, which eventually became extinct, and a relatively light-boned "gracile" type (*Australopithecus*) from which the larger-brained genus *Homo* arose. The appearance of the first species of *Homo* – *Homo habilis,* around two million years ago – may have been due to further climatic cooling.

HANDY MAN

Homo habilis is believed to have used simple tools, hence its common name, "handy man." However, it is not yet clear which, if any, of the currently known australopithecines is the direct

ancestor of the genus *Homo*. Around 1.8 million years ago, two taller and more upright species, *Homo ergaster* and *Homo erectus*, appeared. *Homo erectus* was the first hominin to become widespread throughout the world and fossils of this species have been found in Italy, Georgia, India, China, Java and Indonesia, as well as Africa. The earliest modern human remains, about 160,000 years old, were found in Herto, Ethiopia. *Homo sapiens* had arrived and was poised to take over the world.

EARLY MAN *Australopithecus africanus* was one of the most recent australopithecines, and was more robust than earlier species, such as *A. afrensis. A.africanus* became extinct 2.5 million years ago.

Human relations

In recent geological history the climate in East Africa has been massively altered by tectonic plate movement. East Africa was once relatively flat with a warm, humid climate probably supporting extensive rainforest, very similar to Amazonia today. Then, about 50 million years ago, the Indian and Asian continental plates collided, triggering the massive uplift of the Tibetan Plateau, which has been forced upward by 2 miles (5 km) during the last 20 million years. The plateau deflected moist air away from Africa toward India, progressively drying out East Africa. This distinct climatic split between Africa and Asia coincides with the split between Asian and African apes, the latter of which eventually evolved into humans. The oldest known primate fossils date from Africa around 55 million years ago. These small, lemur-like creatures were generally suited to life in warm habitats and had adapted to life in trees. Their first appearance is linked to the development of tropical forests, which provided a rich diet of fruit and insects. Anthropoids – monkeys and apes – first appeared around 35 million years ago, and split into two groups, one evolving mainly in South America (New World monkeys), and the other in Africa and Asia (Old World monkeys and apes).

This latter group underwent a further split: one lineage, the Cercopithecoidea, gave rise to species such as proboscis monkeys, macaques and mandrills; the other lineage, the Hominoidea, led to the gibbons and the great apes, which includes the tree-dwelling orangutans and the ground-dwelling Hominidae: gorillas, chimpanzees and humans.

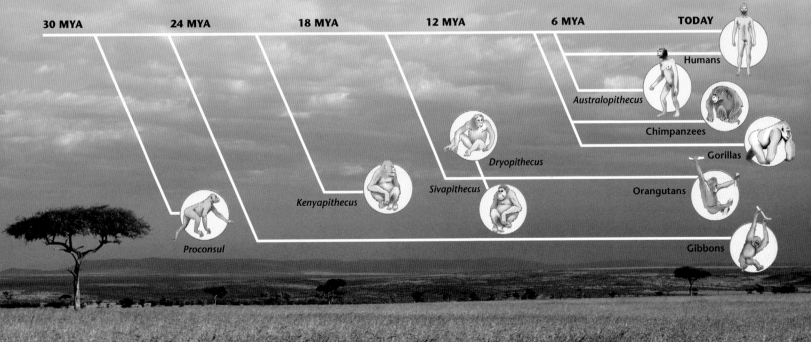

30 MYA 24 MYA 18 MYA 12 MYA 6 MYA TODAY

Proconsul

Kenyapithecus

Sivapithecus

Dryopithecus

Australopithecus

Humans

Chimpanzees

Gorillas

Orangutans

Gibbons

Humanity's Dominion

The last 11,500 years of the Earth's history, the Holocene Epoch, began with the retreat of the great continental ice sheets. Within this short, warm interglacial episode humans have risen to dominance and are now the most abundant large terrestrial vertebrate species on Earth. But for nearly two million years before this, humans struggled to survive through the ages of ice.

THE ICE AGES

The evolution of humans from the appearance of the first erect hominin species, *Homo erectus* and *Homo ergaster*, to the rise of modern humans, *Homo sapiens*, occurred during the Pleistocene Epoch, which began 1.8 million years ago. This epoch was characterized by the onset of worldwide cooling and the ebb and flow of ice sheets that covered up to a third of the northern landmasses. During interglacial periods, however, Earth's climate was sometimes even warmer than it is today, and the sea rose to cover low-lying areas. These cycles of glaciation are thought to be caused by variations in the amount of the Sun's energy that reached the Earth – the variations themselves being caused by the elliptical orbit of the Earth and the degree to which it wobbles on its axis.

During glacial periods, tundra reached as far as the Mediterranean, vegetation zones moved south and sea levels were up to 300 feet (90 m) lower than today. As regions of tundra grew in front of the expanding ice sheets there was a rapid evolution of large vertebrates

CLIMATE COOLING Tundra vegetation, which includes mosses, lichens and sedges, has an extremely short growing season. The main large animals that survive there today are the migratory reindeer, muskox and their predators.

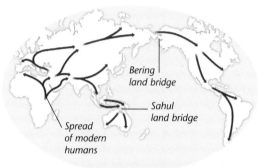

Bering
land bridge

Sahul
land bridge

Spread
of modern
humans

ON THE MOVE It is generally accepted that modern humans arose in Africa about 160,000 years ago. *Homo sapiens* spread out to Europe and Asia as *H. erectus* had done before them. However, *H. sapiens* were more successful and eventually reached Australia via Indonesia and the Americas by island hopping or by crossing a land bridge that joined Alaska to Siberia.

such as the mammoth and woolly rhinoceros, which adapted to the colder conditions.

OUT OF AFRICA

Until recently, two rival theories held equal weight in explaining the rise of *Homo sapiens*. One – the multiregional hypothesis – suggested that humans developed simultaneously right across the Old World, from ancestors that already walked upright. The rival "Out of Africa" theory (see left) maintains that humans evolved in Africa, and only then spread to other continents. Today, this scenario seems by far the most likely, as it is supported by the fossil record and genetic evidence. In genetic terms, all living humans are very similar, with the biggest variation being present in African populations. This is exactly what would be expected if humans first evolved in Africa, and then spread around the world. This genetic similarity also indicates that all races of humans evolved from a single fairly recent ancestor, and that – for some time – the human population was very low, perhaps numbering just a few thousand individuals.

A BRUSH WITH OBLIVION

It is thought that modern humans had their own brush with global extinction around 74,000 years ago, following the eruption of a supervolcano at Toba in Sumatra, which blasted nearly 720 cubic miles (3,000 cu km) of molten rock and ash into the atmosphere, lowering global temperature by several degrees. This, together with the release of billions of tons of sulphuric acid, would have caused immense climatic upheaval and massive damage to ecosystems. The human population would have been significantly reduced. However, even without such a catastrophe there were many other factors, including disease and predation by larger carnivores, that kept human populations low.

INCREASING NUMBERS

To be successful, which in evolutionary terms means leaving descendants, species must take what they need in the way of food and other resources and, as a result, they have an impact on their physical environment. Human beings have the capacity to change their environment to such a degree that it no longer sustains them, forcing them to move elsewhere. It was once thought that humans in the past might have lived in harmony with the environment, but it is simply that humans in small numbers do little damage while increasing populations have larger and longer-lasting effects. Around 50,000 years ago, at the beginning of the Upper Paleolithic,

LARGE VERTEBRATES American bison and other large herbivores roamed the tundra in massive herds, preyed upon by gigantic cats, wolves and hyenas. But their numbers were to be decimated by humans.

VIOLENT EARTH The formation of the Rift Valley in Africa was accompanied by major volcanic eruptions and earthquakes. The supervolcano that erupted at Toba in Sumatra, 74,000 years ago, was particularly devastating.

or Late Stone Age, the number of humans began to increase. This period, which is associated with the development of distinctive cultures, increased technology and more effective hunting techniques, is often called the "Great Leap Forward."

A GREAT LEAP FORWARD

The tools that humans made became increasingly more complex and varied. Artwork in the form of cave paintings, beads, carvings and figurines gradually appeared. As *Homo sapiens* colonized the world they encountered other hominins such as *Homo neanderthalensis*, a heavily built species, adapted to colder conditions, that lived in Europe from 250,000 years ago. The two species lived alongside each other in Europe for around 10,000 years and although it has been suggested that there might have been some interbreeding there is little clear evidence as yet. What is certain is that the Neanderthals went extinct around 30,000 years ago. *Homo sapiens*, meanwhile, continued to thrive and quickly became the world's most successful large predator. Their hunting prowess was soon to have devastating consequences for Earth's megafauna.

The Hunter-gatherers

Toward the end of the Pleistocene Epoch many large vertebrates suddenly became extinct. This wave of extinctions, which took place in various parts of the world, coincides almost exactly with the arrival of *Homo sapiens*. But is it really possible that a relatively few humans equipped with primitive weapons could cause the extinction of so many species?

SCRAPING A LIVING

For most of their time on Earth humans have lived as hunter-gatherers. They kill and butcher prey for meat, hides and other useful byproducts, and they collect plant material such as fruits, seeds and tubers. Killing large prey at close range is a dangerous business and humans may initially have scavenged on the kills of other predators. Later, as their weapons became more effective from a distance (using spears and bows and arrows) and as they developed more cooperative hunting techniques, they would have been able to tackle large prey themselves.

KILLERS ABROAD

Humans arrived in Australia between 46,000 and 50,000 years ago and within 5,000–10,000 years, a relatively short time, many large marsupials such as giant wombats and giant kangaroos became extinct, as did the enormous flightless bird *Genyornis newtoni*.

Within just a few thousand years of humans colonizing North America a

KUNG BUSHMEN Using ancient techniques and primitive weaponry, the Kung Bushmen of northeastern Namibia are still deadly hunters.

wide range of animals became extinct. These included two types of mammoth, mastodons, elephants, several species of camels, 10 species of horses, giant ground sloths, and a further 20 or so genera of large mammals, including predators such the saber-toothed cat, a giant wolf (*Canis dirus*) and an enormous vulture (*Teratornis*) with a 30-foot (4 m) wingspan. From North America humans headed south, and here again it was not long after that the large species, collectively known as megafauna, died out. Among the victims were a species of ground sloth (*Megatherium*) 16 feet (5 m) long and a giant armadillo (*Glyptodon*). As had been the case in Australia, it was the large species that suffered the most.

LOST GIANT The egg of *Aepyornis* was larger than those of the dinosaurs. The massive bird became extinct soon after humans reached Madagascar.

Analysis of the extinctions worldwide showed that it was predominantly the megafauna that suffered. All herbivores with a body mass over 2,200 pounds (1,000 kg) became extinct, as did up to 80 percent of those with a mass of 220–2,200 pounds (100–1,000 kg). Smaller species under 22 pounds (10 kg) and especially those less than 11 pounds (5 kg) were largely unaffected, as were plants and marine species.

GLOBAL WARMING?

The climate at that time was becoming warmer and many of the species that vanished were adapted to extremely cold conditions. Vertebrates, especially larger species, are susceptible to changes in climate affecting vegetation and habitat, as they need more of it. Any reduction

in the numbers of the herbivorous species, for whatever reason, would also greatly decrease the numbers of predators. Some have suggested that it was climate change that decimated the Pleistocene megafauna, but there are problems with this theory. Many of the species had already survived up to 20 cycles of glaciation and warming without going extinct and the extinctions took place at different times in different regions.

OVERKILL?

Or could it be humans that caused these extinctions? There is certainly evidence that supports a Pleistocene overkill theory. Skeletal remains suggest that large prey had fallen into dug pits or been driven over cliffs and into ravines by human-made fires. Also, recent studies using computer modeling show that even with a low human-population growth rate and a

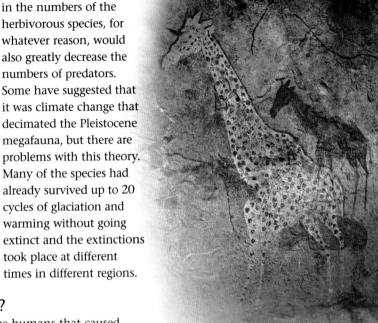

ROCK ART Throughout millennia humans have decorated their cave dwellings with often spectacular paintings of the animals that they hunted for food.

low level of hunting, the effects are easily enough to push large, slow-breeding species to extinction without the effects of climate change. The reason why smaller species are better at surviving is because they need fewer resources and breed more quickly.

AFRICAN MEGAFAUNA

It is easy to see how populations of large animals that might already have been stressed by the warming climate and fragmented habitats could have been exterminated by humans. The fact that the megafauna of Africa survived where it perished everywhere else might be explained by the fact that, in Africa, these species had evolved alongside human beings and would have been very wary of them. Large animals in other parts of the world would have been less wary of the small, ape-like aliens.

The spectacular demise of the Pleistocene megafauna may represent the very beginning of a human-induced mass-extinction event that was to continue at an increasing pace following the development of farming.

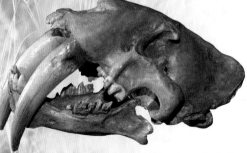

SAVANNA MEGAFAUNA Before the arrival of modern humans, North America was home to a spectacular range of huge animals, including mammoths, dire wolves and the mammoth-hunting saber-toothed cat (*Smilodon*).

Human hunting techniques became much more sophisticated in the Late Pleistocene Period. Spears and bows and arrows allowed hunters to kill from a distance. Many excavations have found large animal remains in association with human artefacts. It was not just prey animals that fell victim to the human hunters, competing predators were also killed.

The First Farmers

The Holocene Epoch, from 10,000 years ago to the present day, is a warm and relatively stable interglacial period in which *Homo sapiens* has brought about massive changes to the landscape and environment. It was the advent of farming that first triggered the beginning of the rapid human-population growth that has continued at an exponential rate to the present day.

SHIFTING TRENDS

The number of humans that can be supported by an area of natural habitat depends on how it is used. A single hunter-gatherer might need to range over nearly 640 acres (260 ha) of tropical forest to find enough food to support himself. Clearing a little of the land at a time for growing crops before moving on – an ancient technique known as shifting cultivation – can sustain a large family or tribe of 15 or more people on the same area. Agricultural practices developed independently in several parts of the world and took a slightly different course in each, influenced by the species available and the climatic conditions that prevailed.

THE FERTILE TRIANGLE

Archaeological evidence shows that the earliest farming occurred around 9,000 years ago in what is known as the fertile triangle – a region of the Middle East spanning from the eastern shores of the Mediterranean Sea, including the regions bordering the Nile, Euphrates and Tigris rivers. From here it is likely that farming people spread out into Europe and elsewhere, taking the new techniques with them.

RIPENING SEED The founder crops of the new Stone Age (Neolithic), which originated in the fertile triangle, included emmer wheat, bitter vetch, chickpeas, barley, flax, peas and lentils.

It is probable that agriculture began as a means of dealing with periods of shortage. During the year there would have been times when certain types of food were scarce and growing edible plants nearby or rearing the captured young of herd animals – sheep, pigs, goats and cattle – would have ensured survival. As groups of humans grew in size, the role of farming became more and more important and eventually became the main way of life. The remains found at some archaeological sites such as Abu Hureyra, on the banks of the River Euphrates, document the transition from hunting, where more than 80 percent of the bones found are of wild antelope, to herding, where the bones are mostly those of sheep and goats. Once having started down this route it is hard to turn back. More people need more food; improvements to agriculture produce more food; more food means more people and so on. The more land that is taken up for farming and the more intensive that farming becomes, the greater will be any damage to the environment.

FOUNDER CROPS

One of the very earliest crops to be domesticated was the ancestor of einkorn wheat that grew in great quantities in a hilly region that is now in southeastern Turkey. It might have taken many centuries for people to change their habits from collecting wild plants to cultivating them. The process of domestication led to larger seeds and stiffer stems, making harvesting easier.

In Mexico, at about the same time (9,000 years ago), squashes and gourds were being cultivated, followed by a thousand years later by corn, which was domesticated from the wild plant teosinte. Agriculture was also developed in the Far East, where millet and rice were brought into cultivation around 8,000 years ago.

DOMESTIC LIVESTOCK

The domestication of dogs, probably from the Asiatic wolf, for use as camp guards, hunting partners and a source of meat preceded that of livestock, but the manner in which this happened is the same. Young orphaned animals would have been taken alive on hunting trips and were reared to eat later.

OVERGRAZING Goat herds belonging to Masai farmers go to water in the Amboseli National Park in Kenya. Overgrazing by herds of goats and sheep is accelerating the process of desertification in vast areas of Africa and Asia.

The animals provided many other useful materials such as hide, wool, bone, horn and dung. Later, as beasts of burden, they provided the power that was needed to cultivate larger and larger areas of land. Domestication of livestock brought humans into direct conflict with predatory species and wild herbivores. The former were killed and the latter lost their habitat.

SHRINKING FORESTS

The cultivation of crops needs land and the clearance of forests and other natural types of vegetation led to the creation of artificial agro-ecosystems, which were not only less diverse, they were also less durable. In the past 10,000 years, more than one-third of the world's original forest has been felled and, in modern times, the process continues for cattle ranching and the growth of cash crops such as soybeans. As trees are cleared, wind and rain gradually erode the soil away and ultimately lead to desertification.

By modifying their environment, humans were able to multiply to such an extent that they overexploited the resources available. Some classic historical examples of nonsustainable growth and the overexploitation of finite resources include the demise of the human populations of Easter Island in the Pacific Ocean (*see* right) and Chaco Canyon in New Mexico.

END OF A CIVILIZATION

Only 150 square miles (400 sq km) in area and covered by forest, Easter Island was colonized by the Polynesians around 1,600 years ago. The human population grew to more than 7,000 individuals and the forests were felled to make way for cultivation and for wood to make boats, houses and as fuel. Large tree trunks were also needed to move the huge ceremonial stone statues, which the islanders quarried and moved to platforms by the coast. In 1722, the first European visitors found a treeless landscape inhabited by a few hundred people. The soil had become eroded and, as there were no large trees left from which to make sea-going canoes, emigration was impossible. Inter-clan warfare broke out and the islanders had to eke out a miserable existence, which terminated in cannibalism.

The Age of Discovery

Humans have explored just about every part of the Earth's surface and our growing numbers inflict an ever-increasing strain on planetary ecosystems. Habitat loss and fragmentation is the single biggest cause of extinction, but biodiversity is also threatened by introduced species – "aliens" that become established in areas outside their natural range.

SPACE INVADERS

Around the world, natural vegetation has been choked and dominated by weeds, and all manner of native animal species have been driven to extinction by introduced species. It has been estimated that 40 percent of all species extinctions in the last 400 years are the result of the accidental or deliberate introduction of alien species. The value of the losses and damage caused by them today runs to several hundred billion dollars per year.

Although the Romans had explored and colonized land from the Rhine and Danube rivers to North Africa, and from Britain to the Middle East, trans-oceanic exploration was not possible until the 15th century, when shipbuilders in Europe produced the first truly ocean-going ships. The early explorers trying to find new lands, trade routes and treasures really were sailing into the unknown and many took live animals such as goats as a source of fresh meat. Whenever a large enough island was encountered some goats would be released, the reason being that if anyone was shipwrecked on the island or if the ship was to return to the island to take on fresh water, they would find familiar food to eat. Goats, like many

successful invasive species, breed quickly. They are tolerant of a wide range of climatic conditions and eat a range of foods. It was not long before the flora and fauna unique to these oceanic islands was damaged irrevocably. Some 2,000 species of Pacific island birds – about 15 percent of the world total – have gone extinct since humans colonized the Pacific. Along with goats, sailors also took cats to control mice and rats on board and all these species escaped to wreak ecological havoc. By the late 19th century it was recognized that rats were a serious problem on Mauritius, Fiji, Hawaii and other oceanic islands and the small Indian mongoose was introduced to control them. Sadly, the mongoose became – and remains – a serious problem by eating endemic birds, reptiles and amphibians.

STOWAWAYS

As worldwide commerce increased, more and more nonindigenous species were transported far and wide. One of the commonest routes is via ballast water taken on to stabilize ships when they are not carrying cargo and then discharged at other ports. It is estimated that around 3,000 species – bacteria, plankton, marine invertebrates, aquatic plants, algae and even shoals of fish – are carried around the world in this manner. Many of the species will not survive, but some do and become serious pests. Zebra mussels, a European freshwater species, were transported in ballast water to the lakes and rivers of Canada and the United States. They were first seen in 1988 and since then have spread and become a very serious pest, fouling pipes, boats, power plants and cooling systems, and altering the lake and river communities by displacing native species and consuming so much plankton that other species drastically decline in numbers.

SHIP RAT Black rats have been introduced via shipping to countries all over the world, including remote oceanic islands. They breed up to six times a year, and by eating native species and competing with them for food they have contributed to innumerable extinctions.

CASTAWAY Goats can survive in nearly all habitats, in low and high altitudes. They are extremely destructive herbivores that will eat almost any type of vegetation, including saplings. On the Galapagos Islands, they changed the landscape from a low-wooded area to a grassland in less than a decade.

ISLAND THREAT A lack of native mammals leaves the Hawaiian ecosystems vulnerable. Native species have not evolved defences against the mammalian predators that have been introduced in the last 300 years.

OUT OF CONTROL

One of the reasons why some species do particularly well and often better in the areas they invade is because they often leave behind the parasites and predators that controlled them in their original habitat. The brown tree snake, a Southeast Asian species, was flown by accident to the Pacific island of Guam on military planes in 1950. In the absence of predators, the population of the snake rose very quickly and in 20 years it brought about the almost total extermination of all Guam's native forest birds.

There are countless examples from all over the world, but if there is one place that has suffered more than any other from alien introductions, it is Australia. Between the years 1840 and 1880, the European settlers released more than 50 species of nonindigenous vertebrates including foxes, pigs and cats, which between them caused economic losses of Aus $600 million. Rabbits were introduced for sport hunting in the late 18th century. By 1910, they had spread across more than half the continent, inhibiting regeneration of plants and competing with native wild animals and domestic livestock.

GREAT ESCAPE Rabbit-proof fencing was built and maintained at great expense to exclude rabbits of Queensland from New South Wales and South Australia. Rabbits are now found on both sides.

DEAD AS A DODO

The dodo, related to pigeons, is probably the best-known example of an extinction brought about by humans and their menagerie of mammalian camp followers. The island of Mauritius, in the Indian Ocean, was explored by the Portuguese as early as 1505 and settled by the Dutch in 1598. Contrary to some accounts, the birds were tough and foul-tasting and their demise was brought about by the destruction of the forest habitat and the introduction of pigs, dogs and rats, which ate the dodo's eggs. The dodo was extinct by the 1680s. On the neighboring island of Rodrigues, a closely related species, the Rodrigues solitaire, went extinct around 80 years later.

The Agricultural Revolution

Mechanization in the 20th century meant that fewer people could produce more food for more people, and the advent of selective breeding and the use of fertilizers increased yields dramatically. World food production is now approaching six billion tons per year, but increasingly intensive farming is having a very damaging effect on the environment.

A GROWING PROBLEM

From simple subsistence farming, still practiced in some areas, agriculture has become a global, multibillion-dollar enterprise controlled by a few massive international companies. The human population has increased exponentially in recent years and so have agricultural yields. Despite this fact there is colossal wastage and more than 800 million humans are hungry or undernourished today. To feed the world population as it heads toward eight or nine billion in the next 25 years or so will require a further massive increase in food production.

IMPOVERISHED LANDSCAPE

As natural habitat is converted for agricultural use, complex, species-rich ecosystems are replaced by simple, species-poor agro-ecosystems. To date, humans are using just over one-quarter of the total land area for growing crops and in doing so have cleared 25 percent of the world's grassland and 30 percent of the world's forest.

Tropical forests cover around 6 percent of the total land surface area, down from 14 percent in historic times. Several studies have shown that these habitats

harbour 60–80 percent of Earth's total biodiversity. Earth's tropical forests are under immense pressure not only from subsistence farming in areas where the human population is still increasing rapidly but also from timber extraction, ranching and large-scale agriculture. Malaysia, for example, has already lost 60 percent of its forest cover, and recent studies on the island of Singapore have shown that it has lost 95 percent of its natural habitat in just over 180 years, causing catastrophic levels of extinction.

MONOCULTURE

In the Amazon, the number of cattle increased from 26 million to over 55 million head in the years 1990–2000 and recent demand for soybean, which is used in all manner of products, has resulted in huge areas being taken for plantations. Agricultural expansion and colonization, fueled by cheap land and high market prices, is encroaching on the rainforest year by year. A similar situation has arisen in Southeast Asia with palm oil. The oil is used to make a range of foods including margarine and is also used to make biodiesel fuel in response to environmental concerns over the consumption of fossil fuels. Millions of acres have been given over to palm oil plantations, contributing to the deforestation that could result in the loss of 20–25 percent of all the world's species within the next century.

DESERTIFICATION

When natural vegetation is cleared for agriculture it becomes vulnerable to drought and soil erosion with billions of tons of soil blowing away in the wind or being washed from the land. Over time the fertility of the land decreases and overgrazing and intensive cultivation

BIOCONTROL DISASTER The introduction of cane toads into Australia to control sugarcane pests was disastrous. The enormous toads did not eat the pests but ate most other things and have spread throughout northern and eastern Australia. The tadpoles dominate freshwater communities and, like the adults, they secrete toxins that can kill a wide range of species.

DEATH OF A SEA

The Aral Sea in central Asia is a textbook example of an environmental catastrophe produced by farming. In the Soviet era, planners decided to divert water from the region's two river systems in order to irrigate cotton on a massive scale. With so much of its water siphoned off, the Aral Sea began to shrink. Today it is divided in two by a spit of dry land, and fishing vessels have been left stranded far from its shores. Before 1960, the Aral's inflowing river deltas were home to over 70 kinds of mammal and 319 types of birds. Less than half of these remain, and increasing salinity has killed off over 20 species of fish.

leads to a fall in yields and, ultimately, desertification. Agriculture now takes 70 percent of the available fresh water, and while irrigated land can be very productive, it eventually becomes useless due to salination of the soil. It is estimated that around 15 million acres (6 million ha) of land are lost every year to desertification and one-sixth of the world's population will be directly affected by it. The Aral Sea disaster is a classic example (see box, left).

WHEAT On average, the USA harvests over 60 million tonnes of wheat each year, yet it is still only the third largest producer. China produces (and consumes) nearly twice that quantity.

INFERTILE EARTH

A major limiting factor to increasing crop yields is a lack of nitrogen in the soil, and the extensive use of fertilizers has allowed cultivation of more and more degraded and marginal land. Also, excess nitrogen and phosphorus from the soil ends up in wetlands, rivers and watercourses, where the enrichment causes drastic changes to

communities and greatly reduces species richness. More than half the artificial fertilizer that has ever been produced has been used in the last 20–25 years.

Despite the fact that there are countless food plants still available, 80 percent of the world's humans are now dependent on just three crops: wheat, rice and corn. The change from hunting-gathering to farming traded a varied and nutritionally rich but unpredictable diet for a plentiful diet of lower quality. It also led to the development of urbanization and industrialization. The problem is growing.

PESTICIDE

The development of herbicides and pesticides contributed enormously to our ability to produce food on an increasingly industrial scale, but it was not long before problems arose. Many non-target species were affected and the pests rapidly became resistant. The harmful effects of biocides on the environment encouraged the use of biological control techniques where other species are introduced to control pests. Biocontrol can be very successful, with minimal or no environmental damage, but there have been cases where it has gone spectacularly wrong.

The Industrial Revolution

From the 18th century onward, a dramatic change took place in technology as engineers began to unlock the staggering potential of fossil fuels. Ironmaking rapidly expanded, the first factories sprang up and the first industrial cities appeared. This breakthrough transformed human society – for better or for worse – and had far-reaching consequences for the environment.

FOSSIL FUELS

Until the 18th century, iron was smelted by burning charcoal, a fuel produced from wood. It was a time-consuming process, and it yielded iron only in small quantities at a time. But in 1713, the English ironmaster Abraham Darby successfully produced iron in a blast furnace, using coke, a fuel derived from coal. In the years that followed, coal was also used to power steam engines – devices that could be put to work in factories, railways and mines. The Industrial Revolution quickly became self-perpetuating, because powered machines made it easier to extract and carry the coal that they needed to work.

Coal was not only used a fuel. New industries grew up that produced coal-based chemicals, such as oils, dyes and paints. These in turn needed a transport system of roads, railways and canals. More and more people were drawn into cities from the countryside. The process began in Britain, but gradually rippled outward to create the "industrial world."

THE OIL INDUSTRY

A second wave of industrialization took place in the mid-19th century with the exploitation of oil. More versatile than coal, it spurred the development of the internal combustion engine, followed by cars and aircraft. It also spawned yet more industries, producing plastics and agrochemicals, including the synthetic fertilizers and pesticides we currently use to squeeze more food out of the land. It is hard to imagine a world without this oil-based economy, but it is one that cannot last for long. Oil was formed from the decay of marine plants and animals over 300 million years ago. It is a finite resource – one that is rapidly running out.

NEWCOMEN ENGINE The early 18th century steam engines of Thomas Newcomen were essentially large pumps used for draining mines. These machines allowed coal mines to be deeper and reach more and more coal.

ACID RAIN Smelting nickel and other ores in the Nadezhda Metallurgical Plant in Norilsk, Russia. The plant has spouted 2 million tons of sulfur dioxide into the atmosphere every year since 1950. Acid rain in the region is destroying hundreds of thousands of acres of forest and tundra.

OIL SLICK An oiled jackass penguin waits to be rescued after a tanker spill off South Africa. The only penguin found in Africa, it has become endangered by oil spills and overfishing.

POLLUTION

Chemical industries in particular have caused grave problems for the living world. They generate hundreds of toxic compounds, including persistent organic pollutants (POPs). These compounds include pesticides such as DDT, dioxins released by combustion and industrial processes, and polychlorinated biphenyls (PCBs) – synthetic compounds used in electrical equipment. Once they find their way into the environment, these pollutants are passed from animal to animal in food, eventually becoming concentrated in the bodies of the top predators. Traces of nearly 300 such chemicals have been detected in human tissues: none were present a hundred years ago.

GREENHOUSE GASES

Since the beginning of the Industrial Revolution, the human population has soared, and so has the amount of energy that we use. The current use of primary energy for heating, transportation and the generation of electricity is 400 million million million joules per annum – the equivalent of more than 13 billion tons of coal, and a figure that may more than double in the next 50 years. Whenever fossil fuels are burned, their carbon ends up in the air, as carbon-dioxide gas. The consequences of this are now well established, and they make uncomfortable reading.

The Earth's climate has always changed and the processes controlling it are immensely complex and difficult to assess. However, one fact is certain: carbon dioxide, together with other gases such as methane and nitrous oxide from agriculture, increase the insulating power of the atmosphere, making the planet warm up. These gases have already contributed to a rise in global temperature of 1.1°F (0.6°C) in the last 150 years. The northern hemisphere has recently experienced the warmest conditions for over 1,000 years and measured levels of carbon dioxide and methane in the atmosphere are higher than at any time in the last 500,000 years. Predicting the future is difficult, but it is, likely that the average global temperature will rise by between 2.7°F (1.5°C) and as much as 9°F (5°C) in the next 100 years.

THROWAWAY SOCIETY The United States generates over 235 million tons of waste each year. Most of the waste is buried in landfill sites, which is far from ideal as they can leach toxins into local water supplies and emit methane – a powerful greenhouse gas.

CHANGING CLIMATE

The results of all these changes will be extremely far-reaching. Weather patterns will become more unpredictable and very possibly more extreme; some areas will become much drier than at present, some wetter. Vegetation zones will shift northward and species adapted to mountainous regions may have nowhere to go. Large areas of productive coastal land – where vast numbers of people currently live – will be at risk of flooding as glaciers and the polar ice sheets continue to melt. By the year 2100, the mean sea level could rise by up to 30 inches (80 cm).

FACING FACTS

Today, we understand a great deal more about our environmental impact than people did in the early days of industrialization. Future advances in technology have the power to damage the environment still further, but also to mitigate the effects. Scientists are actively pursuing less damaging ways of producing energy, and have had some success in repairing the harm already done. But even so, we will have to adapt to survive, and we will do so without many thousands of species of plants and animals that will not be able to acclimatize. Even if we are not entirely responsible for global warming, the continuing growth of industrialization will take a terrible toll on the living world.

Harvesting Nature

It is self-evident that the overuse of anything that has a finite supply will ultimately lead to shortages. The overuse of land for crops results in the decline of soil fertility and diminishing yields. Excessive hunting and fishing has led to innumerable extinctions. Sustainability is not difficult to understand, but politics and profits too often override science and common sense.

SUPPLY AND DEMAND

Any species that is not domesticated or cultivated must be harvested from the wild. The maximum sustainable yield of any species is simply the number of animals you can take without affecting the ability of the population to recover.

Nowhere are the dangers of over-harvesting seen more clearly than in marine ecosystems. The largest source of protein for humans comes from marine species, and millions of people rely on fishing for their livelihood, but the industry is facing real dangers.

DRASTIC DECLINE

A hundred years ago it was thought that Atlantic cod were so abundant and so prolific that nothing humans could do would ever cause a decline in their numbers – indeed it was once said that it would "baffle all the efforts of man to exterminate." We now know that this is far from the truth. Cod numbers have declined by more than 90 percent since the 1850s because of increased fishing, especially on spawning grounds.

COMMERCIAL FISHING A handful of fish species account for more than 25 percent of the total world catch – Alaskan pollock, Atlantic herring, Japanese anchovy, Chilean jack mackerel and skipjack tuna – but stocks of these species are declining.

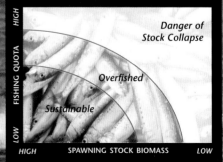

STOCK COLLAPSE

Intensive fishing of low-spawning stock leads to collapse. In the last 100 years up to 30 percent of global fish stocks have been overexploited and around 50 percent are now fully exploited.

Danger of Stock Collapse

Overfished

Sustainable

HIGH — FISHING QUOTA — LOW

HIGH — SPAWNING STOCK BIOMASS — LOW

DIGGING DEEPER

Stocks of the few commercial species are declining and there are few big fish left to catch. In some cases a total ban will need to be implemented if stocks are to recover to levels where they can be safely harvested once more.

Sadly, the tendency for humans is to harvest as much as they can on the basis that if they don't, someone else will, and political pressure can result in fishing quotas being set higher than recommendations based on scientific study. Recently, fishing boats with enormous bottom-trawling gear, 200 feet (60 m) wide, have began targeting deep-sea fish species, whose numbers are now also declining very rapidly. A recent study of five deep-sea species, some of which are of no commercial value in any case, shows that they are close to extinction. Bottom trawling is also very destructive to the seafloor communities, which may take many years to recover.

Another major problem with fisheries is "bycatch" – the slaughter of large numbers of non-target species such as

BUSHMEAT In many parts of the world, the growing trade in bushmeat for basic human subsistence is driving several species of primate toward extinction. These mangabeys were hung up for sale by a roadside in Gabon.

mammals, seabirds and turtles. More than 300,000 dolphins, porpoises and whales die every year in this way.

FAIR GAME

Humans hunt other animals not just for food and raw materials but also sometimes to reduce the numbers of pests or dangerous species or simply as a sport. There has always been a conflict between humans and wildlife. Species that attack domestic livestock or eat crops have been exterminated all over the globe as a result. One example is the white-necked mangabey, once considered to be a serious crop pest in parts of West Africa and is now an endangered species, and there are thousands of other similar instances.

A wide range of species, including reptiles, rodents, birds, antelopes and even buffalo, hippos and elephants, are ending up in cooking pots as an important source of protein and are being sold as a source of income in areas with little employment. What may have been a sustainable traditional

practice with little impact is now a serious problem due to the growing numbers of humans and the fact that natural habitats are shrinking.

One of our closest living relatives, the bonobo, or pygmy chimpanzee, is being hunted to extinction in the Congo basin. The fact that it is a protected species means little to unscrupulous poachers or people who are themselves struggling to survive.

SHELL SHOCK All eight species of sea turtle are endangered. There is a huge demand for turtle flesh in the burgeoning Asian market. Several species range across many political boundaries, making them difficult to protect.

Unfair Trade

Attitudes to trade in wildlife products are slowly changing in many parts of the world as people become more aware of the environmental damage being done and the pain and suffering caused. However, the illegal international trade in wildlife still runs into billions of dollars each year, involves thousands of endangered species and leads to innumerable extinctions.

MIRACLE CURES

The huge Asian market is responsible for the extirpation of many species. The Javan rhinoceros, for example, is now regarded as one of the "living dead" (global extinction of the subspecies is seen as inevitable). Sadly, practitioners of traditional Eastern medicine believe that powdered rhinoceros horn has a range of medicinal properties for curing ailments as diverse as back pain and fever. And so it is with many species whose wool, fur or skin, or body parts, such as gallbladders, blood or even penises, are thought to be especially useful for some purpose of other. Bear bile, for instance, is highly regarded in traditional Eastern medicine for the treatment of stomach and liver problems, impotence and a range of other complaints.

Traditionally, bears were hunted for their gallbladders, but a

MIRACLE CURE? The increase in China's population has raised demand for traditional medicine. Even many non-Asian communities are now supplementing their Western style of medicine with traditional Chinese cures using tiger parts.

decline in numbers led to the appalling practice of bear farming. Thousands of wild bears are kept for their entire lives in cramped cages and are "milked" for their bile through catheters twice a day. The bears may suffer in these atrocious conditions for years before they die.

Around 24 million seahorses are taken from the wild and dried for use in medicines to treat anything from skin complaints to heart disease and bone fractures. There are no scientific studies that support any of the claims made for these "natural medicines" – people simply believe that they are effective. As the human population grows, so does the demand, which is now so high that the populations of many seahorse species, especially the larger ones, are dwindling rapidly.

SHARK FINS

Another inexcusable trade involves sharks, whose fins are used to make a traditional Chinese soup, popular at weddings and New Year celebrations. The trade, which is biggest in Hong Kong, China, Taiwan and Singapore, is responsible for the deaths of over 150 million sharks each year. The nutritional value of a shark's fin is minimal and, although

SHARK ATTACK The high price of shark fins is affecting sharks of all kinds. To save space in boats and to meet the growing demand for this "delicacy," it is easier to cut off the dorsal fin and throw the shark back in the sea to die.

some insist that the taste is unique, most of the soup's flavor comes from stock and seasoning.

EXOTIC PETS

But the East does not hold a monopoly on the barbarous exploitation of wild animals. Europe and the United States provide a huge and diverse market for wildlife products, with massive demand for pets and fashion accessories. As many as 25 million fish, crustaceans, anemones and other invertebrates, as well as 1,000–2,000 tons of coral, are collected every year, especially from reef habitats, to supply marine aquaria in the U.S. and Europe. Often, the harvesting process and the transport results in high levels of mortality, so there is a great deal of wastage. In the U.K. alone, more than 100,000 specimens of one species, the clown anenome fish, made popular in the animated movie *Finding Nemo*, are imported each year. Advocates of the trade say that it provides much-needed income for the areas where collecting takes place

RHINO HORN Rhino horn is prized for use in traditional Chinese medicine. In the Middle East it is used for making ceremonial daggers, demonstrating the wealth and influence of its owner. The rarest horn has the highest price.

and provides an incentive to maintain the health of reef ecosystems. Critics state that the trade is quickening the destruction of biologically rich reef ecosystems by encouraging the use of cyanide fishing, where unscrupulous traders use sodium cyanide to harvest reef fish. An estimated 330,000 pounds (150,000 kg) of dissolved poison is released on some 33 million coral heads annually.

The exotic pet trade is responsible for the death of millions of birds, reptiles, amphibians and other species. The United States imports around two million live reptiles annually, and Europe imports nearly half a million wild birds.

Many pet owners are unaware of the suffering and damage their hobby causes. Black-market traders continue to flout the international laws that limit the trade in rare and endangered species. The problem is likely to increase as traders exploit the anonymity of the Internet to reach their customers.

FASHION VICTIMS

Wearing fur is far less common than it once was, but the fashion has enjoyed a recent revival. Polar bear rugs, gorilla hand ashtrays and elephant foot umbrella stands are no longer socially acceptable as souvenirs and are banned in many countries. But illegal trade in wildlife products does continue. Many items are seized at customs, reptile skin accessories and tortoiseshell curios being among the most common.

BEHIND BARS
Many "exotic species," such as this Capuchin monkey, are targeted for the pet trade. Up to half of the wild animals trapped for export in the pet trade die in transit.

Unnatural Selection

Humans are relatively large animals. When we look at a landscape we are aware of mammals, birds and reptiles – relatively large, back-boned species like ourselves. We give little thought to the countless billions of smaller creatures such as insects, worms and microorganisms that actually contribute far more to the survival and health of global ecosystems.

THE FURRY AND FEATHERED

In a recent survey, nine out of 10 people questioned said they would be happy to pay money in their taxes to save the giant panda from extinction; one in 10 said they would pay to save the Eurasian hazel dormouse. Nobody was interested in wasps or dung beetles.

It is not an accident that wildlife organizations select large, attractive animals – the so-called charismatic megafauna – as flagship species. Furry creatures are more attractive to humans than scaly ones, and the face of a panda is sure to open more wallets than that of an equally endangered crustacean or snake. Why are we sympathetic to some species and yet completely indifferent to others?

CONSERVATION ICON The giant panda is undoubtedly the most famous of all endangered animals. It is threatened by habitat loss in its native China. Only massive conservation efforts have saved this bear from global extinction.

INDISPENSABLE RECYCLERS Dung beetles often roll dung into balls to bury at a nesting site. In doing so they increase pasture yields, reduce pest populations and return valuable nutrients to the soil.

LOVABLE ROGUE

Take a closer look at two creatures: the dung beetle and the domestic cat. What is their value? The cat is one of our most popular pets. It is difficult to quantify the cat's value in terms of the amount of joy that it gives its owner. It is useful in that it rids our homes of mice. But there is also a very dark side to the cat's relationship with humans.

Cats have been introduced around the world by settlers from Europe. Feral and pet cats present a growing threat to wildlife, especially on islands. Around the world, cats are responsible for killing billions of small mammals, birds and reptiles and have so far been responsible for the extinction of more than 30 bird species. The sad case of the Stephens Island wren illustrates the problem. In the 1890s a lighthouse was built on Stephens Island, in New Zealand. One day, in 1894, the lighthouse keeper's cat, which was named Tibbles, brought home a small flightless bird. In the next few weeks it brought back several more. The lighthouse keeper, David Lyall, sent some of the specimens to experts to be identified and the news came back that it was a new species of songbird. However, no sooner had the bird been discovered as a species than it went extinct. Tibbles had killed them all! Nowadays, conservation bodies are trying to remove cats and rats from oceanic islands in the hope that the fauna of some will recover. With larger areas the task is immense. There are now around 21 million feral and domestic cats in Australia alone, causing losses of native birds and mammals and endangering species such as the Norfolk Island parrot, the greater bilby, the little tern and many others.

UNSUNG HERO
When you think of a dung beetle, if you visualize anything at all, it is likely to be the common Egyptian dung beetle renowned in mythology. In fact, there are literally thousands of species of dung beetle, belonging to the family Scarabaeidae, and their value to global ecosystems is immeasurable. By burying dung they increase grazing on pasture that would otherwise remain covered; they recycle nitrogen into the soil that

GLOBAL PEST Cats, like humans, are switching predators. When their major food source runs out they simply switch to another source. Also, they breed rapidly and, especially in island habitats, they can cause extinctions.

CHANGING ATTITUDES Rather than being appreciated as refuse removers, red kites in England were hunted to extinction as vermin. However, they were recently reintroduced and populations are increasing.

would otherwise be lost to the atmosphere; they reduce the incidence of cattle parasites; and they reduce pest flies that breed in dung. The estimated value of all these free "services" runs to several billion dollars. When colonists first brought cattle to Australia the dung remained on the pasture and vast areas of land quickly became poisoned. In the 1960s, dung beetle species that had evolved alongside European cattle were introduced into northern Australia with spectacular results. When the beetles were established, dung that had taken several years to disappear previously was now recycled into the soil in less than 48 hours!

VALUABLE "PESTS"
The "services" that many animals provide often go unappreciated and are only recognized when the animal is lost. The Sumatran tiger is currently ranked among the "living dead" and, without concerted conservation efforts, it is likely to disappear entirely in the next decade or so. When the tiger was first decimated in its native Sumatra by European hunters, the wild boars that were the tiger's chief prey multiplied rapidly and soon destroyed the palm

trees. As a result, the island's great palm oil industry totally collapsed, causing terrible poverty.

The rest of this book is given over to a small percentage of the myriad endangered species and the threats they face from human beings. It is an "unnatural selection" of spectacular mammals, beautiful birds, amazing reptiles, fascinating fish and just a sprinkling of insects and other small invertebrates. As relative giants of the Earth, it is the larger furry and feathered creatures that we will notice disappear and, in many ways, it is the larger species that are most vulnerable (because we notice them). But it is worth reflecting that although many species of charismatic megafauna will be lost and lamented, innumerable creatures will vanish unnoticed – unless, perhaps, their extinction leads to some terrible consequences for you and I.

CULTURAL CHOICE
There is a strong cultural element affecting the way we treat other species. Killing and eating a dog may seem more natural to some people than the force-feeding of geese and ducks with huge quantities of grain to produce pâté de foie gras. But neither of these species is likely to be threatened by extinction, nor are the many species that we domesticate for use as food and products such as leather.

"It seems that you cannot have a deep sympathy with both man and nature."
– Henry David Thoreau, Walden; *Life in the Woods,* 1854

"For what are the whales being killed? For a few hundred jobs and products that are
not needed, since there are cheap substitutes. If this continues it will be the
end of living and the beginning of survival."
– attributed to George B. Schaller (1933–)

THE LOST
AND THE LAST

When we look at a trilobite fossil or the reconstruction of a dinosaur we are fascinated but do not mourn their passing. They belong to a distant past of which we were no part. The same may be true for the more recent demise of giant sloths and mammoths, since living humans never knew them. However, some of the species illustrated in this book will, in the next 50 years, have slipped from being vulnerable to critically endangered, and some will have become extinct. Precisely how many is anybody's guess, but doubtless they will seem as strange to our grandchildren's eyes as a dodo or a moa does to ours.

Many people are worried about the loss of countless numbers of species through habitat loss and degradation, industrial pollution and our overconsumption of natural resources, but what if someone had predicted this situation 150 years ago, when there were far fewer humans than today? It is highly unlikely that anyone would have paid attention or that the course of our history would have been any different. Even today, for a sizeable part of the human population, worrying about the fate of a few animals seems a ludicrous luxury. For them, the problems of finding enough food and clean water are more pressing concerns.

Monotremes & Marsupials
Monotremata & Marsupialia

Separated from other continents for over 40 million years, the massive landmass of Australia is full of animals that evolved in isolation and live nowhere else on Earth. Among them are rare species of egg-laying monotremes and pouched marsupials.

SPINY DEFENSE When attacked, the long-nosed echidna rolls up into a spiny ball. This endangered monotreme loses many of its eggs to predators introduced to New Guinea.

ISLAND ISOLATION

The monotremes are one of the most ancient mammal groups. Instead of giving birth to live young like all other mammals, they lay eggs. These hatch into helpless babies that then feed on their mother's milk. There are two main kinds of monotremes – the unique duck-billed platypus of eastern Australia and about four species of echidnas (spiny anteaters), three of which are found only in nearby New Guinea.

STRANGE MAMMAL

When the platypus was first discovered by European explorers in 1799, its appearance was so bizarre

FOREST DWELLER The rare long-footed potoroo falls victim to introduced dogs and red foxes.

that incredulous scientists thought the preserved skin must be a hoax. Today, the platypus is one of Australia's most famous inhabitants, relying on quiet freshwater streams and billabongs (pools). It is well protected, but the clearance of bankside vegetation, canalizing of waterways and water pollution are all causing a gradual decline in its population.

Platypus eggs are eaten by introduced red foxes and rats, as well as by native predators such as lizards. Many echidna eggs suffer the same fate. Sadly, echidnas are also rather slow and cumbersome, which makes them very easy to hunt. Local people pursue them with dogs in remote parts of New Guinea, where their flesh is regarded as a great delicacy.

BORN AT AN EARLY AGE

The 290 or so species of marsupials are named for the marsupium – a pouch-like flap of skin where the tiny young suckle and grow after being born at an early stage of development. A number of small, mostly tree-living marsupial species are found in New Guinea and South America, and one plentiful species – the Virginia opossum – occurs in North America. But most marsupials are found in Australia, where they have diversified into almost every habitat from wettest rainforest to driest desert.

BACK FROM THE "DEAD"

The better-known marsupials include kangaroos, wallabies, koalas, wombats, bandicoots and possums. Some of these, especially the larger kangaroos

REDISCOVERED Believed for many years to be extinct, the dibbler was refound in 1967. It is a nocturnal predator of mice, lizards and large insects.

UP IN FLAMES

Occasional wildfires are vital in Australia's outback as they remove dead vegetation and encourage new plant growth. But the blazes, whether caused accidentally by tourists or deliberately for agricultural management purposes, are getting larger and more frequent, placing many native species in danger.

and the ringtail possum, are coping so well with human interference that they have achieved pest status in certain areas and their populations have to be culled. However, other marsupials face a growing range of threats – nearly 20 species have died out in Australia in the last 200 years alone, and many more are endangered.

The threatened marsupials include small wallabies, such as the mala, as well as numerous active hunters such as the kowari, mulgara, dibbler and red-eared antechinus. Their habitats have been devastated by introduced rabbits, which wreak havoc on native vegetation, and by excessive sheep and cattle grazing and fire-burning land management schemes. They are also killed by introduced foxes, cats and dogs. Small in size and rarely seen, these marsupials seldom attract the funds lavished on photogenic species like koalas.

SUCCESS STORIES

Some endangered marsupials manage to survive against all the odds. Leadbeater's possum, a small, gliding species, was rediscovered in 1961 in the state of Victoria, having been presumed extinct for 60 years. The dibbler, a shrew-like insect-eater with a pointed snout, was likewise refound after an interval of 80 years, in the extreme southwest of the Australian mainland and on a couple of offshore islets. It depends on scrubby coastal heaths and sandy shrubland, where it scurries around after dark. Just a few hundred dibblers remain in the wild, but there are plans to boost this relict population with zoo-bred animals.

EXTINCT

The largest marsupial predator of modern times was the thylacine, also known as the Tasmanian wolf or tiger. Resembling a medium-sized dog, this striped carnivore died out in mainland Australia around 4,000 years ago due to competition for food with introduced dingoes. A small population survived in Tasmania, but the species was hunted by farmers who thought it took their livestock (in fact, wallabies and kangaroos were its main prey). The thylacine was extinct in the wild by 1930, and the last captive individual died in Hobart Zoo in 1936.

HUNTING UNDERWATER
The platypus dives for up to three minutes, using sensory organs in its duck-like bill to detect the electrical fields created by its shrimp and insect prey. Fully protected, it nevertheless is suffering from damage to its habitat.

Insectivores Insectivora

Strictly speaking, an "insectivore" is any creature that eats insects. But the term is also used to describe this large group of small, mainly nocturnal mammals, which hunt a wide variety of invertebrate prey, including spiders, worms and snails.

SENSE OF SMELL

The order Insectivora contains about 360 species, including the hedgehogs, shrews, moles, desmans, otter-shrews, moonrats, tenrecs and solenodons. Their superb sense of smell is used to locate food, whereas their eyesight and hearing are much less well developed. Most species are secretive, alert, agile and nocturnal, making them difficult to identify and study in the wild. Some scurry on the ground, some are expert burrowers, and others are powerful swimmers found in freshwater habitats.

Water shrews, desmans and otter-shrews, the most aquatic insectivores, are greatly affected by changes to their waterways and by poor water quality. The delicate balance of aquatic food chains on which they rely is upset by industrial effluent and fertilizer runoff from fields, the clearance of bankside vegetation and damming for irrigation and hydroelectric power plants.

DESMANS IN DANGER

The Russian desman has felt all these pressures in its stronghold of the Don,

THE MINK MENACE

American mink that have escaped from fur farms have now established breeding populations in many parts of Europe and Asia. These fierce predators take all kinds of prey up to the size of rabbits (in the picture below, one has just caught a muskrat in its native Canada). Mink have partly webbed feet and usually hunt in wetlands, with serious consequences for local populations of water shrews and desmans. One conservation solution is to trap and remove the feral mink.

SNIFFING AROUND
Resembling a large shrew, the Cuban solenodon uses its trunk-like snout to root out insects and small lizards. Unusually for an insectivore, it also eats fallen fruit and other plant matter.

MOUNTAIN TORRENT The Pyrenean desman inhabits crystal-clear, fast-flowing streams high in the Pyrenees mountains. It is threatened by water pollution, predation by escaped American mink and the construction of hydroelectric plants.

Volga, Ural and Dneiper river basins in Central Asia. Its prey – insect larvae, frogs, water snails, crayfish and small fish – has become much scarcer due to watercourse clearance schemes and the diversion of water for agriculture. It is also hunted for its thick fur, used for gloves and hats, and for its base-of-tail musk glands, an ingredient of perfumes. Fortunately, the species is an associated beneficiary of habitat restoration intended primarily to save the famous giant fish of the region, the beluga sturgeon, whose eggs are harvested as the culinary delicacy called caviar.

DESERT MOLES

In contrast to the desmans, several insectivores occur only in arid habitats. Grant's golden mole, for example, is a desert dweller of the Namib and the surrounding area in southwest Africa. It "swims" through the soft, loose sand using its broad feet and hunts a range of small prey, from locusts to lizards. Particular threats to this vulnerable species are mining and the spread of roads and railways through its formerly silent, pristine habitat.

RARE AND RESTRICTED

Shrews are among the best-known insectivores. With a rapid metabolism, they can be said to "live fast and die young." Several species, such as North America's short-tailed shrew and the Eurasian shrew, remain widespread and common. But deforestation threatens

many tropical species. The secretive Malayan water shrew is one of the most restricted and critically endangered of all mammals. It is found only in the Ulu Langat (Langsat) Forest Reserve of Selangor, in southwestern peninsular Malaysia. Even in this forest haven, it is affected by water pollution and logging.

SOLENODON CAPTURE

There are only two types of solenodon: the Cuban and Hispaniolan, named after their Caribbean island homes. The former species was sighted only sporadically during the last century and by the 1970s it was suspected of being extinct. However, a healthy male

MINIATURE DIVER Water shrews, such as this Eurasian water shrew, are hit hard by declines in water quality, which can seriously affect supplies of their invertebrate prey.

was captured in 2003, studied and released. This celebrated individual, nicknamed "Alejandrito," was only the 37th specimen ever caught. He revived interest in a species endangered by introduced brown rats and mongooses.

DECLINE OF THE OTTER-SHREW

Wetland drainage in West and Central Africa has pushed the giant otter-shrew, or giant potamogale, dangerously close to extinction. The size of a large pet cat, this little-known nocturnal aquatic insectivore has possibly never been photographed alive in the wild. It suffers from being unable to find prey in water that is muddied and cloudy due to soil washed off logged hillsides during heavy rain. It is also trapped for its soft fur, and drowns in fishing nets.

Bats are the only mammals capable of true, powered flight, using their flapping wings. They are a huge and varied group – about 1,050 of the world's 4,700 species of mammal are bats. But, because bats are mostly small, secretive night-fliers that hide during the day, their lifestyles, population numbers and threats are often mysterious.

MEGABATS

Not all bats are easy to overlook – the 170 or so species of megabats can be highly conspicuous. They are known as fruit bats from their chief food source, or as flying foxes due to their long muzzles and dog-like faces. A number of species, including the Egyptian fruit bat, Indian and Malayan flying foxes and several epauletted bats, raid crops, plantations and orchards, reaching pest proportions in some areas. However, other fruit bats are threatened, mainly by habitat destruction.

The best-known example is the Rodrigues flying fox, whose population crashed to just 70 to 100 in the 1970s. Restricted to the Indian Ocean island of Rodrigues, the species declined due to the clearance and degradation of its forest habitat, and to hunting by the islanders for food.

MICROBATS

Whereas megabats occur only in Asia, Africa and the Pacific, microbats live almost worldwide in many different habitats. They include hundreds of species of nocturnal insect-eaters, which fly silently and are difficult to identify and follow. We know very little about many of them, and new species are still being discovered. In

NATTERER'S BAT This scarce bat hunts over woodlands, parks and hedgerows. It feeds mainly on moths and flies, but insect densities are falling as a result of pesticide use, causing starvation. The species is also affected by destruction of its roost sites.

addition to this lack of data, one of the main problems in conserving bats has been their association with darkness, spells, Dracula and witchcraft. Public sympathy *for* bats has long been lacking.

UNDER PRESSURE

Today, up to 100 species of bats are endangered and many others are declining. Intensive farming methods, such as the removal of woods, heaths and hedgerows to create larger fields or the spraying of crops with insecticides, have devastated their supplies of small insect prey. Large-scale commercial logging (rainforests are especially rich in bat species) and the draining of wetlands are also to blame. Bats fall prey to domestic and feral cats, and to mink that have escaped from fur farms.

Vampire bats are persecuted across Central and South America, partly through fear and partly because their

FRUIT THIEVES

In the tropics, fruit bats may come into conflict with orchard owners or farmers, who sometimes respond by attacking them at their roost sites. The bats may gather to feed in very large groups, so can cause serious damage to a ripe fruit crop in a single night. Big fruit bats, such as the Queensland tube-nosed bat (below) of Australia, must land in order to eat; the smaller species are able to hover in front of hanging fruits.

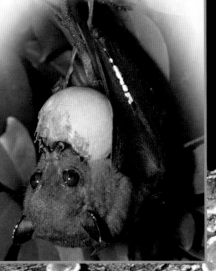

OUT OF THE SHADOWS The ghost bat is vulnerable due to disturbance of its cave roost sites by mining and tourism. Named for its pale appearance, it is also called the false vampire bat from the mistaken belief that it laps blood from larger animals.

COMPETITION FOR NEST SITES

Tree holes are a vital resource for many woodland bats, which use them for daytime roosts and as breeding sites. A shortage of suitable holes – for example, due to the practice of removing old or rotten trees that usually have more cavities and crevices – can be a major factor limiting bat populations. Bats also face stiff competition for holes from animals such as squirrels, tree rats and woodpeckers. Eurasian starlings (right) have become much more common in the last 50 years due to the spread of urban areas, and they often oust bats such as noctules from their holes.

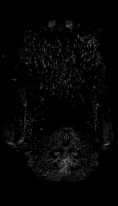

RAPID RECOVERY
Captive breeding has boosted numbers of the Rodrigues flying fox to over 3,000, an increase of 30 times in as many years.

in its home area straddling the border of Thailand and Myanmar (Burma).

CHANGING PERCEPTIONS

Since the 1970s, bats have slowly been recovering from their bad press, and now they are increasingly seen as fascinating, sociable mammals that deserve conservation. There is also a greater awareness that some fruit bats play an important part in pollinating flowers, and that insectivorous bats can help to control agricultural pests.

Bats have benefited in other ways, too. Most species roost by day (and, in

temperate regions, hibernate through the winter) in tree holes, caves, old mines and roof spaces of buildings, protected from extremes of weather and predators. Although this behavior makes them vulnerable to human disturbance, bats and their roosts are now protected by law in a growing number of countries, and they are also being helped by the erection of artificial "bat boxes."

habit of lapping blood from livestock can spread diseases such as rabies. In fact, bats themselves may suffer from the spread of certain new diseases. The Solomon flying fox's population fell from 50,000 to nearer 14,000 in just 10 years during the 1990s due to an infection brought to the Solomon Islands by imported domestic animals. Its small range made it very vulnerable to this kind of threat.

The tiny bumblebee bat – another restricted-range species and the world's smallest mammal – is under threat from deforestation and armed conflict

GROUND FEEDER
The greater mouse-eared bat mostly hunts on the wing, but also searches for prey on the forest floor. It is threatened across its entire European range

Prosimians Primates

An ancient group of mammals, the prosimians include the lemurs of Madagascar, bush babies and pottos of Africa, and Asian lorises. Like their fellow primates, monkeys and apes, most species live in trees and rely on forests for survival.

PRIMITIVE PRIMATES

Prosimians are closely related to the monkeys and apes, but they have more primitive features such as a simpler jawbone design and teeth (the word "prosimian" means "before apes").

Another important difference is their dog-like snout and superior sense of smell. Except for a few lemurs, they are nocturnal, with large eyes and excellent night vision. There are about 85 species of prosimians, although some authorities also place the eight species of huge-eyed tarsiers from Southeast Asia within this group.

By far the greatest problem facing prosimians today is forest destruction. However, bush babies (galagos) and pottos are mostly of low conservation concern, so are not discussed here.

ACROBATIC LIFESTYLE

Madagascar's lemurs make up slightly more than half of all prosimian species. Over the past 30 million years, they have evolved to fill a wide variety of ecological niches on this island, which elsewhere are usually filled by various types of monkeys or birds. Some lemurs never leave the high forest canopy, while others occupy lower levels of the forest or may forage on the ground. All lemurs are acrobatic, with lithe bodies and long, dextrous limbs.

Several lemurs are poorly known or have very restricted ranges, with some scientists speculating that, as more research is undertaken, up to 20 new species may be described over the next few decades. For example, in 1982 biologists in northeast Madagascar discovered a new species – the golden-crowned sifaka. Confined to a tiny enclave of hillside rainforest, it is one of the world's rarest primates.

HANGING AROUND
The indri is an endangered day-active lemur found on Madagascar's east coast, where the rainforest is so fragmented that it can barely sustain viable populations.

FRAGMENTED HABITAT

Sifakas, named for the sound of their barking calls, are also known as leaping lemurs. Verreaux's sifaka bounds with huge leaps among the unique "spiny

FAMILY AFFAIR Most lemurs, including these ring-tailed lemurs, live in groups dominated by females. "Ring-tails" are at risk from deforestation and hunting.

DANCING SIFAKA Verreaux's sifaka hurries between the thorny trees of its arid habitat using a rather ungainly sideways hopping motion, arms aloft. As with other species of lemur, its infants hitch a ride on their mother's back.

thicket" habitat of thorny didier trees in the arid south of Madagascar. It is vulnerable due to habitat destruction – its thickets are cleared for firewood and charcoal production and to make way for commercial forestry, leaving small, fragmented areas that are at risk from fire. The same problem affects many other lemurs, which increasingly are hemmed in to small pockets of habitat surrounded by useless barren hillsides or agricultural land.

GHOST OF THE FOREST

The strangest prosimian is surely the aye-aye. Its wide eyes, pointed ears and thin, bony fingers lend it a goblin-like appearance. On each hand the middle

DEFORESTATION

Cut adrift from Africa 65 million years ago, Madagascar developed a unique range of wildlife, including lemurs, in total isolation from the rest of the world. Around 150,000 of the plant and animal species in this evolutionary hothouse live nowhere else. Yet this amazing ecological richness is at risk because Madagascar is one of the world's poorest countries, and its exploding human population places huge pressure on natural resources. Over 90 percent of its virgin forest has been lost to logging, mining and agriculture.

finger is especially lengthy. This is used to tap trunks and branches and then, after the aye-aye has gnawed the bark with its rodent-style teeth, to winkle out grubs. Filling the ecological role of woodpeckers, the aye-aye was believed extinct until 1957, when it was refound in the island's northwest and east. Nocturnal, solitary and with a natural low population density, the aye-aye is known mainly from its large stick nests and eerie nighttime calls – sounds that local people associate with evil spirits, leading to the species' persecution.

ISLAND HOPES

Conservation organizations have targeted more than 100 Madagascan hotspots that harbor lemurs, as well as rare birds, reptiles and fish, aiming to double the island's protected area network in 25 years. Ecotourism to protected zones is growing rapidly, boosting the local economy and helping people to appreciate the value of their native wildlife. There are also several lemur captive breeding programmes.

MEDICINE THREAT The slender loris is caught for the exotic pet trade and to supply body parts used in Chinese medicine. Its large eyes are adapted to hunting insects at night.

ASIAN PROSIMIANS

Lorises are smallish prosimians that move stealthily through the forest at night, occasionally grabbing an insect, lizard or other small creature, and also feasting on buds, fruits and birds' eggs. They live alone or in pairs, and by day sleep in a tree hole or snug leaf nest. As well as being affected by forest clearance, lorises such as the slow and the slender loris are hunted for their body parts, which are ingredients in Chinese medicine. Their plight is overshadowed by that of more photogenic Southeast Asian species such as the orangutan and tiger. But lorises, together with thousands of other species, benefit hugely from the efforts to establish protected rainforest reserves for those better-known mammals.

BUSHMEAT TARGET
Many mandrills are destined
for the cooking pot – a tragic
end for the world's largest
monkey. Their fearsome
teeth, used in threat displays,
provide no defense against
determined human hunters.

Monkeys Primates

More than 240 of the 350 different primates are monkeys, and most are declining. The great majority live in the tropics, where their treetop ways of life place them at extreme risk from one of biodiversity's greatest perils – rainforest destruction.

OLD AND NEW

There are two main groups of monkeys: Old World and New World. They are distinguished not only by their world range, but by anatomical differences, particularly nose shape. Across the Asian, African and American tropics, more than half of all monkey species are seriously suffering, mainly at the hands of loggers who clear forests for lumber and then turn the land over to crops, settlement or livestock farming.

MONKEY BUSINESS

Old World monkeys face another grave threat – tens of thousands are killed for meat each year. The bushmeat trade is worst in West Africa, especially in war-torn countries, where poverty drives people to kill monkeys to feed their family or for barter at the local market. Even bigger, aggressive species such as baboons may end up on the slab.

Monkeys are caught alive for sale as pets, and some species, such as the rhesus macaque, are trapped to supply research laboratories. A more unusual threat for primates is hunting for their fur coats; this affects the snub-nosed monkey of mountains in China and Africa's black-and-white colobus.

UPS AND DOWNS

Conservation efforts to save monkeys focus on protecting habitat, especially rainforest, and captive breeding. The golden lion tamarin is a notable success story. Since the 1960s, this dimunutive, flame-maned species has been bred in several zoos worldwide, with nearly 200 released back into the wild in Brazil's Atlantic coastal forests by 2005.

Confusingly, in spite of the risk of future extinctions, the number of monkey speciesis going up, not down. Sometimes what was thought to be one species is now known, due to genetic studies and more detailed field observations, to be two or more.

ZANZIBAR RED COLOBUS Huge areas of forest on Zanzibar have been cut down for lumber, development and farming, pushing numbers of this monkey below 1,500.

ORPHANED BABIES

Many young monkeys are orphaned when they are caught for the pet trade or their parents are killed for bushmeat. The lucky ones, such as this baby mustached monkey, end up being cared for. However, there often is little hope for their eventual release. Monkeys have extended parental care and complex social relationships within and between families, and this is very difficult to recreate in captivity and "teach" to orphans. Humans can help to a point, but once a monkey's family life is disrupted, its ability to function in the wild is uncertain.

CLINGING TO SURVIVAL Like several other New World monkeys, the woolly spider monkey has a prehensile (gripping) tail. Critically endangered, it is down to the last few hundred in the wild.

Gibbons Primates

No primates are more acrobatic than gibbons, which perform death-defying leaps through the trees and feed, sleep, mate and give birth high in the forest canopy. All gibbons live in Southeast Asia, where they face growing threats, yet many aspects of their biology, lifestyle and habits are still not known.

COLORATION In several gibbons, the sexes may be different colors. This pileated gibbon is a female – adult males have totally black fur. Considered vulnerable, pileated gibbons occur in Thailand, Cambodia and Laos, where their numbers have crashed due to habitat loss.

THE LESSER APES

Like the great apes, the gibbons, or lesser apes, are tailless primates with grasping hands and feet. They belong to a single family, Hylobatidae, which means "dwellers in the trees."

According to different authorities, the number of species in the gibbon family varies from nine to 15 or even more. These forms probably all arose from a single ancestral species within the past few million years. Changing climates and sea levels altered the map of Southeast Asia, varying the pattern of islands and habitable forests. In this moving patchwork, different gibbon populations adapted to the local conditions, an evolutionary process known as geographic speciation.

EFFORTLESS SWINGING

The gibbons' main way of moving is by brachiation, or arm-swinging. Each hand has four long fingers that arch together like a hook, with the thumb set low on the side of the palm; the knuckles touch the ground if standing upright. A gibbon reaches forward for branches using alternate arms and gains momentum by swinging its body like a traveling pendulum, making brachiation a very energy-efficient way to move. It is impressive to watch, too, as the gibbon's handholds may be as much as 10 feet (3 m) apart.

LIFE IN THE TREES

Gibbons are mostly herbivorous, eating fruits, leaves, flowers and buds, along with some insects, grubs, birds' eggs, honey and occasional small vertebrates such as tree lizards. Their dependence on native trees puts them at grave risk from logging and the encroachment of agriculture and palm oil plantations into forests throughout Southeast Asia.

Another hazard stems from gibbons' breeding system and slow reproductive rate. Most gibbons are monogamous. The dominant female and male in each family forge a strong bond and raise their offspring for 14 to 18 months in the group's home range – which extends up to 125 acres (50 ha) in the case of the largest species, the siamang. A family's ties are reinforced by a range of loud calls, which echo across the canopy, mainly at dawn and dusk.

MIGRANT HUNTERS

Hunting for bushmeat affects some species of gibbon, such as the critically endangered crested, or concolor, gibbon and the white-handed, or lar, gibbon. Gibbon meat is consumed in China and gibbon bones are also ground into a traditional Chinese medicine, which is said to ease rheumatic and arthritic pain. Much of the hunting is the work of incomers who specialize in the job

TAKING IT EASY During the heat of the day, gibbons rest on a big branch or propped up against the trunk. Pictured is the agile gibbon, whose Sumatran population is in freefall.

VANISHING FORESTS

Deforestation, seen here in Borneo, hits gibbon populations very hard. Gibbons are so arboreal (tree-living) that some individuals hardly touch the ground through their entire lives. They cannot cross extensive clear-cut areas and families require large territories, rarely thriving in small, isolated fragments of forest. Displaced groups end up fighting over whatever poor habitat remains, and suitably tall sleeping trees are often in short supply as loggers tend to take the big trees first.

CANOPY LIVING A forest's sunlit upper layers provide gibbons, such as this Javan gibbon, with most of their food. They forage in bursts of activity, after dawn and in late afternoon.

and also sell the orphaned babies as pets. Logging roads give them easier access to the forest. Local people tend to respect forest wildlife, including the gibbons with their close-knit family life.

CRISIS IN JAVA

The silvery, or Javan, gibbon, the only species found on the island of Java, is now a critically endangered species. It has been protected since 1924, but law enforcement is difficult as swathes of rainforest are removed and increasing human populations create rising pressure on the land. In common with other gibbons, it makes a spectacular zoo exhibit and is bred in captivity, although there are fewer than a dozen breeding pairs worldwide.

A recent report revealed that Javan gibbon numbers are higher than previously thought, perhaps over 4,000. The study advised that local conservation measures and bigger reserves, especially in central Java, are more likely to save the species than captive breeding programs in centers scattered around the world, notably in Perth, Australia, and Santa Clarita, California.

KING OF THE SWINGERS Gibbons, such as this white-handed gibbon, have long, dextrous limbs and flexible joints. Many youngsters are caught for sale as "comical" pets, especially in Thailand.

Great Apes Primates

Chimpanzees, gorillas and orangutans are almost at the point of no return, so the extinction of our closest living relatives is a real and terrible prospect. Some scientists predict that great apes will virtually disappear from the wild by the mid-21st century.

ALMOST HUMAN

People who spend just a few minutes with great apes in their natural habitat are astonished by their similarity to ourselves. They form close-knit families, show problem-solving intelligence, use tools and (in the case of chimpanzees) even make them, plan for the future, play and learn. They occasionally wage battle with their neighbors, cherish their young and form sneaky alliances within their groups to improve their ranking. So it is tragic that these close relatives of humans are in such danger.

DIRE STRAITS

In the 1990s, genetic studies led to the recognition of two distinct orangutan species: the Sumatran and the Bornean. This brought the total number of great ape species to six, the others being the chimp, bonobo (pygmy chimpanzee) and the western and eastern gorillas. All six are classed as endangered.

Great apes are awkward to count as they are so wide-ranging and wary, but most populations appear to be falling. In particular, the Sumatran orangutan numbers under 3,000 and the eastern gorilla's mountain subspecies numbers 600 at most. Great apes breed slowly, with young depending on their mother for 3–4 years (up to 7 years in orangs), putting a brake on any recovery.

NOWHERE TO GO Captive and orphaned Bornean orangutans are being rehabilitated for release, but saving tracts of rainforest is this species' only long-term conservation solution.

AFRICAN APES

Chimps, bonobos and gorillas live in parts of West, Central and East Africa, a highly unstable area, both politically and economically. It has long been illegal to kill them and sell their meat, or capture their young, but much of their range is suffering from guerrilla warfare and lawlessness. This makes enforcement difficult and also causes terrible human poverty, which worsens the trade in bushmeat (carcass parts are openly on sale at many markets) and

BONOBO
Unlike other great apes, bonobos do not yet have any self-sustaining captive populations, and the only protected part of their small range is Salonga National Park in the heart of the Congo basin, Democratic Republic of Congo.

GORILLA GROUP Mountain gorillas may be the rarest kind of great ape, but they are also valuable earners of tourist revenue, ensuring a high level of protection compared to the rest of their family.

TOOL USER The intelligence and learning skills of chimpanzees are second only to human beings. This unfortunately makes them irresistible to unscrupulous pet traders, collectors and zoo owners.

accelerates the rate of deforestation as desperate people try to settle new land. Baby apes are caught as exotic pets or for illegal commercial use, which invariably causes the death of the mother as she tries in vain to save her infant. Some African apes, especially gorillas, are also killed as "trophies."

ORANGS IN PERIL

Restricted to fast-disappearing forests on the islands of Borneo and Sumatra, orangutans are probably in even worse trouble. Their numbers are plummeting, and some experts estimate viable wild populations could be gone by 2020. Habitat loss is horrendous as yet more forest is cleared for rice paddies, oil-palm plantations and other cash crops or for commercial logging. The present level of legal protection of both the orangutans and their habitat, even in national parks, is insufficient and the laws are often ignored. There is a flourishing illicit trade in baby orangutans to supply disreputable zoos and pet dealers. It is thought that the overall losses could be as high as three orangutans per day – every day.

SILVERBACK
Poaching driven by poverty, civil unrest and corruption is the worst threat facing the western lowland gorilla. The individual pictured here is a mature male, or silverback.

Anteaters & Relatives Xenarthra

The xenarthrans, or "strange-jointed" mammals, include three main families – sloths, armadillos and anteaters. These fascinating creatures look very different from each other, but they share an unusual backbone and all have specialized diets. Some are in dire need of conservation due to human persecution and habitat loss.

UNUSUAL ANATOMY

What makes the 30 or so species of xenarthrans stand out is the atypical design of the joints between the vertebrae of their lower backbone, or spinal column. They were formerly placed in a group called the edentates. This means "toothless," but only the anteaters truly have no teeth.

On the outside, however, the long-snouted anteaters, tree-climbing sloths and shuffling, armor-plated armadillos look totally unrelated. They also have very different habitats and behavior, although they are all fussy eaters in their own separate ways.

ALL-AMERICAN SPECIES

The xenarthrans occur only in the New World, with most species in South and Central America. Several species are a familiar sight, particularly the nine-banded armadillo, which ranges through much of Latin America into the southern United States. Others are classed as vulnerable, including the tree-preferring southern tamandua, or lesser anteater, and the giant anteater. Both are at risk of habitat clearance

UPWARDLY MOBILE The southern tamandua is a fast climber thanks to its sharp claws and gripping tail. As farming eats into its savanna and forest habitat, it faces the twin dangers of a shrinking range and increased persecution.

UNLOVED GIANT

By far the largest armadillo, at 5 feet (1.5 m) long and up to 110 pounds (50 kg), the giant armadillo is in decline across its wide range, from Venezuela to Argentina. Many farmers kill it for its meat and body plates, and because of the belief that it raids crops. It actually eats ants and termites, but its tunnels do cause damage.

BIG NOSE
Giant anteaters were once plentiful in South America's grassy plains, but are increasingly vulnerable to hunting and habitat damage. They use their incredibly long snout and tongue to fish ants and termites from their nests.

as pampas (grasslands) and scattered open woodlands are cleared for crops and livestock.

TASTY FLESH

The giant anteater and the armadillos are generally ground-living and walk slowly, so make easy targets for hunters with guns or dogs. Their meat is prized as a traditional delicacy. In addition, these less mobile xenarthrans are common victims of fast-moving "slash-and-burn" fires set to remove scrub and shrubland to create farmland.

Considered a valuable trophy, the giant anteater is also killed for its fur and long claws – adapted for ripping open termite mounds – which are used for decorative items such as necklaces and bracelets. Similarly, the armadillo's bony armor plates and leathery skin represent a cash crop for the tourist trade, being fashioned into baskets, containers, bags and utensils.

TROUBLE IN THE TREES

Apart from the giant anteater, the other three species of anteaters regularly forage in the branches, and all four species of sloths are entirely tree-living. These xenarthrans are

PROTECTIVE ARMOR The three-banded armadillo rolls up into an impenetrable ball when menaced. Sadly, its bony plates – and delicious meat – make it attractive to hunters.

seriously at risk from deforestation for lumber extraction, agriculture and charcoal production.

Sloths are famed for their extreme slowness. They hang upside down with their large, hook-like clawed limbs, leisurely chewing leaves, buds, flowers and fruits. An individual may remain in the same tree for days, and come down to the ground perhaps just once a week, to defecate or cross a clearing.

When loggers turn up with their noisy chainsaws, sloths are usually the last animals to flee. Some of the more enlightened tree-fellers allow wildlife representatives to capture the sloths carefully and take them away for relocation. But sloth meat, like that of anteaters and armadillos, is a handy dish, and sloths still hanging on to felled trees may well end up in the pot. Some sloth body parts are used in local medicines. Orphaned young sloths that are too small to bother cooking might be given to children as pets. But when the novelty wears off the hapless young sloth is abandoned to its fate.

MANED SLOTH This endangered species has been decimated by the clearance of Brazil's coastal forests. It has a few strongholds in protected reserves.

RESCUE EFFORT
All remaining bushman hares live on private land, so efforts to save this species rely on the cooperation of farmers. They are encouraged to set aside areas for the hares.

Rabbits & Hares Lagomorpha

One in four of all rabbit and hare species are in danger, mostly from hunting and habitat damage. Yet the abundant European rabbit has become one of the world's most destructive animals. Widely introduced, it wrecks the local plants and wildlife.

LEAPING MAMMALS

Sometimes mistakenly called rodents, rabbits and hares belong to a separate mammal order of around 80 species. Its name, Lagomorpha, means "leaping form" and refers to the long, powerful hind legs typical of the group. Also in this order are pikas, or conies, which resemble dwarf rabbits with short ears. Most lagomorphs prefer open habitats such as grasslands, scrub and hillsides, but a few live in forests.

Rabbits and hares, like rodents, are much-hunted herbivores that rely on incredible alertness, impressive speed and a rapid breeding rate to survive their natural predators. They have long been hunted by people, too, who value their fur and rich, gamy meat. But in the past century there have been many added threats, including predation by feral cats and dogs and loss of habitat. This has made a few species extinct and has pushed several others to the brink.

DOWN IN THE VALLEYS

One species under great threat is the critically endangered bushman hare, also known as the riverine rabbit. In the past 50 years it has lost more than two-thirds of its specialized habitat in the south-central Karoo, South Africa. It depends on ribbon-like seasonal floodplains along narrow river valleys in this otherwise arid region, and many of the plains have been ploughed for crops or grazed by livestock. Not only do the cattle graze grasses to the ground, thus accelerating a process of desertification, they also remove scrub, which exposes the hares to extra predation.

RAPID BREEDING The release of European rabbits in Australasia was a fatal error. In the absence of natural enemies, the fast-breeding rabbits could build a vast population, whose feeding activities transformed the landscape.

In the Great Basin of the southwestern U.S., another specialized lagomorph, the pygmy rabbit, is under pressure. This diminutive species relies on a few species of sagebrush for more than 90 percent of its food, as well as for shelter. Such a highly restricted diet has made it vulnerable to habitat degradation by poor livestock management, wildfires and deliberate land clearance.

MOUNTAIN RABBITS

The lagomorphs of upland regions are generally safe from the spread of farming. However, montane habitats are often fragile, and thus easily damaged by human activities. This has proved to be the case with the Amami rabbit, which lives in high-altitude old-growth forest on just two islands, Amami and Tokuno, in Japan's southern Ryukyu archipelago. The population of this unusual rabbit, with its black fur and smallish limbs, has plunged due to attacks by introduced mongooses and clear-cut logging of the forest.

Also endangered is Mexico's volcano rabbit, known locally as *zacatuche* or *teporingo*. It lives in tall bunch grass under scattered pine trees high on volcanic peaks, to the south and east of Mexico City. Although this marginal

PYGMY RABBIT The smallest of its family, this rabbit is able to fit in the palm of a hand. It has lost much of its specialized habitat through agricultural development, especially sagebrush burning to create new pasture for livestock.

landscape is not of much use to people, its proximity to the sprawling giant of the nearby metropolis inevitably puts it under pressure. The coarse grass is harvested for thatch and brushes, and feral dogs prey on the rare rabbits.

RABBIT INVASION

Several lagomorphs are considered to be farming pests, but none has caused as much devastation as the European rabbit. Native to Iberia and southern France, it has been taken to many new regions, partly to provide food and partly as a game animal for shooting. Introduced rabbits are now a huge pest in Australia and New Zealand, where they overgraze vegetation and massively disrupt the ecological balance.

Mouse-like Rodents Rodentia

It may seem curious that mice and rats deserve conserving. But just a handful of the 1,150 species in this huge group, which includes voles, hamsters, gerbils and lemmings, are true pests. A surprising number of them are close to extinction.

GNAWING TEETH

Rodents are by far the largest order of mammals, accounting for over two out of five species. Their main feature is their ever-growing, chisel-like incisors adapted for nibbling and gnawing. Rats, mice and their kin (myomorphs) make up the largest rodent group. They occur around the world in many habitats, from jungles to deserts and tundra, and some species are aquatic.

RAT VERSUS RAT

Some mouse-like rodents are pests that eat crops and stored foodstuffs, create spoilage with their droppings and urine, and cause damage by gnawing electrical cables and burrowing under floors, in walls and under roofs. But more than 100 myomorphs face grave threats. Apart from habitat loss, these rodents suffer from predation by pet and feral cats and dogs, and introduced species such as red foxes, mink, cane toads and mongooses.

Some threats come from their own kind – the black and brown rats and house mice that invariably accompany people moving to new areas. The 3-pound (1.4 kg) Malagasy giant rat, a rabbit-sized species from Madagascar, is under intense pressure from marauding packs of introduced black rats that compete for its food and kill it and its young.

DISTURBED SLEEP

Changing agricultural and forestry practices affect numerous mouse-like rodents. The garden, hazel and edible dormice of Europe prefer hedgerows, copses and woods, and are well known

ISLAND RARITY Now extinct on mainland Australia, the greater stick-nest rat lives only on Franklin Island, off the coast. Its distinctive nests were all too often wrecked by cats, foxes or cattle trampling.

DOMESTIC PET Familiar around the world as a pet, the golden hamster is endangered in the wild. Its range in western Asia is under threat from periodic droughts and exhausted soils caused by overintensive farming.

for passing the winter in hibernation. Removing ancient hedges and planting fast-growing lumber removes the native trees that provide food, sheltering holes and hibernation sites for these dormice. Again, there are dangers from domestic cats and various other introduced carnivores. Once a sleeping dormouse is discovered and disturbed, then even if the predator loses interest and leaves, the unlucky dormouse is likely to perish.

FRUITS OF THE FOREST Garden dormice are active only from May to September, feeding up before they hibernate. Their numbers are falling in much of northern Europe.

INTENSIVE AGRICULTURE

Modern farming methods have demolished populations of harvest mice in Eurasia and North America. Sprayed chemical weedkillers and pesticides effectively create an "agri-desert" with few insects, wildflower seeds and shoots for the mice to eat, and these toxins accumulate in the rodents' bodies, too. At harvest time, giant, fast-moving combine harvesters give the mice almost no time to escape to safety, and many mice and nests are destroyed.

VICTIM OF PROGRESS
The Eurasian harvest mouse thrives in small, traditionally managed grain fields, so has declined steadily since new, intensive farming methods spread after World War II.

Squirrel-like Rodents Rodentia

Not all squirrel-like rodents live in trees. Ground squirrels such as marmots and prairie dogs are burrowers, chinchillas brave icy mountains and beavers spend much of their time in water. Many dangers, particularly deforestation, hunting and intensive farming, threaten this charismatic group.

WHISKERS AND TAILS

About 380 species belong to the seven families of sciuromorphs, or "squirrel-shaped" mammals. Together with the mice and their relatives (see pp. 70–71) and the cavy-like species, they make up the huge rodent order, which represents over 40 percent of all mammals.

Sciuromorphs have several features in common, including long, sensitive whiskers and well-furred tails, as well as the long, gnawing incisors shared by all rodents. Some of them are well known, such as gophers, chipmunks and North American gray squirrels, which achieve pest status in many areas. But more than 30 species are at the other population extreme, varying from rare to critically endangered.

RED PERIL

The Eurasian red squirrel ranges across Europe and Asia, feeding on nuts, seeds, fruits, bark and sap. In parts of Europe, especially England, it has been displaced by the larger gray squirrel, introduced from eastern North America, and it is now placed in the vulnerable category. The reasons for this shift include not only the gray's superior strength, aggression and dietary adaptability, but also changes in how woodland is managed. One solution is to cull gray squirrels that encroach into its strongholds.

VULNERABLE LEAPER

Deforestation is the major threat faced by most species of tree squirrels, especially in the tropics.

SQUIRREL RIVALS
Eurasian red squirrels cannot compete with introduced American gray squirrels. Their numbers crash whenever this alien invader spreads into their native woodland or forest.

GRACEFUL GLIDES Despite its name, the Scandinavian flying squirrel is in fact just a glider, using a flap of skin between its front and rear legs. It prefers forests with a mix of old trees.

One of the largest, with a nose-tail length of almost 3 feet (1 m), is the Indian giant squirrel. It can leap more than 16 feet (5 m) and consumes various foods from bark and buds to birds' eggs and grubs. Its populations have shrunk by an estimated one-third in recent years due mainly to forest clearance and fragmentation, worsened by hunting for its meat and luxurious fur.

GLIDING MAMMAL

Another threatened tree squirrel, the Russian or Scandinavian flying squirrel, is an attractive rodent of northern conifer forests. Its gliding skill helps it avoid ground predators and having to cross snowbound clearings. But it is declining across its wide range, partly due to altered habitats as different patterns of tree species are planted, and to logging before the trees are old enough to offer the squirrel hollow cavities for nesting.

GROUND SQUIRRELS

The main home of ground squirrels is grassland, so the conversion of this fertile, open landscape to farming has put a

DEMAREST'S HUTIA Thanks to its tree-climbing ability, this Cuban species is less critical than ground-living hutias. But its large size makes it a tempting target for poachers.

SILKY COAT Chinchillas are captured for their meat and, above all, their supersoft fur, which keeps them warm at high altitudes. They live in colonies of as many as 100, surviving on a meager diet of grasses and leaves.

few species in real danger. In several parts of the world, burrowing squirrels such as gophers and prairie dogs have been the subject of mass eradication campaigns by farmers and ranchers. The animals' tunnels undermine the soil, banks and irrigation ditches, causing subsidence and potholes. Also their feeding destroys both crops and root systems. The black-tailed prairie dog, once present in vast numbers across North America's Great Plains, is now classed at lower risk.

CAVY RODENTS

Alongside the squirrel-like rodents are the 190 or so mainly New World species of cavy rodents, which include guinea pigs, hutias, chinchillas and porcupines. Various members of this group are threatened, too. Chinchillas, so popular as a pet, are vulnerable in the wild, surviving only in a small region of the rocky Andean foothills and coastal mountains of Chile. Hutias are large, vole-like rodents unique to Caribbean islands. Heavy hunting and urban development mean most species are endangered or already extinct.

The European Beaver

Found in scattered locations across Central and Northern Europe, this rodent was formerly much more widespread. Hunting for its prized fur and for "castoreum oil" from its anal gland (used as an aphrodisiac) drove it close to extinction in the mid-19th century. More modern threats are those facing many wetland animals – water pollution, the draining and reclamation of marshes for farming, and water abstraction for irrigation and human use. Several countries now have beaver conservation programs, such as reintroduction projects along the upper Rhine, in Sweden and in Britain.

NATURAL HEAVYWEIGHT Larger than its American counterpart, the European beaver weighs up to 77 pounds (35 kg), making it the second biggest rodent after the capybara of South America. Its thick, glossy fur is susceptible to pollution: detergents that leach into rivers destroy its waterproofing oils.

DAM BUILDER In parts of its range, as here in Sweden, the European beaver constructs stick-and-mud dams to create a shallow pool for its "house," called a lodge. In other areas, especially the lowlands of Central Europe, it digs a simple bank burrow. Ironically, human-made dams are one of the threats this species faces.

Baleen Whales Cetacea

By far the largest animals on Earth, baleen, or great, whales have long occupied the conservation spotlight. Their tragic plight after over a century of mass slaughter was recognized by the 1986 moratorium on large-scale whaling. A recovery in their populations appears to be underway, but other threats have since emerged.

FILTER FEEDERS

The 12 species of baleen whales make up the smallest group in the Cetacea (whales, dolphins and porpoises). They have unique feeding equipment: large comb- or brush-like straps of a springy "whalebone" material hanging from the upper jaw. Called baleen plates, these almost have the consistency of plastic.

To feed, a baleen whale opens wide, gulps a vast mouthful of water, and squeezes its chin and cheeks to push the water out through the plates. The plates' fringed borders trap small food items such as shrimp-like krill, little fish or squid.

HOW MANY WHALES?

Since the internationally agreed ban on whaling, it is believed that baleen whale populations are mostly stabilized or gradually recovering. But this is by no means certain. For example, stocks of the huge sei whale, the last species to be heavily exploited, remain in doubt.

Moreover, estimating the numbers and distribution of whales is notoriously complex and far from accurate.

Modern technology such as satellite tracking and radio beacons helps, but data collection still relies on sporadic (and not always reliable) sightings from trawlers, cargo-carriers and

BREACHING
Humpbacks breach often, perhaps to rid their skin of parasites or as a form of sonic display. Tours to see this vulnerable species are popular around the world.

passenger ships, and is complicated by the migrations of most species. Recent estimates for the blue whale, the world's largest animal at up to 150 tons and 100 feet (30 m) long, range very widely, from 4,000 up to 15,000.

COLLISION COURSE

Most baleen whales are considered to be endangered. The North Atlantic right whale is critical – its numbers are probably below 300 and might never recover. One projection puts its extinction within 200 years from now. Like the North Pacific right whale, southern right whale and bowhead,

it swims slowly at the surface when feeding, so runs the gauntlet of collision with propellers and ship hulls. Also it tends to stay near to the coast, where there is more boat traffic.

The gray whale faces even greater risk from coastal water traffic, being an even more inshore species. Its long journey up the west coast of North America to the cold, food-rich Bering and Chukchi seas for summer feeding, then back to warm Baja California for breeding in winter, may clock up a maximum of 12,500 miles (20,000 km) – the longest migration of any mammal.

Recovery is held back by the whales' slow breeding rate. Typically, a female baleen whale does not mature until at least five years old, and has a calf every two to three years. Decades may pass before any upward trend in numbers.

THE WHALING DEBATE

Despite the ban on commercial whaling, killing under license still occurs for "scientific research." This is controversial, because conservationists argue that a few long-standing whaling nations abuse their privilege. Limited traditional kills by age-old methods are also permitted in a few areas, such as Arctic Canada and Polynesia. Outright poaching takes place, too, but is rare.

MOTHER AND CALF Humpbacks migrate to tropical seas to give birth. They were heavily hunted along their migration routes – more than 100,000 were slaughtered from 1900 to 1940 in the southern hemisphere alone.

Other threats include tangling and drowning in fishing nets, and marine pollution, especially dumped industrial waste, oil spills and floating plastic debris that sticks in the digestive tract. Stocks of the baleen whales' prey are dwindling due to mechanized fishing fleets that hoover up krill and fish. Oceans are also becoming noisier, and this interferes with communication and navigation by whales, particularly the toothed species (*see* pp. 76–77).

WHALE WATCHING

A holiday highlight for many people is a whale-watching trip to see these ocean giants in their natural surroundings; here, tourists watch a gray whale in Baja California, Mexico. If managed correctly, this tourism can be carried out in an eco-friendly manner while raising funds for conservation. Most countries have regulations that prevent boats getting too close, tempting the whales with food or interfering with mothers and their calves. But not all boat operators follow the code. And for the whales, which live for 60, 80 or even 100 years, the long-term behavioral consequences of whale watching remain unknown.

TELLTALE Whales can be recognized by their "blow" and by their fluke shape as they dive, with notches or scars identifying individuals. Blue whales like the one pictured below have the largest flukes, at 20–23 feet (6–7 m) across.

Toothed Whales Cetacea

This fascinating group of mammals includes dolphins, porpoises and some whales. They live in both seas and fresh water, and vary from the tiny vaquita porpoise to Earth's largest predator, the mighty sperm whale, which is 1,000 times heavier.

ACTIVE PREDATORS

There are 70 species of toothed whales, which belong to the order Cetacea together with the baleen whales. Apart from the sperm whale, they include the distinctively tusked narwhal, the beluga, or white, whale, 20 species of oceanic, deep-diving beaked whales, 30 species of oceanic dolphins, five river dolphins and six porpoises. Their common names can be confusing: the killer whale (orca) is in fact the largest member of the dolphin family.

All toothed whales are carnivorous, taking mainly fish, squid, shellfish and similar prey. Their conical, pointed teeth, which last for a lifetime, grip slippery prey with ease. Many species are highly social, hunting in groups known as pods or schools.

POLLUTED SEAS

Some toothed whales are holding their own, but as a group they share many of the problems faced by baleen whales (*see* pp. 74–75), such as competition by fishing fleets for their prey, poisonous oil spills and collisions with boats.

Chemicals and floating waste harm these whales and dolphins even far out in mid-ocean. They may suffer diseases due to a weakened immune system, caused by polluted water or through ingesting toxins in their prey. Bits of discarded plastic bags and similar items are mistaken for fish, swallowed, and block the gut, causing eventual starvation.

DEEP-SEA DIVER Sperm whales dive to the inky depths to hunt squid and octopus, staying down for up to two hours. Growing numbers are stranded on land, for reasons that remain unclear.

Thousands of the smaller toothed whales and dolphins die each year after drowning in nets set for fish (they are air-breathers, so suffocate if trapped underwater). They chase the same targets as fishing vessels, such as tuna, thus swimming straight into danger. Experiments with dolphin-friendly nets that have trapdoor-like flaps or "pingers" that give off warning sounds are helping to reduce this accidental death toll in some areas.

UNDERWATER SOUNDS

Most toothed whales socialize vocally using many different clicks and calls. They also navigate and hunt with a sophisticated echolocation system, similar to that of bats and ships' sonar. But rivers and oceans are becoming ever noisier – ship engines and marine navigation devices cause vibrations, seabed mineral prospectors detonate underwater explosions and submarine sonar sends out immensely powerful bursts of sound. All of these acoustic hazards could affect the behavior of whales and dolphins. Internal injuries caused by underwater sound energy might explain why increasing numbers are washed up dead on beaches.

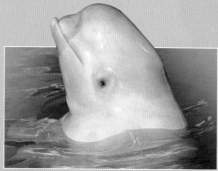

WHITE WHALE In the St. Lawrence estuary of eastern Canada, a toxic cocktail of industrial chemicals accumulates in the beluga's body, potentially affecting its breeding. Nicknamed the sea canary, it is famous for its eerie song.

THE VAQUITA

Measuring just 4–5 feet (1.2–1.5 m), the little vaquita porpoise is the smallest toothed whale and also has the most restricted range, at the northern end of the Gulf of California. It is in serious danger from nets set for sharks and shrimp, thought to kill 20 or more yearly. Pollution, increased boat traffic and prospecting for oil are further threats. With a declining population of perhaps fewer than 250, its future looks bleak.

RIVER DOLPHINS

The river dolphins possess extra-long, flexible, sensitive beaks suited to finding food in soft, muddy riverbeds. All five species are acutely theatened by changes to their

BUOYANCY AID
Formerly, sperm whales were hunted for their spermaceti organ, in the head, which contains a thick oil that helps their buoyancy. The oil was used as a lubricant and fuel.

RARE GLIMPSE The Chang Jiang river dolphin is wary and easily frightened, diving at the slightest provocation. This makes it hard to estimate its range or numbers.

freshwater habitat. Dams used for irrigation or hydroelectricity block the seasonal movements of the dolphins and their prey, and extraction of river water for human use or crops concentrates pollutants and reduces food supplies.

In some areas, people respect these dolphins as river cohabitants, but newcomers hunt them for their edible meat, as fish bait or as competitors for local fish stocks. Another serious danger is capture in fishing nets, while dredging and river straightening upset the local ecology. As a result, the Amazon river dolphin is vulnerable, the Ganges river dolphin is endangered and the Chang Jiang river dolphin is critical, with fewer than 100 left. Efforts to conserve the latter include attempts at captive breeding, so far unsuccessful, and setting aside a protected oxbow tributary of the Chang Jiang River.

NATIVE HUNTING

Traditional native, or aboriginal, hunting for toothed whales continues in some areas, with little effect on their numbers. The Inuit of the far north take narwhals and use many body parts: the raw skin is a delicacy rich in vitamins, the sinews make strong threads, the tusks are carved and the blubber is rendered for oil.

Dogs Carnivora

Domestic dogs may be our best friends, but wild members of their family, including wolves, coyotes, dingoes, foxes and jackals, are in various forms of conflict with humans. Several of these impressive carnivores could soon vanish forever.

HISTORY OF PERSECUTION

The 36 species of dogs, or canids, are placed in the order Carnivora. Largest is the gray, or timber, wolf. Long ago, it was the world's most widespread big land carnivore, ranging all around the northern regions. But the wolf's size and notorious reputation are the source of its main problem – which also, to a varying degree, affects other canids. It is persecuted for supposedly attacking humans, spreading diseases such as rabies and taking livestock. As a result of centuries of shooting, snaring and poisoning, the wolf is largely restricted to remote areas, especially mountains.

WIDE-RANGING African wild dogs wander over huge areas, so few protected reserves are big enough to contain their packs. This leads to road casualties and clashes with local farmers and villagers, although in truth these dogs rarely attack livestock.

CRITICAL SITUATIONS

Among the rarest canids are the red and Ethiopian wolves and the African wild (hunting) dog. The Ethiopian wolf

SAVING THE RED WOLF

The red wolf of southeastern North America is considered by some to be a subspecies of the gray wolf, and by others a full species in its own right. It was classed as endangered in 1967 and assumed to be extinct in the wild by the 1970s. In 1987, eight captive-bred individuals, from a founding captured group of only 14, were reintroduced to the hilly Alligator River area of North Carolina. Here they have produced an established population of more than 50. Further reintroductions have occurred in the Great Smoky Mountains. By 2005, there were about 200 red wolves.

ETHIOPIAN WOLF
Unlike its northern relatives, this wolf has a very restricted range in a specialized alpine habitat. Measures to help it include vaccinating domestic dogs to prevent them from transmitting diseases.

occupies three small areas of a high-altitude ecosystem, which have been greatly fragmented and degraded by overfarming, thereby reducing its main prey of rodents and hares. This wolf also suffers attacks by domestic and feral dogs, catches diseases such as distemper from them, and is disturbed by the droughts and human conflicts that have afflicted its homeland. Its total wild population is probably under 500, and its future, like that of human residents of the area, is desperate.

PACK HUNTERS

Most canids live in family groups, or packs, in which young of the main breeding pair (known as the alpha female and male) are raised with the help of subordinate pack members. The African wild dog shows the most extreme version of this system, and also hunts in coordinated groups. Some of the dogs pursue the prey directly, while others split away and approach from the flanks or lie in ambush.

It may be one of the world's most efficient pack hunters, but the African wild dog encounters a wide mix of hazards: damage to its savanna habitat; a reduction in wild game prey; road traffic; and persecution for taking cattle or goats. Its population numbers fewer than 5,000 – one-twentieth of that of a century ago.

BLAST THREAT In California, the endangered San Joaquin subspecies of the kit fox has been disturbed by mining and by oil and mineral prospectors, who set off explosions to locate underground reserves. Today, efforts are being made to avoid working near the foxes' dens.

CONTRASTING FORTUNES

Foxes inhabit open grassy or arid habitats the world over, and the red fox has taken the gray wolf's place as the planet's most wide-ranging land carnivore. Almost endlessly adaptable, it has now been introduced to most continents, thriving equally well in urban areas. In some places, its success threatens, by competition for food, its rarer relatives such as Ruepell's fox.

In southwestern North America, the kit and swift foxes are under increasing pressure. Grazing of farm animals on poor grasslands has removed the food and ground cover needed by their prey (mostly rodents). And more highways and vehicles mean more roadkills.

WARMING RISK Arctic foxes are locally common in polar regions, except for mainland Scandinavia, where fewer than 150 survive due to a long history of hunting. In the future, global warming may harm the species' icy environment.

Bears Carnivora

These heavyweight, mostly vegetarian carnivores have always had an uneasy relationship with people. Persecuted as crop pests and livestock raiders, they suffer, too, as circus performers and the providers of body parts for traditional medicine.

DIFFERENT DIETS

Bears are magnificent mammals with a superb sense of smell yet relatively poor eyesight and hearing. Contrary to popular opinion, only the polar bear is exclusively a meat-eater, and six other species have a varied diet. These are the brown (grizzly), American and Asiatic black, spectacled, sun and sloth bears. The final member of the bear family, the giant panda, hardly ever eats meat, consuming over 98 percent bamboo shoots, buds and leaves. Bears are a highly endangered group – only the American black bear is not at risk.

SYMBOL OF CONSERVATION

The giant panda was adopted by the World Wildlife Fund for Nature in 1961 as a worldwide symbol of conservation. It is found in the wild in a fairly small area of hilly bamboo and mixed forests in southwest China, with about 1,000

individuals spread over 25 separate populations in Szechuan, Shaanxi and Gansu provinces. Threats include the rapidly increasing human population, which requires land for settlement and farming, plus some logging. Poachers receive the death penalty, but pandas are still occasionally hunted for pelts to sell on the illegal market.

SHRINKING RANGES

The spectacled bear lives only in South America, where urban sprawl and the spread of agriculture have forced it to retreat to cloudforest refuges high in the Andes mountains, usually above 3,300 feet (1,000 m). It is very herbivorous and raids crops such as corn, which brings it into conflict with farmers. In Southeast Asia, the sun bear is also attacked for stealing crops. This is the world's most tree-living bear, and logging is fast reducing its range.

Brown bears require vast tracts of untouched wilderness, and this is why their strongholds lie in remote Siberia and Alaska. The southern brown bear subspecies found in Europe, western Asia, China and the

PANDA RESERVES The Chinese authorities have set up several breeding colonies, notably at Woolong, with around 100 young born yearly. But infant mortality is high: fewer than half of the cubs survive more than six months.

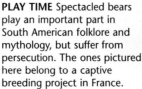

PLAY TIME Spectacled bears play an important part in South American folklore and mythology, but suffer from persecution. The ones pictured here belong to a captive breeding project in France.

rest of North America are much more susceptible to human disturbance.

With a population of perhaps 25,000, polar bears are not in any immediate danger. But in the longer term, global warming poses a serious threat. Polar bears rely on broken sea ice for resting, hunting and traveling. As ice melting patterns change and sea ice shrinks, the bears and their seal prey may be corralled into ever-smaller areas.

GRIM TRADE

In some parts of Asia, bear body parts, such as bones and the gallbladder and its bile fluid, are valued ingredients of local medicines. Asiatic black bears, in particular, are kept alive in cramped cages where it is impossible to turn around, while tubes drain out the fluids. This species' paws are also used to make a soup delicacy in countries such as Thailand and Korea. Outside protected areas, the bear is in trouble.

DANCING BEARS

The cruel entertainment of bear dancing dates back to medieval times, and still continues in parts of India. Although it has been illegal since 1972, up to 800 Asiatic black (pictured) and sloth bears are held in captivity for this purpose. They are caught as cubs, thus depleting wild numbers.

FEARS FOR THE FUTURE
Polar bears depend on a cold Arctic climate and extensive sea ice. Global warming is predicted to cause a 30 percent fall in their numbers over the next 35–50 years.

Mustelids & Relatives Carnivora

The mustelids are a huge group of lethally efficient carnivores with viciously sharp teeth and an acute sense of smell, found all over the world. They include stoats, mink, ferrets, polecats, badgers, otters and their kin. Mustelids have been hunted for centuries for their luxurious pelts and their perceived nuisance as raiders of farm stock.

IMPORTANCE OF SMELL

Mustelids are the second-largest family in the mammalian order Carnivora, with around 67 species worldwide. They are mostly flexible, long-bodied, shortish-legged predatory loners with keen senses and very sharp teeth. The family ranges from the least weasel, often weighing under 5 ounces (150 g), to the powerful 30-pound (14 kg) wolverine of the far north and the 65-pound (30 kg) giant otter of the Amazon basin. All of them use their superb sense of smell to find prey, and mark their territories with strong-smelling oily musk.

SUPERSOFT FUR

Through the ages, mustelid fur has been prized above all others. It is dense, long and strong, yet soft and water-repellent, especially in the cold season. Valued most highly are the pelts of the sable,

BONE CRUSHER Wolverines have strong jaws able to crunch through frozen flesh and bone during winter scavenging. They are persecuted for killing livestock such as sheep and goats.

mink, fisher and stoat (particularly its white winter coat, or ermine). Also hunted are the yellow-throated marten, which like the sable is endangered, and the marbled polecat, now vulnerable.

In the past 30 years, the trade in wild-caught mustelid fur has declined, and instead species such as mink are farmed commercially. Even so, illegal poaching occurs in remote regions where human survival, let alone law enforcement, is very difficult. Wearing fur has become controversial in some countries, but there is sufficient demand to ensure that poaching and farming of mustelids will continue for the foreseeable future.

MULTIPLE THREATS

Mustelids are commonly trapped and poisoned (*see* panel, left) to keep their populations artificially low. Usually the targets are martens, polecats and stoats, but other species may also be hit. In Britain, for example, Eurasian badgers are being culled since they are thought to spread bovine tuberculosis

ODD ONE OUT The red panda's scientific relationships are much debated, but it is often grouped in the raccoon family, which is distantly related to mustelids. It is at risk from clearance of its Himalayan forests.

among cattle herds. Many mustelids are scavengers, so they are attracted to feed on roadkills, frequently becoming casualties themselves.

In North America in the 20th century, federal campaigns to exterminate prairie dogs (*see* pp. 72–73) pushed black-footed ferrets, which prey on nothing else, to the brink of extinction. Their numbers crashed to 30 by 1985, and they were extinct in the wild by 1987. Since then, small numbers of captive-bred ferrets have been reintroduced in Wyoming.

OTTERS' PLIGHT

Unlike the majority of mustelids, otters are semiaquatic and mostly fish-eaters. They are at the top of aquatic food chains, so are affected by waterborne pollution, which kills off their prey and causes a buildup of toxins in the predators' bodies. Other threats include excessive water abstraction and being entangled in fishing nets. The sea otter, the world's smallest marine mammal, is threatened by damage to inshore kelp beds, where it dives for shellfish and crabs. These are easily degraded by pollution, especially oil spills.

TRAPPED AS PESTS

Mustelids are sworn enemies of fishery managers, gamekeepers and poultry farmers worldwide. While it is true that these predators can be a nuisance, the losses blamed on them are probably exaggerated. Two of the chief methods by which mustelids are culled include poisoned baits and gin traps. The latter often lead to a slow death, as shown by the cruel fate of this beech marten.

Cats Carnivora

Few threatened animals capture our imagination like tigers and other big cats. But despite all the conservation funds lavished on them, several remain in dire straits. Many less well-known cats are also in trouble due to habitat loss and persecution.

STEALTHY HUNTERS

The world's 38 different cats, or felids, show little variation in basic body design and behavior. Most cats, apart from lions and cheetahs, are loners, and most hunt by stealth, stalking their prey for a surprise attack.

Almost half of all cat species are listed as threatened to some degree. The bigger cats – especially the tiger, lion, cheetah, jaguar, leopard, snow leopard and puma (also known as the cougar or mountain lion) – are persecuted through fear. They suffer revenge attacks for livestock kills, too, although often other animals may be to blame, such as feral dog packs.

Many cats prefer forests or grasslands, where they use their camouflaged coats and stalking skills to greatest effect. But as these habitats vanish, to be replaced by fields of crops, grazing livestock and settlements, cats inevitably come into closer contact with people. And as cats need large home ranges, they tend to roam outside protected areas.

JUNGLE CAT

Since the 1970s, the tiger has had a double image: it has been perceived as both a dangerous man-eater and a rare species in serious trouble. So, despite protection laws and official sanctuaries, such as Ranthambhore in India and Chitwan in Nepal, the species is still poached and persecuted. Its saleable body parts include the bones, ground into traditional medicines or carved into dagger handles; the beautiful

TRAPPED FOR FUR After ocelot populations were decimated by hunting for fur, the margay (above) was one of the next small cats to be targeted. It suffered greatly in the 1970s and 1980s, but is now protected in most areas.

striped coat; the teeth and claws, prized as trophies; and the internal organs, again used in medicines. These trades are so lucrative that wildlife experts in Asia have been bribed to overestimate tiger numbers, hoping that the cats will be subject to looser regulations and reduced anti-poaching patrols.

Today, five of the eight known tiger subspecies remain (the Caspian, Javan and Bali tigers have already gone).

SPECIES WORTH SAVING African lions are a major cultural icon for Africa and one of the continent's most valuable ecotourism species. But as with all other big cats, the cooperation of local people is vital to safeguard its future.

ENDANGERED FELINE
The Bengal tiger is the most numerous tiger subspecies, with perhaps 3,000–4,000 in the wild. But even in the 21 tiger reserves in India, it is not safe and still declining.

Largest and rarest is the magnificent Siberian tiger of eastern Asia, of which a 2005 survey found just 350–400 wild individuals. Smallest is the Sumatran tiger, with a fragmented, fast-declining population of fewer than 500.

OTHER BIG CATS

The tiger is not alone. The clouded leopard of Southeast Asia, for example, is threatened by loss of its rainforest habitat and by hunting for its fur, meat, teeth and bones. The elusive snow leopard of the Himalayas and Central Asia is endangered due to the loss of its mammal prey to human hunters and because agriculture is encroaching into the lowland corridors it requires for mating trips and dispersal of young.

African lions are classed as vulnerable and often still eradicated for attacks on farm stock, but occur across a wide range. By contrast, the Asiatic lion subspecies survives only in the Gir Forest Reserve area of northern India. Critically endangered, its precarious population is around 350, and the whole reserve area is under pressure from surrounding farmland and water pollution. In 2005, seven Asiatic lions mysteriously died from poisoning – a severe setback for such a rare species.

SMALLER CATS

The small cats may have lower profiles, but many are equally at risk. Species such as the ocelot, Geoffroy's cat and margay, all from South America, were heavily hunted for their beautifully patterned coats. Trade in their body parts is usually now illegal, although occasional poaching continues. In the 21st century the chief danger to these and other small cats is habitat loss, especially rainforest deforestation.

LACK OF PREY Eurasian lynx inhabit remote forests of Scandinavia, Russia and Central Asia. Overhunting has depleted numbers of deer, their main prey, causing lynx to decline in many areas. Roadkills are another problem.

Seals & Sea Lions Pinnipedia

Despite the outrage caused by graphic images of their endearing pups being brutally clubbed, seals and sea lions are still widely persecuted. Additional dangers to these agile swimmers include toxic waste and drowning in fishing nets.

LAKE SEAL With a population of just 270 in 2004, the Saimaa ringed seal is one of the rarest seals in the world. Named after the lake in Finland that is its sole home, it has a viable future only because of intensive conservation.

FIN FEET

Pinnipeds (the name literally means "fin feet") include 33 species of seals and sea lions, plus the walrus. In general, seals lack ear flaps, and their rear flippers, which face backward, provide the main thrust for swimming. By contrast, sea lions possess small external ear flaps and swim mainly with their front flippers. On land they can raise the front of their body on these flippers, folding their rear flippers underneath the body to waddle. Seals do not use their flippers out of water, so have to hump or squirm along.

All pinnipeds are wholly carnivorous, taking prey such as fish, squid, krill, shellfish and crabs, depending on the species. Some hunt marine reptiles and mammals – the powerful 1-ton Steller's sea lion preys on sea otters and smaller seals. Pinnipeds haul out onto land to rest and breed, choosing quiet beaches, mudflats, rocky shores or ice floes. For this reason, most species live inshore, although elephant seals may stay in the open ocean for many weeks.

MARINE POLLUTION

Like other coastal animals, seals and sea lions are affected by the growing problem of marine pollution, and this has many forms. It includes oil spills, human sewage, diesel fuel from ships, and floating bits of plastic garbage that are mistaken for fish and eaten, causing great pain

CALL OF THE WILD
The New Zealand sea lion has the smallest range of the world's five sea lion species, and it is also the rarest. It is a frequent victim of drowning in squid fishing nets.

SURFACE SWIMMER Most pinnipeds, such as this Galapagos sea lion, feed close to the water's surface, where they risk fatal encounters with fishing hooks, nets and longlines, and ships' propellers.

and sometimes starvation. The worst pollutants, however, are toxic chemicals from industry and agriculture, which leach into rivers and thereby reach the sea. These deadly substances enter food chains, becoming concentrated in the bodies of top predators such as seals – a process known as bioaccumulation.

Another form of pollution is fishing nets and gear, which can entangle and drown seals and sea lions, especially since the animals and people are often hunting the same shoals. Young pups suffer the most from these underwater deathtraps, perhaps because they are less experienced. Fishing bans during the pupping season are one solution, and are already helping to stall the long decline of the Saimaa ringed seal.

CULLS AND POACHING

Pinnipeds are often blamed for taking "excessive" amounts of fish, squid and krill, although the evidence that they actually affect commercial fisheries is

REMARKABLE COMEBACK The Galapagos fur seal was ruthlessly hunted in the past for its warm coat. Now it is protected by the marine park authorities and is part of a new economy on the Galapagos Islands based on ecotourism.

inconclusive. They are persecuted by fishing interests worldwide, occasionally through organized culls of pups. Such mass culls are only sanctioned for non-threatened species such as Canadian harp seals and South African fur seals, but remain controversial nevertheless. Ironically, hyperefficient fishing fleets do more lasting harm to fish stocks – and thus to seals and sea lions – than the other way around.

Certain pinnipeds are permitted to be caught for traditional uses, for example by the Inuit and Aleut people in the far north, but this activity seems to do little damage. Unregulated poaching is a different story: several rare seals are illegally killed for their meat, blubber, skins and fur, causing their populations to nosedive. There are also less practical uses for seal body parts. In Asia, the testicles of male fur seals are a valued ingredient in aphrodisiacs.

DISEASE OUTBREAKS

In biological terms, pinnipeds have many similarities to dogs, and they are susceptible to various dog-type diseases, especially distemper and brucellosis. Unusually severe outbreaks of these diseases among colonies of seals have made headline news since the 1980s. It is suspected that toxic pollutants may have weakened the seals' immune system, leaving them prone to illness. Harbor and gray seals suffered several epidemics of phocine distemper virus in the North Sea during the 1980s and 1990s, while the same disease killed more than 10,000 rare Caspian seals in just two months in 2000.

The Walrus

Unlike other pinnipeds, the walrus is almost totally hairless. It relies on an extra-thick layer of blubber (fat under the skin) to keep warm in its Arctic home. The species is safe in its Pacific range, but is declining in the Russian Arctic and the North Atlantic, where it formerly occurred as far south as Cape Cod in North America. Walruses have not recovered their original numbers or distribution since their mass slaughter during the 18th and 19th centuries. They presented a tempting and highly valuable target: the fat burns in lamps, the meat is rich, the skins make tent shelters and kayak covers, and the ivory tusks can be carved into tools, weapons and decorations.

STATUS SYMBOLS
The walrus's tusks are extra-long upper canine teeth, and reach 3 feet (1 m) in older males. Their chief function seems to be symbolic, as a sign of breeding maturity. Licensed aboriginal hunts in Canada and Alaska can sell on the tusks, and some now argue that this trade could provide a sustainable alternative to elephant ivory.

FUTURE THREATS
Walruses live in large herds, and are most at risk from hunters when huddling together on the shore or sea ice to rest or molt their skin. But in the future, oil and mineral exploration, and ice caps melting due to global warming, are likely to pose worse threats to the species.

Dugongs & Manatees Sirenia

"Sea cow" is an apt common name for these big, barrel-shaped vegetarians, found mainly in tropical seas and rivers. Sluggish and mild-mannered, they munch through beds of water plants in the shallows, where they encounter increasing hazards.

DOCILE GRAZERS

One of the smallest mammal orders, the Sirenia contains just four species. Most frequent warm, shallow coastal waters and also wander upstream into estuaries and freshwater lagoons.

The dugong occurs along most shores of the Indian Ocean and Southeast Asia, to the more northern coasts of Australia. It has relatively short front flippers and a crescentic tail, not unlike a whale's. The three manatee species are the West Indian, Amazonian and West African. Compared to the dugongs they have

relatively long fore flippers and a rounded tail. The Amazonian manatee is the only sirenian virtually confined to fresh water.

DANGERS IN THE SHALLOWS

Manatees and dugongs, or sirenians, were perhaps never very common. But with a total world population for all four species estimated at fewer than 150,000, they are now in trouble. All are vulnerable and trade in them or their body parts is restricted.

Sirenians face dangers common to many river and inshore marine species. Among the worst of these are chemical pollution, the accidental consumption of garbage items such as plastic strips, falling water levels as water is extracted for irrigation or human use, drowning in fishing nets, clearance of "untidy" waterside vegetation, and barrages and hydroelectric schemes that disrupt currents and tidal flows.

The meat, oil, hides, teeth and bones of sirenians have long been used by local peoples, and this hunting still continues, although it is mostly illegal. In particular, dugongs are killed around

SEABED FORAGING The most pessimistic forecasts suggest that dugongs may become extinct by 2030. Their numbers are declining rapidly, although the species has an important stronghold in Western Australia.

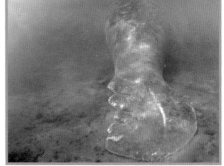

INJURED BY BOATS

A sirenian's digestive tract produces lots of gas, making its body very buoyant. Manatees and dugongs therefore tend to rest floating at the surface, and, with their laborious movements and sluggish reactions, frequently collide with vessels of all kinds, from barges to powerboats. So-called "watercraft-related mortality" is a major problem in busy waterways, especially in Florida. This photograph shows a West Indian manatee with a boat-damaged tail.

New Guinea and Amazonian manatees are caught by riverside tribespeople. The West African manatee is a meaty delicacy in Sierra Leone and Nigeria.

VALUABLE REAL ESTATE

A major problem affecting sirenians is the dramatic spread of industrial, residential and tourist developments along tropical coasts where they live. This invariably leads to much greater boat traffic, which heightens risks such as pollution by fuel and fumes, noise disturbance, and lethal strikes by hulls and propellers. Since captive breeding of sirenians is impractical, their best hope for the future will be to set aside large tracts of waterways and coastal strips as sanctuaries, such as Western Australia's Shark Bay World Heritage Site. Around 10,000 dugongs live in the Shark Bay area – more than one-tenth of the global population.

MANATEE GATHERING In general, coastal development spells disaster for sirenians. But these West Indian manatees have learned to take advantage of warm water discharged by a power plant at West Palm Beach, Florida.

OUT OF TIME
Manatees evolved over millions of years to fill a highly specialized niche in their environment. In just a few decades, their habitat has changed so much that their survival is in doubt.

Elephants Proboscidea

Until the 1990s, scientists recognized two species of elephant, but careful studies have shown that there are three – and all are in danger. Poaching for their tusks, clashes with local people and loss of habitat seriously threaten these great mammals. Often adopted as symbols of conservation, elephants are also victims of political debates about how to save them.

ONE BECOMES TWO

There are two species of elephants in Africa. The African savanna elephant is slightly larger, with a big male scaling 7 tons and standing more than 13 feet (4 m) at the shoulder. Its tusks curve forward and outward, and it prefers more open habitats. The African forest elephant is darker, with smaller, more rounded ears, and straighter, more parallel tusks. These are adaptations to moving through thick vegetation in the forests of West and Central Africa.

DOMESTICATION

Asian elephants have smaller ears and tusks than their African cousins. They occur in 13 countries – India, Nepal, Bhutan, Bangladesh, Sri Lanka, Myanmar (Burma), Thailand, Laos, Cambodia, Vietnam, China, Malaysia and Indonesia. Unlike in Africa, these elephants have long been partly domesticated for lifting and carrying heavy loads, felling and dragging timber from forests, and ceremonial duties.

MATURE MALE
Old "tuskers," like this African savanna elephant, are most at risk from poaching. As a result, long tusks are almost nonexistent in the herds of some African game reserves.

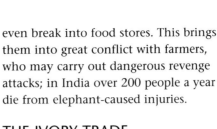

MINERAL LICK African forest elephants visit favored wetlands to ingest essential minerals, but this faithfulness to specific places can put them at risk from the guns of waiting hunters.

Since Asian elephants are not widely bred in captivity, capture for domestic work puts pressure on wild populations, which are classed as endangered.

NOT ENOUGH ROOM

Habitat encroachment is a big problem for all elephants as farmland, grazing livestock and human settlements spread. As their natural areas shrink and their traditional movement routes are blocked, elephants may cause such immense damage to the landscape that the land and its plants take years to recover. Elephants also raid crops, push through fences, destroy buildings and

even break into food stores. This brings them into great conflict with farmers, who may carry out dangerous revenge attacks; in India over 200 people a year die from elephant-caused injuries.

THE IVORY TRADE

Another threat, particularly in Africa, is poaching for elephants' ivory tusks. The ivory trade has been illegal in many regions since 1989–1990, but the illegal market is so active, and the rewards so great, that corruption among officials and park rangers is common. Once an elephant population has been reduced, its recovery is slow. The elephant has the longest gestation of any animal, at 22 months, and a calf depends on its mother for three to four years. Just a few years' poaching can devastate a herd.

Some African nations have too many elephants for their available land. They wish to undertake controlled culls that would save the habitat, reduce conflict with people and supply ivory for legal trade under license. This might reduce the need for illegal ivory and also bring in funds for further conservation. But other countries push for a total ban on all forms of hunting and culling.

A BURNING ISSUE

The long-running debate about the trade in ivory continues into the 21st century. Some governments approve a total ban, supported by public burning of seized poached ivory or old stockpiles. Countries that prefer this policy include the Democratic Republic of Congo, Kenya, Tanzania and Uganda. However, since 1997 controlled ivory sales have restarted in a few African countries; nations that would favor some form of controlled ivory trade include Botswana, South Africa, Zambia and Zimbabwe.

BEASTS OF BURDEN Asian elephants, seen here carrying tourists in India, have a long shared history with humans. Today, their total population of around 45,000 is vulnerable partly because too many youngsters are being taken from the wild to work for people.

Horses Perissodactyla

Horses and donkeys may hardly seem under threat as they thunder along racetracks, pull people around or pull carts. But most of their wild relatives are in real trouble, including two zebra species, wild asses across Africa and Asia, and a close cousin of the domestic horse.

WILD HORSE Named after a Russian explorer, Przewalski's wild horse was saved only by captive breeding. It has been released in two remote areas of Mongolia: Hustai National Park and the Gobi Desert.

WARY HERBIVORES

The horses belong to the perissodactyl (odd-toed hoofed) mammals. Also in this group are the rhinos and tapirs (*see* pp. 94–95). Horses are distinguished by a single hoof-tipped toe on each foot, and evolved as very swift, long-legged herbivores of open country. As they graze on grasses and other low-growing plants, their keen senses of sight, hearing and smell are ever alert to the slightest hint of danger.

Domestic horses, from miniature ponies to massive draft horses, are all included as one species, *Equus caballus*. Their wild relatives in the 10-species family Equidae include Przewalski's wild horse, the wild asses of Africa and Asia, and three zebra species. Domestic donkeys, or burros, were bred from wild asses 6,000 years ago, while domestic horses came from now-extinct Asiatic wild horses known as tarpans.

WILD ASSES

Although they superficially resemble donkeys, wild asses have paler, sandy coats and are much tougher and faster. The African wild ass of Eritrea, Ethiopia and Somalia in northeast Africa is now critically endangered: fewer than 500 survive. In this region wracked by human poverty and conflict, African asses are still hunted for their meat, hides and body parts, used in local medicines. They are also seen as competitors with livestock, so are driven away or killed by farmers. But it is the farm animals that are damaging this arid habitat through overgrazing.

Similar threats confront the Asiatic wild asses, particularly the kulan, onager and kiang, which live in equally fragile habitats vulnerable to drought and grazing pressure.

DISTINCTIVE STRIPES

Herds of zebras count among the great wildlife spectacles of Africa, but these much-loved horses face many of the difficulties of wild asses. They are still hunted for their attractive hides, catch diseases spread by domestic horses and lose grazing to herds of cattle. Of the three zebra species, only Burchell's (also called the plains or common) zebra is out of danger. The mountain and Grevy's zebras are both classed as endangered.

Grevy's zebra is native to East Africa and numbers fewer than 2,500 in the wild, including 400–500 in a private reserve managed by Kenya's Lewa Wildlife Conservancy. National parks, this time in South Africa, likewise

BARREN LAND Onagers eke out an existence in the arid habitats of Iran. Just two small and highly isolated populations remain, so a chance event such as an outbreak of disease could cause extinction.

play a major part in conserving the rare Cape subspecies of mountain zebra. There are many mountain and Grevy's zebras in zoos worldwide, offering the prospect of future reintroductions.

ROAMING FREE AGAIN

Przewalski's wild horse is a very close cousin of domesticated horses. Stocky and strong, it has a large head, thick neck and shortish legs. For many years this species was extinct in the wild, with a mere 31 in captivity in 1945. However, breeding programs raised this figure to more than 1,500 by the early 1990s, when reintroductions began into the species' native habitat of steppe and thornbush in Mongolia. Field surveys in 2005 and 2006 were cautiously optimistic, revealing that the captive-bred horses are adapting well to freedom and have established their own breeding units.

THE QUAGGA PROJECT

Quaggas were a subspecies of Burchell's zebra with a brownish color and fewer, fainter pale stripes. The last one died in 1883. Since 1987, the Quagga Project has picked the most quagga-like zebras to be translocated to designated zones for selective breeding. The aim is to recreate quagga-like herds from characteristics hidden in the gene pool of Burchell's zebras.

DRIVEN AWAY
Cape mountain zebras lost much habitat after the arrival of European settlers. They survive mainly in protected areas, such as De Hoop and Gamka Mountain reserves.

Rhinos & Tapirs Perissodactyla

With their unique nose horns and prehistoric-looking "armor-plated" skin, rhinos seem out of place in the modern world and are one of the most threatened of all mammal families. Tapirs, often described as living fossils, may also be on the way out.

MALAYAN TAPIR Common until as recently as the 1930s, this species has lost most of its range due to deforestation. Relict populations cling on in isolated pieces of forest.

BULKY BUT FAST

Along with horses (*see* pp. 92–93), the rhinos and their relatives the tapirs make up the order Perissodactyla, or odd-toed hoofed mammals. Many rhino-type animals lived on Earth in earlier eras, but there are just five living species of rhinoceros. Only the largest, the African white rhino, has anything like a viable population, with 11,000–12,000 surviving into the 21st century. The Indian (greater one-horned) rhino is endangered, while the black, Sumatran and Javan rhinos are all critically endangered.

Rhinos are mostly solitary, apart from mothers and calves. Claimed to have a bad temper, they are in truth peaceful vegetarians that charge only as a last resort, when despite their huge bulk they move with amazing speed, often outpacing a human sprinter. Their fearsome reputation made rhinos a prized trophy of big-game hunters during the colonial period in Africa.

KILLED FOR THEIR HORNS

Sport hunting pales into insignificance compared to the present-day pressures of habitat loss and the trade in rhino horn. In Africa, the rhinos' savanna and bush habitat is degraded by overgrazing and converted to crops. The Sumatran and Javan rhinos are forest browsers, and suffer the great

DECIMATED
Black rhinos, seen here with attendant oxpeckers, have been hit hardest by trade in rhino horn. In 1970, there were 65,000; by the mid-1990s, just 2,500 were left.

RHINO BODYGUARDS

Constant 24-hour armed guards have been assigned to some rhinos, such as this black rhino in Zimbabwe. Even this desperate measure may not stop the killing, however, because the stakes are high enough for poachers to murder the guards if necessary. Park officials are also bribed to give the poachers access.

scourge of tropical deforestation. A few rhinos are killed annually in revenge attacks for raiding crops or through fear of charging. But poaching for their horns is the overriding danger.

Rhino horn is neither bone nor true horn, but composed of tightly matted and glued hair, and grows through the animal's life. It is sold as a trophy, for making drugs used in Asian medicine and for carving into dagger handles in the Gulf region, especially Yemen. Such is the demand for this commodity that many thousands of rhinos have been poached, in defiance of armed patrols and international trade restrictions.

LIVING FOSSILS

Forming a separate family within the Perissodactyla, the four tapirs are big, pig-like herbivores of riverine rainforest in Southeast Asia and Latin America. Remarkably, tapirs have changed little for over 30 million years, and yet due to human activities have become endangered in only the last 100 years or so. In Latin America, Baird's and mountain tapirs are endangered and the lowland tapir is vulnerable; the only Old World species, the Malayan tapir, is also vulnerable. Tapirs are pressurized by commercial logging and by hunting with rifles or dogs for their highly prized meat.

FLEXIBLE TRUNK All tapirs have trunk-like snouts. This Baird's tapir is native to Central America, where vast tracts of its rainforest habitat are being cleared to make way for cattle ranching and other development.

The Indian Rhinoceros

Hunting for sport and rhino horn has long threatened this species, which is found in the monsoon-drenched region of northeastern India, Nepal and Bhutan. To deter the poachers, India and Nepal created a corps of several hundred heavily armed guards. However, a more intractable problem is geography – the rhino's fertile habitat of floodplain grasslands and adjacent swamps and forests is prime farming land, and during the 20th century much of it was cleared to grow rice and other crops. This forced the rhinos to forage in cultivated areas, causing conflict with farmers; every year, some rhinos ended up being killed as pests.

WEAKENED POPULATIONS
Like all rhinos, Indian rhinos breed slowly – the female is pregnant for 15–16 months and the calf is dependent on its mother for 2–3 years. This means numbers are slow to recover from pressures such as habitat loss. The depleted populations suffer from inbreeding.

PROTECTED ZONES
Indian rhinos have staged a recovery in reserves such as Chitwan (above), Dudhwa, Jaldapara, Pobitora, Kaziranga and Orang, some of which were originally established for tigers. Tourism contributes to the local economy, encouraging people to value the rhinos as an asset.

Pigs & Hippos Artiodactyla

Somewhat unfairly, pigs, hogs and boars have a reputation as dirty, greedy animals and are usually viewed only as a convenient source of protein and hides. Overhunting, together with habitat loss, has endangered half of the pig family as a result. Confined to swamps and forests in West Africa, the increasingly rare pygmy hippo is also a frequent hunting victim.

BAD PRESS

Pigs and hippos are members of the order Artiodactyla, or even-toed hoofed mammals, along with the camels, deer, giraffes and cattle. They are intelligent creatures with fascinating social behavior, yet suffer from an image problem, which means that they very rarely feature in popular conservation campaigns. Mostly they are incidental beneficiaries of protected reserves and other programs aimed at higher-profile groups such as primates and big cats. If wild pig populations were managed sustainably, instead of being hunted to extinction, they could provide a useful long-term resource for local people.

In Africa, the hippopotamus (larger of the two hippo species) is generally respected, if only because its massive bulk means that it is safer left well alone. It earns valuable tourist revenue, and remains widespread and common. But the status of its vulnerable smaller relative – the pygmy hippo – could not be more different.

FOREST HIPPO

Measuring just 5 feet (1.5 m) long and weighing around 550 pounds (250 kg), the pygmy hippo is more adapted for land than its hulking semi-aquatic relation. It is also far more solitary, with a very restricted distribution in West Africa, mainly in Liberia, as well as in Guinea, Ivory Coast, Sierra Leone and Nigeria.

By day the pygmy hippo rests along a forested stream or in a dense swamp, emerging at night to feed on grasses, reeds and fruit. Despite legal protection, it is threatened by logging, marshland drainage, water pollution and, above all, hunting for its pork-like flesh for the thriving trade in bushmeat.

YAWNING DISPLAY
This pygmy hippo is baring its lower canine teeth to intimidate an attacker. The species' habitat is difficult to patrol, hampering attempts to protect it in the wild.

ADAPTABLE OMNIVORES

The 19 species of pigs, hogs and boars are all native to the Old World. Some of them – notably the wild boar, the ancestor of domestic pigs – have been introduced to other continents. They are stocky-bodied and short-legged, with elongated sensitive snouts to sniff out and grub up all types of food. At least seven species are threatened.

Largest of the pigs is the giant forest hog of Central Africa, which weighs up to 610 pounds (275 kg). Although familiar to peoples of tropical African forests and subject in many of these cultures to superstitions, the giant forest hog was not known to Western science until 1904. Its chief threats are the removal of its habitat by agriculture and human settlement, and hunting for its meat, hides and male tusks. At the other end of the size scale, the pygmy hog is now critically endangered. Poaching and the loss of its grassy floodplain habitat have restricted it to just two protected reserves, Manas and Barnadi, in Assam, northeast India.

ASIATIC PIGS

The forests and wooded wetlands of Southeast Asia are home to several rare and declining pig species. The almost hairless babirusas of Sulawesi and the nearby Togian, Mangole and Taliabu

MUDBATH Babirusas are often caught when they leave the safety of the trees to wallow in mud. In males (right) the upper canines grow, not downward, but up through the top of the mouth and curve back toward the eyes.

islands, all in Indonesia, are classed as vulnerable. Around 4,000 babirusas are left in the wild, but whereas these pigs were formerly considered to be a single species, recent research has suggested that they in fact make up three separate species. This means that each distinct geographic form of babirusa includes only a fraction of the total number, increasing the level of threat.

Babirusas are hunted by islanders and by packs of feral dogs. They are rapidly losing their rainforest home to large-scale commercial logging, which opens up the formerly virgin landscape and makes further poaching easier.

FEEDING PARTY Like most pigs, giant forest hogs are social and the males have elongated canines that grow outside the mouth as tusks. These are valued as symbolic decorations and trophies, causing additional hunting pressure.

Another forest pig, the "punk-haired" Visayan warty pig of the Philippines, is critically endangered. Its remnant populations survive on just two of the six islands it formerly inhabited – in tiny pockets of forest on Negros, and in the western mountains of Panay. The species is hardly a conservation priority locally since it often raids the crops and fruit trees of farmers, who are themselves only just managing to survive by shifting slash-and-burn agriculture. However, captive breeding colonies of Visayan warty pigs set up at conservation centers on Negros and Panay may ensure that the species does not vanish from the islands.

SHAGGY HAIR The little-known Visayan warty pig disappeared from 98 percent of its former range during the 20th century. Viewed as a pest, it is trapped and snared by farmers, and interbreeding with free-roaming domestic pigs threatens the genetic purity of the species.

Camels Artiodactyla

For thousands of years camels have lived alongside people in Africa and Asia, as beasts of burden and providers of milk, meat and skins. So have their domesticated South American relatives, llamas and alpacas. But today, their wild cousins are in trouble.

ONE HUMP OR TWO

The camelid family is made up of six species, all of which are long-legged, herd-dwelling grazing animals. They include the one-humped, or Arabian, camel, also known as the dromedary. This species is fully domesticated, with no original representatives left in the wild, although feral herds roam regions of Africa, the Middle East and western Asia, as well as Australia, where they were taken in the 1860s for transport in the bush, and released from the 1930s. The total world population of dromedaries is 15 million, with feral Australian herds numbering 50,000.

The two-humped, or Bactrian, camel is also a common beast of burden, with around two million domestic animals across Central and East Asia. But wild Bactrian camels are endangered, with as few as 1,000 remaining in the Gobi Desert of Mongolia and China.

WILDERNESS HOME

This vast, remote area is the last refuge for free-roaming untamed Bactrian camels. It is open, dusty and high – an incredibly harsh land of windswept steppes and cold deserts up to 13,000 feet (4,000 m) above sea level. The thick coat of Bactrian camels is essential for survival in conditions that range from scorching and sandstorm-ridden on summer days to far below freezing with fierce blizzards on winter nights.

Like dromedaries, wild Bactrians eat all kinds of plants and can go a week or more without water, then drink more than 26 gallons (100 L) in just a few minutes. But despite their remarkable toughness and the extreme inaccessibility of their habitat, for many centuries they have nevertheless succumbed to heavy hunting for their meat and hides. Today, they are also persecuted for competing with cattle for the scarce water and grazing of the desert, while gas pipelines and mining have eaten into their habitat.

THE HIGH LIFE

Four camelids live in South America: the guanaco and vicuña, and their domesticated descendants, the llama and alpaca. They resemble smaller, humpless versions of their Old World relatives. Both the guanaco and vicuña are coming under threat, although as yet not seriously.

Guanaco numbers probably exceed half a million, spread through the high puna (alpine grassland), scrub and forest of the Andes in Argentina and Chile, with a few herds in Peru, Bolivia

PRECIOUS COAT Historically, the main threat to vicuñas was the lucrative trade in their fine, soft wool, which had endangered the species by the 1960s. Since then, wild populations have been better managed.

DOMESTICATION

Wild camelids frequently interbreed with their domesticated cousins, such as this llama, which often live in the same areas. This hybridization gradually dilutes and contaminates the gene pool of the truly wild species, and could eventually lead to their extinction, as has happened already in some other groups of animals. Hybridization is a worrying long-term development: once hybrid animals form part of wild herds, it is difficult to isolate or remove their domesticated traits from the formerly pure-bred stock. Nowadays, numbers of domestic, feral or hybrid animals dwarf wild populations.

POACHING DANGER
Years of hunting have made Bactrian camels very wary of people (a domesticated animal is pictured). Poachers continue to harrass their few surviving herds.

and Paraguay. This species is adapted to grazing and browsing the scant mountain vegetation, but fast-growing herds of sheep and cattle, more suited to lowlands, are degrading the region's thin, poor soil and pushing guanacos into smaller, fragmented areas.

The delicate vicuña is the lightest camelid, at just 110 pounds (50 kg); on average, dromedaries weigh 10 times as much. It has a more northern distribution than the guanaco, grazing the Andean puna at altitudes of up to 16,000 feet (4,800 m). Its main populations are in Peru, Chile, Bolivia and Argentina, with smaller recently established herds in Ecuador. As with the guanaco, the vicuña's habitat is being taken over or damaged by grazing livestock, and ever since the Spanish conquest of South America it has also been caught for its valuable woolly coat. Improved protection in Peru and Chile, driven partly by the needs of tourism, has lessened this trade's impact.

ON TOP OF THE WORLD Guanaco used to have the high slopes and plains of the Andes to themselves, but now herds of domestic stock compete for grazing and bring diseases.

Deer & Giraffes Artiodactyla

Most deer are herd-living woodland browsers. A quarter of all species are under threat, particularly by massive deforestation in the tropics and hunting for venison and hides. By contrast, the giraffe, elegant symbol of Africa, is not yet at risk.

MINIATURE SPECIES The tiny southern pudu lives in temperate rainforests in Chile, which are endangered by agricultural expansion. Other threats include poaching and capture as a crowd-pleasing "mini-attraction" for zoos.

MALE ANTLERS

The 45 species of the deer family form part of the Artiodactyla, or even-toed hoofed mammals. They range in size from the huge moose of North America (known as the elk in Scandinavia) to the diminutive 30-pound (14 kg) southern pudu of Chile, which stands shorter than a domestic Labrador retriever. Without doubt the most impressive feature of deer is the antlers of males (stags), used in clashes during the "rut."

Deer have been hunted over millennia for their antlers, delicious meat and durable hides, and poaching is a major factor threatening several species. They also have many natural enemies, so are typically shy animals that can vanish quietly into cover. Such secretive habits, combined with a preference for thickly wooded or swampy habitats, makes it difficult to gauge their numbers. This explains why there is insufficient data on the status of around 12, mainly tropical or Asian, deer that could be in trouble; at least 10 other species are definitely known to be threatened.

SHRINKING HABITAT

The main hazard to forest deer is the loss and fragmentation of their habitat through commercial logging or because of the spread of crops and ranchland. Access roads into the forest divide the remaining habitat further, cause extra disturbance to the deer and result in numerous roadkill victims. Woodland managers sometimes cull deer due to the damage they do, such as nibbling tree buds, stripping bark or flaying it with their antlers.

Wetland deer, including the marsh deer of southeast South America and the barasingha of the Indus, Ganges and Brahmaputra river floodplains in India, face different threats. They are at risk from drainage and hydroelectric projects, as well as pollution from industrial areas.

A growing threat to these and many other deer is contact with farmed livestock, which compete for grazing and pass on diseases. Some cattle-borne viruses have resulted in mass die-offs in herds of wild deer.

A MIXED BLESSING

The Chinese kept deer over 1,000 years ago, and almost ever since these stately animals have been popular attractions in parks. Capture to supply private collections has arguably benefited and threatened deer in equal measure – it depletes the wild populations, but also creates a captive stock that might later protect against extinction in the wild. Père David's deer, from China, would have died out in around 1900 were it not for its small captive population in England. In East Asia, sika deer are critically endangered, yet thousands of sika exist in parks, ranches and reserves elsewhere, especially Europe and Texas.

LAST SURVIVORS

Giraffes belong to the same hoofed mammal group as deer, but whereas there were once many different species, in modern times there are just two – the long-necked giraffe and the shorter okapi, its rainforest-dwelling cousin of Central Africa. The giraffe is killed for its patterned hide, but not in sufficient numbers to be a threat. However, the okapi lives in a region where logging and the bushmeat trade are rampant, so it could soon become of concern.

MARSH DEER This species' wetlands are being drained to make way for more profitable fields of sugar cane and pasture for beef cattle. It also catches diseases from the farm stock.

SAFE FOR NOW Giraffes remain a common enough sight in protected reserves, although poaching does occur. At one time, they were killed just for their long tails – used as fly whisks and good luck charms.

CONFLICT OF INTEREST Reindeer, or caribou, are generally abundant in northern tundra and taiga, but some subspecies are rare. This forest reindeer, for example, survives at a handful of sites in Finland and neighboring Russia. Local farmers, hunters and conservationists disagree about how best to manage its herds.

SIKA STAG
Common in captivity, sika deer are very rare in the wild due to poaching. The antlers and sinews are ingredients in Asian medicines, and the meat is sold as venison.

Cattle & Relatives Artiodactyla

This large, varied family includes cattle, buffalo, bison, gazelles, antelopes, sheep and goats. Farmed and hunted all around the globe, these herbivores are of immense economic importance, but as many as 50 of the 140 species are under threat.

SHARED HISTORY

Cattle and their relatives make up the family Bovidae, which is in the order Artiodactyla, or even-toed hoofed mammals. They are all herbivores and tend to live in groups for safety against their many natural predators, especially dogs, cats and hyenas. Different species are native to all continents except for Australia. Humans and bovids share a long history. We have domesticated some bovids, such as farm cattle, oxen, water buffalo, sheep and goats, and use almost every part of their bodies. Other species remain untamed, but have been hunted through the ages.

BISON SLAUGHTER

One of the most famous illustrations of disastrous overhunting is provided by the American bison, or buffalo. Before European settlers arrived, an astonishing 50–60 million bison roamed the continent, in woods as well as on prairies. Slaughter by rifle on an almost industrial scale for their meat, hide and coats reduced numbers to a few hundred by 1890. In particular, "Buffalo Bill" Cody and other Wild West characters hunted enormous quantities

of bison to feed the railroad workers and pioneers. Conservation efforts have since boosted the species' population to 200,000 wild and semi-captive animals (*see* panel, right).

The slightly smaller European bison, or wisent, was extinct in the wild by 1920. Captive breeding has enabled reintroductions into Bialowieza Forest Park on the Poland-Belarus border and also elsewhere in the Caucasus.

RIVAL SPECIES Contact with domestic cattle is a growing threat for wild banteng such as these. The livestock compete for food, pass on diseases and readily interbreed, compromising the bantengs' genetic purity.

DESERT SPECIALIST Captive-reared scimitar-horned oryx have been released in Morocco (above) and Tunisia in a bid to reestablish the species in its former haunts across the Sahara.

A THREATENED FAMILY

The list of other bovids at risk is long and spans many regions and habitats. It features wild yaks, saiga antelopes and markhor goats in the Himalayas, argali sheep in Central Asia, forest oxen in Southeast Asia, chamois and ibex in European mountains and numerous African antelopes. Apart from hunting, these bovids are threatened by habitat loss, competition with domestic breeds and susceptibility to their diseases.

Resembling domestic cattle in shape, the banteng of Southeast Asian forests is endangered by logging, poaching and cross-breeding with farm livestock it comes into contact with. Rarer still is the kouprey, of which fewer than 250 survive, mainly in Cambodia. Its rainforest range is rife with warring factions who kill it for food, and it encounters land mines as well as the usual perils facing wild bovids.

In contrast to these forest-dwelling species, the scimitar-horned oryx lives in the central Sahara – one of Earth's driest places. This desert antelope was hunted virtually to extinction for sport, meat and its magnificent curved horns, but it clung to survival in Chad.

LAST WILD HERDS

Most American bison are either captive or have a history of captivity and live on commercial ranches; around 95 percent of bison are privately owned. The only truly wild herds left are in Yellowstone National Park, which straddles Idaho, Montana and Wyoming, and the giant Wood Buffalo National Park in north-west Canada. The former area is a sanctuary for 2,000 of the plains bison subspecies, while the latter is home to 2,500 wood bison. All of the wild herds depend on intensive conservation.

THRIVING AGAIN
Reintroductions to the wild of European bison, seen here in dawn mist in Bialowieza Forest, Poland, have gone so well that some new herds may even require culling.

Ostriches & Relatives
Struthioniformes & various others

Heavier and taller than any other bird, the ostrich belongs to the world's most ancient bird group – the ratites. Its relatives include the flightless emu, cassowaries, rheas and kiwis, plus the free-flying tinamous. One in four of these species is threatened.

LIVING GIANTS

Adult ostriches stand 7–9 feet (2.1–2.8 m) high, with massive, muscular legs that enable the great birds to sprint at up to 45 mph (70 km/h) to escape enemies. The species is adapted for a life in savanna, open woodland or semidesert, where the birds form herds and wander long distances in search of plant food such as grasses. Ostriches became extinct in the Middle East early in the 20th century, but remain locally common across most of their range in Africa. The red-necked ostriches found in arid

HERDING INSTINCT Ostriches are sociable birds, ideally suited to farming. In the wild their main threats include hunting and habitat degradation caused by goats and cattle.

country from Ethiopia west to Senegal are much scarcer than the paler-necked savanna forms in the south.

AN ANCIENT GROUP

Around a quarter of the 57 species in the ratites group are not faring so well. In particular danger are New Zealand's kiwis (*see* box, far right) and cassowaries, which are unique to the rainforests of New Guinea and Queensland in northern Australia. All three species of cassowary sport a protective, horny casque on the head, with wattles of loose neck skin that change color to indicate their mood. Their numbers are falling fast as a result of deforestation, hunting by villagers for food, human

TINAMOU IN TROUBLE As with so many South American forest animals, the solitary tinamou is losing ground to agriculture, the logging industry and creeping urbanization.

settlements encroaching into their forest home, and attacks by feral dogs, which find their chicks easy prey.

FARMLAND PESTS

Emus are native to Australia and, like ostriches, have shaggy, drooping wings that help to regulate heat in the hot climate. In mainland Australia, emus can be so numerous that they are a pest to cereal farmers because they raid

EXTINCT

We know moas only from their fossils, but when New Zealand's first human settlers, the Polynesians, arrived there in around AD 700, the islands were home to 24 species of moa. These long-legged, long-necked, flightless ratites stood up to 10 feet (3 m) high. Moas were good to eat and easy prey, having evolved in predator-free isolation. They were all hunted to extinction by the time Europeans arrived in 1642.

and trample crops. But they have long since vanished from Tasmania, and two other species died out in historic times – the Kangaroo Island and King Island emus. Settlers shot them both to oblivion in the early 19th century.

The common and lesser rheas of South America resemble small emus. They are under pressure due to overhunting and conversion of their rough grassland habitat into rangelands for cattle ranching. But this continent's smallest ratites – the tinamous – are most at risk. Of the 47 species, seven are globally threatened. Tinamous live in grasslands, scrub and forest, and do not flourish in the modified landscapes created through agricultural intensification, where pesticides deplete food supplies. Logging threatens the rainforest-dwelling tinamous.

The Kiwi Family

All four species of kiwi are threatened. Their ancestors reached New Zealand around 40 million years ago, and subsequently lost the power of flight as their new, predator-free home did not require it. Living alongside humans and introduced mammals, however, kiwis are highly vulnerable, losing most of their eggs and young. For species that lay only two eggs a year, this pressure is unsustainable. The main hope for kiwis is that, because New Zealanders identify so closely with them, sufficient resources will be devoted to conserve these strange nocturnal birds.

NORTH ISLAND BROWN KIWI
This species' population fell by over 90 percent during the 20th century, due mainly to the loss of its eggs and chicks to introduced stoats, cats and dogs. In one case, a single dog killed 500 kiwis in the space of just six weeks. Several brown kiwi sanctuaries have now been set up.

GREAT SPOTTED KIWI
Confined to the forested mountains of New Zealand's South Island, this species suffers very high chick mortality. On average fewer than 1 in 10 of its young reach adulthood. Today, conservationists are trapping stoats and other nonnative mammals in kiwi strongholds so that more of these birds survive to breeding age.

NO ESCAPE
Having lost the ability to fly, the southern cassowary, like other flightless ratites, is very vulnerable to hunters and feral animals such as dogs.

Albatrosses & Petrels
Procellariiformes

Among the most skillful fliers of all, the long-winged albatrosses and petrels may spend weeks on end far out at sea and undertake staggering migrations across oceans. But a deadly fishing method, marine pollution and introduced predators at their breeding grounds are driving many species to a critical state.

TUBE-SHAPED NOSES

Albatrosses and petrels are referred to as the tube-nosed seabirds. Supremely adapted to life at sea, this group gets their name from their complex bills, with large, tubular nostrils. Most birds have a poor sense of smell, but the tubenoses' strongly developed olfactory ability helps them to find food at sea and literally to sniff the way back to their colonies on land. Individuals can even identify one other by smell alone.

LIFE ON THE EDGE

Together with their close relatives the shearwaters, albatrosses and petrels are under severe threat from changes in the seas and oceans on which they depend. The worst dangers come from commercial fisheries, marine pollution and introduced predators at their coastal or island breeding sites.

Of the 106 species alive today, at least 55 are globally threatened. An infamous case is the Bermuda petrel, or cahow, believed extinct for 300 years until its rediscovery in 1951. Even under intense protection, the population of just 20 pairs has grown very slowly.

MARINE SCAVENGER
Southern giant petrels have benefited from scavenging garbage and discarded fish thrown overboard, but they are vulnerable to disturbance at their nesting grounds.

FAITHFUL PARTNERS Overexploitation of the Laysan albatross for its feathers decimated its breeding colonies. Despite a ban in 1980, its numbers have been slow to recover due to longline fishing and collisions with aircraft.

The cause for the species' decline was contamination of its eggs with DDT – remarkable as this is an agricultural pesticide that must have washed out to sea, where the petrels ingested it.

HELPLESS CHICKS

Most albatrosses and petrels come to land only to breed. Their chicks are helpless, yet must be left unguarded while the parents are away hunting for fish or squid, so these birds have always favored remote, uninhabited and predator-free islands as breeding sites. If predators are later introduced by humans, the results can be catastrophic. The roll call of animals that have devoured the chicks or eggs of albatrosses and petrels around the world includes rats, mice, cats, dogs, mongooses, pigs, goats and even brown tree snakes.

The situation is worsened by the fact that albatrosses and petrels breed very slowly, raising relatively few chicks per season. Normally, this would not matter due to their long lifespans (of 50 years or more in larger albatrosses). However, if the populations of slow-breeding species decline rapidly due to extra pressures, they often are unable to recover their numbers in time. This is exactly what has happened.

LONGLINE FISHING

One particular fishing method has devastated the populations of no fewer than 17 species of albatrosses. In the southern oceans, tuna are caught by trailing baited "longlines" that stretch for dozens of miles behind boats. These baits snare and drown vast amounts of other wildlife, known as "bycatch," including an estimated 100,000 albatrosses every year. The global wandering albatross population of 28,000 birds could halve in just three albatross generations, largely because of this unsustainable pressure.

OCEAN WANDERER Like many of its relatives, the black-browed albatross spends most of the year at sea, gliding over the waves in search of fish and squid. Thousands drown after getting snared by longline baits and trawlers' nets.

MATING CALL A wandering albatross calls to its mate on South Georgia, one of the species' main sub-Antarctic breeding islands. Its nesting grounds are protected, but out at sea longline fisheries are killing countless birds.

Penguins Sphenisciformes

Unique to southern hemisphere oceans, penguins are superbly adapted for a life at sea, with flipper-like wings, webbed feet and streamlined bodies. These much-loved flightless birds are at risk from changes to their breeding and feeding grounds.

EXTREME SURVIVAL

Penguins have dense plumage and a thick layer of fat to provide insulation against ice-cold waters and windchill temperatures that are among the lowest ever recorded on Earth, and perhaps no group of birds is more closely associated in the popular imagination with harsh environments. But only four species – the emperor, chinstrap, Adélie and gentoo penguins – live on or among the Antarctic pack ice. Most species of penguin breed away from Antarctica on the coasts or offshore islands of Australia, New Zealand, South America and South Africa. One species, the endangered Galapagos penguin, even occurs near the equator.

CROWDED COLONIES

There are 17 species of penguin, which belong to the family Spheniscidae, and all except for the yellow-eyed penguin breed in large colonies. Some colonies may number hundreds of thousands of birds, so the birds rely on calls and visual signals to locate their mates and young. Penguins are long-lived and typically do not reproduce until they are at least three (or, in some species, eight) years old. Their breeding seasons tend to be protracted, too.

BREEDING CYCLES

The larger penguin species lay a single egg, which in the emperor penguin is immediately transferred to the male. He incubates it for two months on his feet to keep it off the ice, and during this time he lives off his body's fat reserves. The smaller penguins usually lay two eggs, but in some species one egg is smaller and only one chick will fledge. The details of breeding vary greatly between the more southern species that are strongly seasonal in their reproduction, and the more northern species that can remain at their colonies throughout the year and breed when conditions are suitable.

FOREST BREEDER Uniquely among penguins, the endangered yellow-eyed penguin breeds in spaced-out territories rather than colonies. Its specialized nesting habitat is under serious pressure, leading to poor breeding success.

ROCKY HOME Rockhopper penguins often nest among boulders and their colonies in the Falkland Islands are a major tourist attraction. But numbers here fell by 90 percent in the late 20th century due, in part, to disturbance.

GOLDEN CREST The macaroni penguin's feather tufts are used in courtship displays. Considered vulnerable, it has to compete with modern fishing fleets for its crustacean prey.

CLIMATE CHANGE

In the past, people exploited penguins for their meat and to produce oil, causing huge losses to penguin populations. Strict protection over several decades has since restored their numbers, but the

MARINE OIL SPILLS

Nicknamed the jackass penguin for the braying calls it makes at its breeding colonies, the African penguin is now vulnerable. Human fishing activities have depleted its prey and oil spillages at sea kill many penguins. Two major spills since 1994 claimed the lives of 30,000 birds, and the species' slow reproductive rate means that its numbers may halve by 2025 without a concerted conservation program. However, African penguins respond well to being cleaned after oiling, so rescued oiled birds (below) can be brought back to full health and eventually returned to the wild.

world's changing climate, triggered in part by human activity, means that the future of some penguin species is now increasingly uncertain. Long-term changes in the extent and distribution of floating ice in the Antarctic could seriously reduce the breeding success of the four species found there.

Significant shifts in ocean currents and water temperatures might also alter the distribution of fish, small crustaceans and other prey, so that the penguins have insufficient food close to their breeding sites.

THE RAREST PENGUIN

Like other ground-nesting seabirds, most penguins breed on islands where they are safe from predators. The introduction of cats and rats to these refuges can present a major threat to penguins. This has been most acute for the yellow-eyed penguin, or hoiho, found only on New Zealand's South Island and several nearby sub-Antarctic islands. It neared extinction due to attacks by nonnative ferrets, cats,

rats and dogs, disturbance by humans, the trampling of its nests by sheep and the loss of its unusual breeding habitat in coastal forests, but now it is benefiting from intensive protection.

In the end, the enduring popularity of penguins offers probably one of the best hopes for their future.

MACQUARIE ISLAND
Royal penguins nest mainly on this island, to the south of Tasmania. Their small breeding range makes them vulnerable to a natural or human-made disaster.

Pelicans & Herons
Pelecaniformes & Ciconiiformes

The pelicans and their relatives are mostly seabirds, whereas herons usually favor fresh water. Human persecution and intense pressures on their habitat have put one in six species of these charismatic waterbirds at risk.

EXPERT FISHERS

Pelicans belong to a varied order of web-footed fish-eaters that also includes the cormorants, frigate birds, tropic birds, darters, boobies and gannets. Most are strictly marine, nesting on islands, cliffs and rocky coasts, but several occur on lakes or marshes.

Herons make up another major order of waterbirds together with the egrets, bitterns, storks, spoonbills and ibises. These medium to large wading birds all have long, robust bills and legs. Apart from a few notable exceptions, such as the northern bald ibis, they are predisposed to more or less marshy freshwater wetlands. They take a wide range of prey, especially fish but also amphibians, small rodents and snakes, as well as some carrion.

LONG DECLINE The northern bald ibis has undergone a spectacular decline over many years. Hunting, pesticide poisoning and the loss of its arid steppe habitat are all to blame.

The robust anatomy and aquatic habitat of both the pelican and heron groups means they are well represented in the fossil record; for example, more than 60 species of extinct heron and stork are known from fossils.

HUMAN HAZARDS
Persecuted by fishers, shot for sport and disturbed by tourist boats, Dalmatian pelicans struggle to coexist with people. These big, heavy birds also die in collisions with overhead power lines.

LIVING TOGETHER

Many of the pelicans, herons and their relatives nest colonially, a habit that helps to warn the birds of danger, and may assist in the transfer of information about feeding areas. However, it can also make these species very vulnerable to localized threats such as pollution incidents or the drainage of a wetland, since entire colonies can be lost. Species at risk because their population is small and concentrated in just a handful of colonies include the Chinese egret, the greater adjutant of southern Asia, and Abbott's booby, which breeds only on Christmas Island in the Indian Ocean.

Once widespread in North Africa and the Middle East, and often pictured in Ancient Egyptian hieroglyphs, the northern bald ibis is now found at a single reserve in Morocco. With fewer than 300 birds left, its status is critical. In 1996, the mysterious death of 40 of the ibises, probably through disease, demonstrated how precarious colonial nesting can be for very rare species.

HUNTING PRESSURE

In the historical past, hunting for food caused the extinction of the Réunion flightless ibis and various other species in the pelican and heron groups, while egrets suffered heavily during the 19th and early 20th centuries because of the trade in their lacy white plumes, used in fashionable hats. Since the craze for

GREATER ADJUTANT This huge stork breeds only in Assam, India, and at Tonle Sap Lake in Cambodia. It is endangered by pollution and the drainage of its feeding areas in swamps, flooded forests and wet grasslands.

GOING HUNGRY Fluctuations in the water temperature of the eastern Pacific cause the fish prey of the Galapagos flightless cormorant to move elsewhere. These events may be natural, or they could be a symptom of climate change.

wearing egret feathers came to an end, the worst-hit species – the snowy, little and great egrets – gradually recovered. Today, hunting is still a threat for a few species, in particular the giant ibis of Cambodia and Laos, but a far greater danger is habitat loss and degradation.

VANISHING WETLANDS

Wetlands and wet forests everywhere are under massive pressure from the rise in human populations. When drained, marshland soils are among the most fertile in the world, and even where wetlands are not directly threatened by conversion to agriculture, they may be damaged irrevocably by water extraction for the irrigation of nearby agricultural land or to supply towns with drinking water. Another problem is the spread of toxic waterborne agrochemicals and industrial pollutants into freshwater drainage systems. The effects of climate change (increased temperature and reduced precipitation) may shrink the planet's wetland areas still further.

By changing the seasonal distribution of their fish prey, global warming also affects seabirds in the pelican group, including boobies, gannets, cormorants and tropic birds. The phenomenon has been blamed for poor breeding seasons in which colonies struggle to raise a fraction of their normal young.

MIGRATION DANGERS

A number of species, such as Europe's white and black storks and East Asia's black-faced spoonbill, are impressive long-range migrants. As is always the case, migratory birds are exposed to risks across a wider geographical area. Not only do their nesting and wintering grounds require protection, but also the places where they rest and "refuel" while on migration. In the case of the black-faced spoonbill, its winter sites on the coast of Hong Kong and Taiwan are at risk from industrial sprawl.

DRYING OUT Swampy reedbeds are a major wetland habitat for herons and bitterns, such as this Eurasian great bittern. But in many countries low-lying reedbeds are a fraction of their original size because they can easily be drained to create prime farmland.

Waterfowl Anseriformes

Ducks, geese and swans are collectively known as waterfowl, or wildfowl, and live in virtually every conceivable aquatic habitat worldwide. Slaughtered for both food and sport, they also suffer from the drainage and pollution of their wetland refuges.

AT HOME IN WATER

The 157 species of ducks, geese and swans make up the family Anatidae, which, together with three closely related South American species called screamers, comprises the order Anseriformes. All these species share a strong affinity for water, with plump, buoyant bodies, waterproof plumage and powerfully webbed feet. In most cases, the downy chicks are able to swim well soon after hatching. Within hours, a brood of chicks follow their mother away from the nest, usually taking to the water for safety, and start to search for their own food.

MIGRATIONS AND MOLTS

Waterfowl are typically strong fliers – in steady, level flight, ducks are among the fastest of birds, and several species can exceed 60 mph (100 km/h). Many waterfowl in the northern hemisphere

BACK TO THE WILD The release of captive-bred Hawaiian geese, such as this one tagged with rings for identification, saved the species. But the restored population's small genetic base means that inbreeding is a problem.

carry out extensive migrations from their breeding grounds in the far north to wintering grounds on lowland fresh waters and the coast. After breeding, almost all waterfowl undertake a rapid complete molt, during which they become temporarily flightless.

HUNTING DANGER

To date, the main cause of extinction among waterfowl has been hunting for food and sport. This fate befell the Labrador duck of Canada and the northern United States, for example, which was shot to extinction by around 1875. Waterfowl are particularly vulnerable during their flightless molt period.

Some waterfowl have also been hit hard by the arrival of predators brought by settlers – notable examples are the extinct Auckland Island merganser and the Auckland Island teal. The latter's much-depleted population of around 600 to 2,000 birds faces extermination by the same cats and pigs that led to the merganser's demise.

WETLAND DEGRADATION

Overhunting remains a big problem for waterfowl, but nowadays they have many other dangers, faced by all birds of wetlands. More and more wetlands are drained for agriculture or urban development; too much fresh water is extracted for irrigation projects; and water supplies are contaminated by industrial pollutants, chemicals used in farming, the silt washed off deforested hillsides and all kinds of refuse.

Today, the most threatened species of waterfowl have restricted global ranges, as suggested by their names – Hawaiian goose, Laysan duck, Campbell Island teal and Madagascar pochard, to name but a few. The last of these has not

CROSS-BREEDING Eurasian white-headed ducks (this is a male) breed with American ruddy ducks, which depletes their gene pool. One controversial solution is a mass cull of all the escaped ruddy ducks in Europe.

been seen since 1991 so may be extinct, while the critically endangered Laysan duck was once the world's rarest bird, with just a single wild female; captive breeding has since boosted its numbers to around 600.

HYBRIDIZATION

Rarely a problem in other groups of birds, hybridization (where two different species mate to produce offspring) can pose a real threat to the genetic purity of rare waterfowl. Many species of waterfowl hybridize freely, often producing fertile offspring. For example, domesticated mallards have frequently escaped and bred with the local species of duck, such as the Hawaiian duck, Florida's mottled duck or the New Zealand gray duck. Escapes from private waterfowl collections can cause similar problems.

The white-headed duck, found only in Iberia and parts of western Asia, is threatened by hybridization with the closely related North American ruddy duck, which established a thriving wild population in western Europe after escaping from captivity in the 1950s.

BRED IN CAPTIVITY

The relative ease of breeding waterfowl in captivity offers a vital conservation tool, used to rescue species such as the Hawaiian goose, or nene. Its population crashed to just 30 by 1952 due to loss of its (unusual for a goose) dry lava flow habitat and predation by nonnative mongooses, pigs and cats. So far, more than 2,500 captive-reared nenes have been returned to the Hawaiian islands.

CLEAN RIVERS The endangered New Zealand blue duck depends on crystal-clear rivers with lush bankside vegetation and plenty of aquatic insects to eat. Loss of this habitat has confined the duck to remote mountain watercourses.

GOING FAST Lesser white-fronted geese may disappear from Scandinavia because of hunting at their wintering grounds beside the Black and Caspian seas. Their Siberian population is also in trouble.

Vultures Falconiformes

These supremely efficient scavengers are a vital part of many food chains around the world, and make an important contribution to human health by disposing of carcasses quickly. So the catastrophic population declines of some vulture species, especially in Asia, is of grave concern to environmentalists and public health officials alike.

OLD AND NEW WORLD

Vultures share carrion-eating habits, bare heads, powerful, meat-cleaver bills and incredible powers of flight, but the 23 species fall into two separate groups that evolved from different ancestors.

The 16 species of Old World vultures, found in Africa, Europe and Asia, are closely related to the eagles, hawks and falcons (*see* pp. 116–117) and belong to the same family, Accipitridae. The seven New World vultures (including the two condors) make up the family Cathartidae, the true status of which is hotly debated. Traditionally, both families are placed in the order of birds of prey: Falconiformes. However, recent genetic studies suggest that the New World vultures are related to storks and so they may not be birds of prey at all.

We have always persecuted vultures by shooting them or by destroying their nests, in the mistaken belief that they pose a risk to livestock.

They are also susceptible to accidental disturbance at their nest sites, and lose out when open country is converted to farmland, which does not supply as

ASIAN VULTURE CRISIS
Vultures feed in groups, so toxins spread through their populations rapidly. Within a decade these white-backed vultures went from being abundant to endangered.

much carrion. But a far worse danger is the contamination of their food sources. This potent threat endangers several Asian vultures, as well as the already very rare California condor, and it is a growing problem for Andean condors.

ACCIDENTAL POISONING

Vultures use their superb eyesight to find food, soaring high to spot distant carcasses and carefully watching the movements of other circling vultures in case they see anything. New World vultures also use their sense of smell, which is unusually well developed for birds. A scavenging lifestyle means that vultures are at risk of ingesting toxins present in the dead animals' flesh. Over time, these poisons can build up in the birds' bodies, eventually causing their death. One of the commonest toxins is lead shot. California and Andean condors have

LETHAL COCKTAIL Post-mortem studies on the bodies of dead Cape griffon vultures show that eating poison baits is a major threat to this species.

both suffered from lead poisoning as a result of feeding on animals shot by hunters or farmers. In Namibia and South Africa, Cape griffon vultures are threatened by eating poison-laced baits left out to kill jackals.

Since the early 1990s, populations of the white-rumped, the Indian and the slender-billed vultures have crashed in India, Pakistan and Nepal. It is estimated that 95 percent of the vultures have gone in just 10 years. So few survive in some areas that carcasses are left to rot in the open, creating a serious risk of disease. This tragedy was caused by widespread use of Diclofenac (an anti-inflammatory drug) to treat sick cattle.

FATAL COLLISIONS

Another significant cause of vulture mortality is midair crashes with big, human-made objects such as electricity pylons or ski lifts. It appears that the

CLEANING UP The carrion-eating activities of vultures are useful as they control the spread of cattle diseases such as brucellosis, to which the birds are immune. Pictured is the lappet-faced vulture, considered vulnerable.

large, slow-flying birds have difficulty in avoiding such artificial hazards. In California's Altamont Pass, collisions with wind turbines are a major threat to the tiny population of California condors. Fewer than 100 of these critically endangered birds remain.

CRITICAL CONDITION By 1987, only eight wild California condors were left, so all were captured to start a breeding project. Captive-bred condors have since been rereleased but the species is still extremely vulnerable.

Eagles, Hawks & Falcons Falconiformes

Super-keen senses and a razor-sharp bill and talons make these aerobatic species the most lethally effective predators of the bird world. Mercilessly persecuted by humans, often for no logical reason, they also suffer from habitat loss and poisoning.

THE RAPTORS

Eagles, hawks and falcons, together with their close relatives such as kites and the osprey, form a large group of around 290 species. They are known collectively as birds of prey, or raptors, and belong to the order Falconiformes, which also contains the vultures and condors (*see* pp. 114–115).

Raptors range in size from big eagles such as the harpy eagle, which weighs up to 20 pounds (9 kg) and snatches

NEW FLEDGLINGS Once the world's rarest raptor, the Mauritius kestrel was rescued by captive breeding. Its numbers grew from six in 1974 to 650–800 in 2000, enabling it to be released at new sites on the island.

sloths from the rainforest canopy, to various diminutive tropical falconets that weigh just a little over an ounce (35 g) on average – less than a common starling – and which feed on small vertebrates and insects. Raptors occur in many habitats worldwide and face many of the same threats as their prey. Chief among these is the loss of habitat, especially tropical forest. Two further distinct threats are persecution by humans and poisoning by pesticides and other agrochemicals – dangers that are probably greater for members of the Falconiformes than for any other group of birds.

SMALL RANGES

Many of the threatened raptor species occupy small geographic ranges, in which habitat loss, fragmentation and degradation have a more significant effect. For example, the destruction of the Mauritius kestrel's favored virgin evergreen forest almost drove it to extinction, reducing the numbers of this small island falcon to just six by the 1970s. Another restricted-range species

FRIEND OR FOE? In the past gamekeepers would shoot or poison any bird with a hooked bill, irrespective of its diet, and raptors such as this red kite suffered terribly. Many countries have since passed raptor protection laws.

is the Philippine eagle, found in rainforests on just four of the 7,000 islands in the Philippines archipelago: Mindanao, Luzon, Samar and Leyte. Widespread deforestation has already removed virtually all of the lowland rainforest; most surviving eagles cling to survival in remote mountain forests above 4,200 feet (1,300 m).

There are many similar instances of endangered raptors that are endemic (unique) to a specialized habitat on an island or in a small region. Their very names often allude to the problem: they include the New Guinea harpy eagle, Seychelles kestrel, Cuban kite, New Britain and Nicobar sparrowhawks, Galapagos hawk, Réunion harrier and Philippine and Javan hawk-eagles.

HUNTING THE HUNTERS

Raptors are magnificent predators, but they inspire mixed reactions in people, varying from admiration to disgust or even fear. Many species are routinely persecuted. The persecution of raptors is often based on the unsubstantiated assumption that, because these birds are predators, they must somehow be competing with humans for resources, or even taking livestock.

In truth, few raptors actively target domestic stock, and even then they usually pick off only weak or injured animals, or scavenge their carcasses. Raptor numbers are naturally held in check by the availability of prey, so a good population of raptors is a sure sign of a healthy ecosystem.

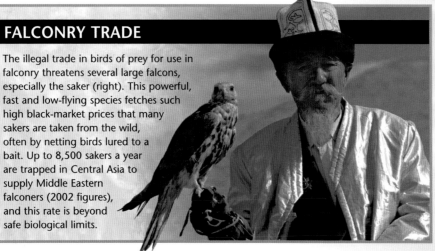

FALCONRY TRADE

The illegal trade in birds of prey for use in falconry threatens several large falcons, especially the saker (right). This powerful, fast and low-flying species fetches such high black-market prices that many sakers are taken from the wild, often by netting birds lured to a bait. Up to 8,500 sakers a year are trapped in Central Asia to supply Middle Eastern falconers (2002 figures), and this rate is beyond safe biological limits.

LETHAL SIDE EFFECTS

Often raptors are harmed accidentally through the ingestion of pesticides. For example, a hawk might catch a rat that has eaten grain sprayed with pesticides; the chemicals pass up through the food chain and accumulate in the body of the predator. The toxins do not always kill raptors outright – usually they cause harm via sublethal effects such as eggshell thinning, which reduces breeding success dramatically.

During the 20th century, DDT caused many raptors to decline in Europe and North America, including bald eagles, Eurasian sparrowhawks and peregrine falcons. A worldwide ban on DDT has been effective in restoring these species' populations. But the spread of malaria in Africa has seen renewed calls for its use to control mosquitoes, once again raising fears for raptor survival.

MARTIAL EAGLE Large eagles such as this one can take prey up to the size of gazelles, so cattle farmers are often tempted to kill them on sight.

PESTICIDE BAN
DDT weakened the eggshells of bald eagles so that entire clutches cracked under the weight of the sitting birds. The eagles' plight finally led to a ban on this pesticide.

Game birds Galliformes

For thousands of years, game birds have played an important part in human history. People raise species such as chickens, turkeys and guinea fowl, sometimes on an industrial scale, and hunt many others all over the world.

LINK TO HUMANS

The first-ever bird to be domesticated, probably in New Guinea or China over 5,000 years ago, was the barnyard chicken, whose ancestor is the red jungle fowl of Southeast Asia. Ironically, wild jungle fowl are now threatened by interbreeding with feral chickens living in forest villages. Many other kinds of game birds have since been reared in captivity. We also deliberately release game birds into the wild to create new populations for sport shooting. For example, ring-necked pheasants are commonly seen in the U.S. and Europe but are not native, originally coming from Central Asia.

WALK NOT FLY

In addition to the groups already mentioned, the game birds include grouse, quails, partridges, francolins, curassows and peafowl. There are 282 species, which occur worldwide, often in extreme habitats such as mountains, tundra or semidesert scrub.

Although many game birds fly well, most do so only reluctantly, preferring instead to walk. Their tendency to stay in one area, along with their preference for upland habitats, may explain why there are numerous small, isolated or relict populations of game birds, often in mountainous terrain. These species with limited distributions are naturally vulnerable to hunting and habitat loss.

VULNERABLE POPULATIONS

Sustained hunting over many years has dramatically reduced the numbers of game birds around the globe, such as prairie chickens in the United States, francolins in Africa, curassows in Latin America and pheasants in Asia. If hunting occurs at the same time as habitat loss, the situation is far worse.

The plight of two francolin species serves to illustrate this state of affairs. The woodland-dwelling Swierstra's francolin has a population of fewer than 10,000 birds at a handful of sites in western Angola, where intensifying deforestation will drive the species to extinction without conservation help. Meanwhile, the critically endangered

DANCING GROUND

A male great argus pheasant clears a patch of forest floor to dance his courtship ritual. In parts of the species' Asian range, particularly Borneo, trapping means this sight is fast becoming a rarity.

Djibouti francolin numbers fewer than 1,000 birds, restricted to just two sites. It is an upland forest species, but the forest is degraded with many dead and dying trees due to a combination of overgrazing by livestock, acid rain, firewood gathering and fungal attack, perhaps related to climate change.

SURVIVAL STRATEGIES

Game birds nest on the ground, so their eggs and chicks are at risk from a wide variety of predators, from dogs and cats to pigs, rodents, birds of prey and crows. Presumably because of this intense predation – the natural form of hunting – many game bird species have evolved life-history strategies to compensate. They lay large clutches of at least five and sometimes up to 20 eggs, to ensure enough young survive.

This ability to produce many eggs rapidly has long been exploited by humans to harvest domestic hens' eggs. It also means that wild game bird populations can be restored quickly, provided conservation measures such as hunting controls are put into place.

SCRATCHING A LIVING Blyth's tragopan is a scarce pheasant of thick mountain forests in southern Asia. Local people snare it for the pot, while slash-and-burn subsistence farming destroys or fragments its fragile habitat.

PAIR DUET Seldom glimpsed, the rare Congo peafowl skulks in lush undergrowth, where pairs sing loud duets. Its rainforest home has been ravaged by war, mining and agriculture.

EXTINCT

The story of the heath hen provides a graphic illustration of how game birds can easily be hunted to oblivion unless their populations are managed properly for this purpose, as happens with some grouse, partridges and pheasants. Heath hens were a race of the greater prairie chicken, found only in scrubby terrain in the eastern United States. European settlers caught them for food; it is claimed that heath hen, not turkey, may in fact have been served at the original Thanksgiving dinner. Heath hen numbers declined steadily until eventually the species was confined to Martha's Vineyard, an island off the coast of Massachusetts. There, a wildfire and a series of harsh winters took their toll, and the last known survivor died in 1932.

Cranes & Relatives Gruiformes

Famous for their graceful courtship dances and epic migrations, the cranes play a major part in folklore and cultural traditions but are now threatened as never before by hunting and habitat loss. Many of their colorful relatives are also at risk, especially the turkey-like bustards and flightless rails.

BEAUTIFUL DANCERS

There are 15 species of cranes, all of which have tall, elegant legs and long, dagger-shaped bills. Their impressively broad wingspans are an adaptation for performing long-distance flights. Cranes mate for life, and breeding pairs perform elaborately choreographed courtship dances to strengthen their bond each year. These ballets are accompanied by far-carrying honking or trumpeting, produced by the birds' specially elongated windpipes, which serve to amplify sounds. But cranes are among the

DOUBLE THREAT The Siberian crane is endangered by habitat loss – both in its wintering grounds in China, Pakistan, India and Iran and at its migratory stopover sites on the way to its Siberian breeding range.

bird families most at risk – nine species of crane are globally threatened and numbers of several others are in decline.

A VARIED GROUP

The cranes are classed with 10 other families of birds, including the bustards, finfoots, seriemas, button quails, kagu, rails and trumpeters.

Together, these form a large and varied order of birds: the Gruiformes. Bustards are stocky residents of flat, open country; the kori bustard of the African savanna is a leading contender for heaviest flying bird – males can weigh up to 42 pounds (19 kg). Other gruiformes resemble herons, wading birds, game birds or waterfowl.

Ornithologists are examining DNA evidence of the relationships between these seemingly dissimilar families. Unfortunately, one thing that they definitely share is the level of conservation concern they elicit.

NEW REFUGES With its huge red bill and bright plumage, the flightless, hen-sized takahe is an impressive rail. Formerly widespread across New Zealand, the bird almost died out due to habitat loss and attacks by non-native animals. In 1985, some takahes were taken to five offshore islands free of predators, where in safety their numbers are growing again.

DOWN TO EARTH The flightless kagu of New Caledonia forages for small prey among fallen leaves and in soft earth. A study of radio-tagged kagus showed that feral dogs pose the main threat to this rare ground dweller.

For example, 46 out of the 135 species of rail and 10 out of the 25 species of bustard are threatened. However, the causes for their conservation status differ between the groups.

RARE RAILS

Rails are small, ground-living, semi-aquatic birds found in a wide range of habitats from swamps to forest, usually among dense vegetation. Perhaps their most familiar members are coots and moorhens, some of which are very widespread. Because rails are generally more at home walking than flying, they often have evolved into flightless species when living in areas without natural predators. They provide an

excellent example of a process known as oceanic island endemism, whereby different sets of unique species evolve on different island groups.

Many remote islands in the Pacific Ocean, plus several in the southern Atlantic, have their own flightless species of rail. These island rails tend to have small, restricted populations, so are vulnerable to sudden changes in their envionment. And, of course, their flightlessness and plump bodies make them a perfect meal for human settlers and their introduced cats, dogs and rats. Fourteen species of rail have become extinct in recent history.

CHANGING LANDSCAPES

In contrast to rails, cranes favor huge open areas of marsh, wet grassland and forest, so their chief threats include the logging of forests, wetland drainage and agricultural intensification. Many species of crane found in the northern hemisphere migrate between their northern breeding and southern wintering grounds. This means they also require protection at their staging grounds – in effect, refueling stations where they can feed and rest – all along their migration routes. Bustards, meanwhile, mainly inhabit arid steppe country, so the spread of farming in

these dusty plains is a problem. Both bustards and cranes have long been hunted by people for food and sport.

STRUTTING ITS STUFF Much of the great bustard's native grassland has gone under the plow or been turned into fenced ranchland. This male is displaying to potential mates.

DANCING ON SNOW
Symbols of good luck, fidelity and long life, Japanese cranes were nevertheless almost hunted to extinction for their plumes. In late winter pairs dance to reaffirm their bond.

Waders, Gulls & Auks
Charadriiformes

These birds mostly live at sea, on coasts and in wetlands. They provide us with some of the natural world's greatest spectacles, often migrating huge distances or nesting in colonies thousands strong. Hunting has already killed off several species, but pollution, wetland drainage and climate change are potentially even more devastating.

GLOBETROTTERS

Waders, gulls and auks are three of the main groups in the Charadriiformes. Other members (not discussed here) of this large and very varied order include the terns, skuas, skimmers and sheathbills. Altogether the order contains almost 350 species, many of which migrate between breeding and wintering grounds, flying thousands of miles annually and often traversing continents or oceans.

Although they share an association with aquatic habitats, the waders, gulls and auks have a strikingly different appearance and lifestyles. The waders, also known as shorebirds, are typically long-legged, long-billed birds that feed on invertebrate prey at the water's edge or in the shallows, and may form large flocks outside the nesting season. They include plovers, sandpipers, curlews, avocets, stilts and oystercatchers. Gulls are aerobatic, strong-billed birds with an omnivorous diet, often featuring vertebrate prey and scavenged food,

FARMING THE PRAIRIE Long-billed curlews have vanished from much of North America's Midwest because wheatfields have replaced the prairie and pools they use for breeding.

and many species live along seashores. Auks, including guillemots and puffins, are among the most maritime of all birds and recall penguins in looks, but unlike them every species of auk alive today has the power of flight.

GAINS AND LOSSES

Around 60 charadriiform species are globally threatened, with the waders under greatest pressure. However, the picture is a mixed one because several

species, particularly gulls, are actually increasing in numbers. In Europe and North America, gulls have benefited from incidental food provision by the waste-disposal and fishing industries, and quickly spread into new habitats such as towns and farmland. A few species of gull have become pests as a result. Their success can threaten other birds: herring and lesser black-backed gulls, for example, prey on the chicks of a wide range of seabirds, and culls are needed to keep them in check.

But not all gulls are thriving. At least six species, including the lava gull of the Galapagos Islands, are at risk due to growing pressures on their habitat. Several others, such as the ivory gull of the Arctic seas and pack ice, are likely to be in trouble in the near future.

DIFFERENT THREATS

The threats to waders, gulls and auks have changed over the last 150 years. In the past, it was direct persecution of individual species that posed the main danger. Once-plentiful birds such as the great auk (*see* panel, opposite) or eskimo curlew of North America were

CONTAMINATED SEAS

Colonial seabird species are vulnerable to marine pollution incidents because so many congregate in one area, sharing the same offshore feeding grounds. Among the Charadriiformes, terns and gulls are sometimes affected, but it is the auks, which spend long periods swimming at sea, that suffer most heavily. Crude oil is one of the worst pollutants. Oil slicks on the surface of the sea prevent auks from fishing and thickly coat their plumage (oiled common guillemot, right). The victims lose their feathers' natural waterproofing, ingest oil during preening, and finally succumb to poisoning or starvation. Marine oil slicks are created by tankers flushing out their tanks and by disasters such as the wrecking of the *Exxon Valdez* in Prince William Sound, Alaska, in 1989.

ISLAND DWELLER Gulls are generally thought of as common birds, and even as pests, but this is not true of every species. Unique to the Galapagos Islands, the lava gull has probably always been rare and is classed as vulnerable.

gradually hunted to extinction. Even after protection measures were put in place in the 1940s, the rare wrybill plover of New Zealand continued to be shot for sport; this little, confiding wader survived, but is still vulnerable.

The chief threat to these groups of birds today is the much wider problem of environmental change. This takes many forms: marine pollution; the development of coastal mudflats and estuaries for industry, tidal barrages and urban expansion; the drainage of freshwater wetlands, often to create agricultural land; river "improvement" projects; and global warming.

LOCAL AND GLOBAL RISKS

A large proportion of the endangered waders, gulls and auks occupy small geographic ranges, which means they are at greater risk from habitat changes such as those just mentioned. Some nest only on certain island archipelagos.

Waders are ground-nesters, and some island-specific species are particularly vulnerable to alien predators introduced by humans.

It is not only restricted-range species that are in danger, however. There is mounting evidence that rising air and sea temperatures have the potential to threaten waders and seabirds that are numerous yet which "live on the edge" in ecological terms. Many waders fly north to breed on the Arctic tundra, where insect food is abundant during the short Arctic summer. However, while circumpolar in distribution, this habitat is critically limited by climate.

Just a few degrees of global warming will probably shrink the area of tundra in favor of forested taiga, massively reducing the breeding grounds of these Arctic nesters.

WARNING SIGN The ivory gull is believed to be at risk from climate change in the Arctic, where it forages among sea ice. Its Canadian population has fallen since the 1980s, which suggests that this process is already underway.

EXTINCT

Regularly described as the "penguin of the north," the great auk was a large, flightless seabird that bred abundantly around the North Atlantic coasts of Canada, Greenland and Iceland, and as far south as Ireland. Last seen in 1852, it was driven to extinction by harvesting for its feathers, meat and oil. Unable to take flight and rather clumsy on land, the great auk was easy sport. As it grew rarer, demand from collectors for its skins and eggs increased until none were left.

ENDANGERED WADER
Introduced mammals are a threat to the Chatham Island oystercatcher, by stealing its eggs and killing adult birds. Its nesting scrapes also suffer from trampling by cattle.

Doves & Pigeons Columbiformes

Flocks of pigeons are a familiar sight in towns and fields, but nowadays many members of their family are seriously under threat. Found worldwide, pigeons and doves are hunted for the pot and affected by the destruction of tropical forests.

TWO OF A KIND

Strictly speaking, there is no scientific distinction between a dove and a pigeon – the words merely reflect different origins (Anglo-Saxon and Norman French respectively). There are 308 species in a single family, Columbidae.

GLOBAL RANGE

In terms of lifestyle and behavior, there are strong parallels between pigeons and parrots, although they are not closely related. Both groups are herbivorous, with many fruit-eating species, and are strong fliers, which has enabled them to colonize large parts of the globe.

PINK PIGEON Numbers of this Mauritian species fell to under 20 in the 1980s, but captive breeding has saved it from extinction.

Many forms are endemic (unique) to particular islands, where they have subsequently been vulnerable to loss of habitat and hunting. Thus both the pigeons and parrots have lots of rare, localized species – around one-third of all pigeons and doves are threatened.

HARD TO SPOT Despite their often gorgeous plumage, fruit doves and pigeons blend in with the foliage of their treetop homes. They usually live quietly in pairs, but flocks gather to feast at large fruiting trees, especially wild figs. Many Southeast Asian species, including this Jambu fruit dove, are at risk from logging.

PIGEON MILK

Doves and pigeons have very small broods, typically of two chicks. This is because the adults feed their young on a rich "milk" secreted by the crop, which contains so much protein and fat that it requires a lot of energy to produce. However, the advantage is that it allows pigeons and doves to breed almost throughout the year, rather than only when food is plentiful.

GOOD EATING

Humans have always killed pigeons and doves for their succulent meat, giving the conservation movement two of its famous icons: the dodo and the North American passenger pigeon. The dodo was a plump, tame, flightless pigeon endemic to the island of Mauritius and for many it has come to symbolize extinction (*see* pp. 38–39).

(*see* pp. 38–39).

EXTINCT

North America's passenger pigeon bred in colonies and is thought to have been the world's most numerous bird. It was regarded as a pest for eating grain, and by 1900 had been shot and trapped to extinction in the wild. Its corpses were even used as fertilizer. The last one lived in the Cincinnati Zoo, and died in 1914.

Passenger pigeons were so numerous before the mass arrival of European settlers that as recently as 1800 their enormous flocks were said to darken the sky. No one imagined the species could disappear, so people continued to shoot it mercilessly for sport.

Numerous pigeons and doves have died out through human history due to overexploitation, but deforestation is an added menace in recent times. The pink pigeon, for example, suffered from destruction of its evergreen forest and scrub habitat during the late 20th century. At one time all the remaining birds lived in a single forest, but their former habitat is now being restored.

LACY PLUMES
The Victoria crowned pigeon lives in small groups, searching for fallen fruit in the rainforests of New Guinea. Deforestation and poaching for the pet trade are the species' main threats.

Parrots Psittaciformes

Parrots are the most threatened group of birds in the world. Every year hundreds of thousands of parrots are caught for the caged bird trade, the majority illegally, and many die before being put up for sale. Combined with rapid deforestation, this unsustainable pressure has put more than one-third of all parrot species at risk.

COLORFUL FAMILY

The 354 species of parrots, parakeets, cockatoos, lories and macaws comprise a well-defined group, and so form a single family, the Psittacidae, within their own order, the Psittaciformes. Many of them are brightly colored, intelligent and have certain apparently human-like characteristics, such as the ability to handle food dextrously with a foot while feeding. Some species are also excellent mimics, for example of the human voice, and are long-lived. All of these characteristics have ensured that parrots are highly prized as pets, and this has played a major part in their downfall. Nineteen species have died out in historical times, while a few dozen more are on the verge on extinction.

TRADE IN PARROTS

Despite the fact that many parrots will breed readily in captivity, most of them are still trapped extensively. This is because by far the greatest diversity of species occurs in developing forested regions of Latin America, sub-Saharan Africa

LONE SURVIVOR
This female Spix's macaw, photographed on a scientific expedition to Brazil in the mid-1980s, was one of the last-ever free-flying individuals of this species. Today, Spix's macaw is extinct in the wild.

PARROT FASHION Macaws are probably the parrot family's most sought-after pets. As a result, nine of the world's 17 species, including these military macaws, are now at risk.

and Southeast Asia, where poverty and lax law enforcement drive a thriving bird-trapping business. Wild-hatched parrots are cheaper than those reared by hand, so demand remains high.

Parrots pair for life and usually raise just one or two chicks each year, which in some species take up to nine weeks to fledge. As with any birds that have a low reproductive rate, thefts of adults from the wild have a drastic effect on populations. Chicks are stolen, too, an act that may cause irreparable damage to the tree-hole nest. Sometimes pairs do not recover from this trauma.

LAST OF THEIR KIND
The history of Spix's macaw offers an important case study. First described in 1832, this handsome Brazilian parrot was known to science only from traded birds for more than 150 years. In the 1980s it was at last located in the wild, but by then decades of trapping and habitat destruction had taken their toll and only three birds remained. These were captured in 1987 and 1988, thus making the species extinct

EXTINCT
North America's only native parrot, the Carolina parakeet, fell victim to rapid economic progress and decades of persecution. During the 1800s most of its riverine old-growth forest in the eastern U.S. went under the plow, and the flocks that survived were treated as crop pests. Hunters and farmers killed the parakeets by the thousands, while yet more were caught alive as pets. The last known specimen of this beautiful species died in captivity in 1918.

in the wild. In 2000, 60 Spix's macaws were known to be alive, of which 54 hatched in captivity.

Conservationists hope to return some Spix's macaws to the wild, but face two serious difficulties. The available gene pool of the species is small, creating the risk of inbreeding, and hardly any of its habitat remains. About 11 square miles (30 sq km) of its dry-country forest is left in the arid Caatinga region of northeastern Brazil – barely enough to support a few pairs. Moreover, there is no guarantee that macaws hatched in captivity have the right knowledge to survive in the wild.

Unlike Spix's macaw and the Carolina parakeet (*see* panel, above), most of the extinctions recorded among parrots to date relate to island forms. They include the Seychelles, Raiatea and Guadeloupe parakeets, Cuban and Jamaican macaws and Martinique parrot, to name but a few. Habitat loss and the pet trade, as well as hunting for food, were to blame.

SHRINKING RANGES Deforestation is not the only type of habitat loss to affect parrots. This orange-bellied parrot is endangered by salt marsh destruction in southeastern Australia, where it spends the winter.

PARROT CONSERVATION
In an effort to avoid any more parrots meeting the same fate, large sums are being channeled into captive breeding and habitat restoration programs, such as the high-profile project to save the kakapo of New Zealand. This rare, dumpy nocturnal parrot (the world's only flightless species) was endangered by introduced carnivores, so its entire population was translocated to small, predator-free offshore islands.

HIDDEN DEATH TOLL
For every parrot on sale in a pet shop, several others are likely to have died en route, and so the caged bird trade is exceptionally wasteful. Heavy mortality occurs between capture and export due to stress, disease and exhaustion, with the birds packed into poorly ventilated cages with inadequate food and water. There is also evidence that, for months after leaving quarantine, wild-caught parrots continue to die from disease and suffer from behavioral problems.

Owls & Nightjars Strigiformes

Among the most interesting yet poorly known groups of birds, at least in the tropics, owls and nightjars live worldwide in forests and many other habitats. Their famously stealthy, nocturnal lifestyle hinders efforts to evaluate their population trends and assess their threats, but it is safe to say that habitat loss presents the greatest single danger.

GENETIC DISCOVERIES

The classification of birds, and indeed all animals, is not fixed, but evolves as new evidence comes to light. Species, families and orders may be grouped in different ways or sometimes are placed in entirely new groups. Until recently, owls and nightjars were treated as two distinct orders: the Strigiformes (owls) and the Caprimulgiformes (nightjars). However, studies comparing their DNA have shown that they share a common ancestor. New classifications therefore "downgrade" these groups to suborders within an enlarged order: Strigiformes.

Exactly when the owls and nightjars separated historically is a mystery, but their origins must be ancient because the oldest owl fossils are around 65 million years old, while the oldest

FISHING OWL
Blakiston's fish owl inhabits thickly forested rivers in Siberia, northeast China and Hokkaido, where logging is endangering this magnificent species. The individual shown has been ringed as part of a conservation project.

FLAGSHIP SPECIES Something of a cause célèbre, the highly publicized decline of the northern spotted owl has brought attention to the loss of species-rich, old-growth forests in the western U.S. and southern Canada.

nightjar-type fossil dates back some 40 million years. That they are related should, perhaps, come as no surprise, given that many of their most obvious characteristics are shared.

HUNTERS OF THE NIGHT

Most owls and nightjars are nocturnal or crepuscular (active around the hours of dawn and dusk), and rest during the day. Their adaptations for a life in the dark include very large, light-gathering eyes, superb hearing and a wide range of eerie, far-carrying calls designed to penetrate the night air. Many species in both groups have beautifully cryptic (camouflaged) plumage, with elaborate and intricate patterning of browns and grays on every feather. This hides them from predators by day; owls usually sit tight against tree bark or among foliage, nightjars "freeze" on the ground.

One of the chief differences between owls and nightjars is their diet. All are predators, but most owls specialize in taking vertebrate prey, especially small rodents, whereas most nightjars feed on invertebrates such as moths, beetles and flies. The groups employ strikingly different feeding strategies. Owls drop on their victims from a perch or quarter the ground at low level to track down prey. Nightjars catch flying insects in midair, using their very broad, gaping mouths like huge scoops.

LACK OF DATA

There are around 204 species of owls and 118 of nightjars (including the owlet-nightjars, frogmouths, potoos and nighthawks). Relatively few are classed as globally threatened, but in part this no doubt reflects the difficulty of studying elusive nocturnal birds. Seldom seen and often found in dense forest habitats, owls and nightjars are usually monitored by counting calling birds in the breeding season.

We have only sketchy details of the behavior of many tropical owls and nightjars, particularly in rainforests, where the greatest diversity of species occurs. Recently, a number of "new" species previously unknown to science, such as Sri Lanka's Serendib scops owl, have been discovered. This is a rare event in the bird world that serves as a reminder of the gaps in our knowledge. Also, several species long thought to be extinct, including the forest owlet of India, have been found alive and well.

HABITAT LOSS

Owls and nightjars face similar threats. By far the most significant are habitat degradation – for example, modification of scrub, grassland and semidesert by cattle grazing – and habitat loss, especially deforestation by logging and the spread of farming. So-called "old-growth" (primary) forest is important for many

FOUND AGAIN Believed extinct for over a century, the forest owlet was located again in northern India in 1997. Its tiny population is threatened by illegal woodcutting, shifting cultivation, forest fires and grazing pressure.

species, such as the northern spotted owl of North America. The plight of this owl turned it into an icon of conservation interests fighting the financial and political power of big international logging companies.

Some of the most endangered owls and nightjars are endemic (unique) to islands. They include species such as the Philippine eagle-owl, Christmas Island hawk-owl and Puerto Rican nightjar. Fewer than 2,000 of the last-named species survive, due mainly to the loss of forest and the introduction of mongooses to the island in 1877. A ground-nester, like all nightjars, it is very vulnerable to predation.

The use of pesticides, such as DDT, has devastated the numbers of some owls and nightjars. Pesticides greatly reduce the density of flying insects, which nightjars depend on. They also travel up food chains and accumulate in the body fat of rodent-eating owls.

FEWER INSECTS European nightjars have become rare in the west of their range due to a loss of heathland for breeding and a reduction in insect prey.

Hummingbirds & Swifts
Trochiliformes & Apodiformes

Masters of the air, these fast-living birds have a special wing structure that permits amazing feats of aerobatics. Hummingbirds dart to and fro in a blur, while swifts hardly ever land, except to nest. Several species are poised on the brink of extinction due to the loss of their habitat, so we stand to lose some of the most wonderful birds that ever existed.

UNIQUE FEATURES

Formerly lumped in the same order, the hummingbirds and swifts are now recognized as being sufficiently distinct on the basis of their DNA that they are split into two groups: the Trochiliformes and Apodiformes respectively. They provide a good illustration of the way in which new DNA profiling techniques have led to major advances in how we classify the world's birds.

One of the most distinctive features shared by these exciting birds is tiny feet, at times giving the impression that they are footless. This adaptation to a highly aerial lifestyle means that hummingbirds and swifts cannot walk, or even hop; indeed, swifts are able only to cling onto vertical surfaces. Another characteristic, unique to these groups, is that the "elbow" joint of the wing is located close beside the body to give maximum flexibility.

Hummingbirds can hover and are the only birds capable of flying backward, while groups of swifts maneuver in tight, fast-moving formations like an air force's display team.

The dull, gray or brown plumage of swifts is as unremarkable as their flight is spectacular, but hummingbirds have gorgeously colored, iridescent feathers that shimmer in the sunlight.

FRENETIC PACE

Relentlessly active, hummingbirds beat their wings up to 80 times per second, and refuel by regularly drinking high-calorie nectar from flowers. Swifts also lead a high-energy lifestyle, spending virtually their entire lives on the wing. They feed by trawling the sky for insect "plankton" with wide-open bills.

Where these birds differ most is their life history. Hummingbirds are short-lived fast breeders, whereas swifts are long-lived slow breeders. In the latter group, each year's breeding season can be a very protracted affair. By contrast, hummingbird chicks grow much more quickly, and many species can produce multiple broods in the same year.

RELATIONSHIP WITH PEOPLE

Hummingbirds are important in the cultural history of Latin America, and the scientists who described these birds gave their various genera (groups) some delightful names, including sunangel, woodnymph, ruby, emerald and hillstar. They are ecologically important, too, because they pollinate many flowers, particularly deep-throated ones such as bromeliads, heliconias and fuchsias. If hummingbird numbers decline in an

BIRD'S NEST SOUP

Swiftlets are small members of the swift family that breed in very large colonies in caves, where they construct a nest of plant scraps and saliva stuck to the cave wall. For centuries their nests have been harvested to make bird's nest soup. This practice can be sustainable if managed carefully, but the populations of several island species, including the Seychelles and Mascarene swiftlets, are highly vulnerable to overexploitation.

TINY RANGE
Critically endangered by deforestation, Colombia's beautiful chestnut-bellied hummingbird lives only on the forested slopes of the Serranía de San Lucas and East Andes.

CROP THREAT
Unique to dry forests in the
northwest of Peru, marvelous
spatuletails are disappearing
fast. They are endangered by
the spread of cash crops such
as coffee and marijuana.

The Honduran Emerald

Two species of hummingbird have died
out in historical times: Brace's emerald
and Gould's emerald, both of which
were last seen in the 1800s. Now one
of their living relatives, the Honduran
emerald, may be on the way out, too.
This critically endangered species lives
within an area of just $4^1/2$ square miles
(12 sq km) in Honduras, Central
America. Although estimates vary, it is
thought that fewer than 200 individuals
survive. The species' population trend
is still downward, so it could already be
too late to avert its demise.

NECTAR SUPPLY
Honduran emeralds (this is a male) display a
glittering blue throat and upper chest, and are
otherwise metallic green. Like all hummingbirds,
they rely on flowers for food, although they
supplement this nectar diet with a few insects.
It is not yet known if they feed from only a few
types of bloom, or are not so fussy, but this may
be of great significance for their conservation.

SPECIALIZED HABITAT
The Honduran emerald is restricted to arid
thorn-forest and scrub, where the dominant
plants are drought-adapted succulents, cacti
and mimosas. Most of this habitat has been
destroyed to make way for cattle grazing,
pineapple plantations and rice cultivation.

area, certain flowers could
therefore vanish, potentially
with an adverse impact on the
health of the wider ecosystem.

The worst threat to hummingbirds
is loss of habitat, especially rainforest
and dry tropical forest. Of the world's
335 species, around 30 are globally at
risk; at least one, the Bogotá sunangel,
might already be extinct. Most of the
endangered species, including the very
rare chestnut-bellied hummingbird of
Colombia, are unique to small areas,
so any damage to habitat within their
range is potentially catastrophic.

Compared to hummingbirds, swifts
are in general at much less risk – of the
102 swift species, just six are threatened.
These highly mobile aerial feeders can
travel daily to different foraging areas,
so are not tied to specific habitats. In
their case, the main danger is the loss
of nest sites and disturbance during the
breeding season (see panel, left).

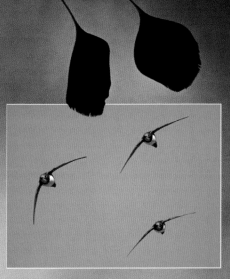

UP IN THE AIR Swifts such as these alpine
swifts feed on the wing, so typically are safe
from the peril of habitat destruction, although
falling insect numbers could be a problem.

Hornbills & Woodpeckers
Coraciiformes & Piciformes

Although not closely related, these groups of forest birds both nest in tree holes and have long, powerful bills, which in the hornbills are hugely expanded to form some of the most spectacular appendages in the animal kingdom. The frightening speed with which the Earth's mature, old-growth forests are being lost presents a grave threat to these colorful birds.

FOSSIL RECORD

Hornbills and woodpeckers are ancient groups that are well represented in the fossil record. The oldest hornbill fossil, found in Morocco, dates from the mid-Miocene, around 15 million years ago. The earliest woodpecker fossils are 25 million years old, but holes in fossilized trees suggest that these birds may have been around for up to 25 million years before that. As the planet's green forest cover is shrinking at a rate not seen for several million years, these groups are coming under growing pressure.

There are 57 hornbill species, which form one of 10 diverse families in the order Coraciiformes; this varied group also includes the kingfishers. With their massive bills that give a front-heavy appearance, hornbills bear a superficial resemblance to toucans, but in fact the latter are related to woodpeckers. The 217 species of woodpeckers, together with the toucans and several other families, all belong to the Piciformes.

HORNY CASQUE
In addition to deforestation, the rhinoceros hornbill is under pressure from hunting for its meat and its upswept casque, used as an ornament and in tribal festivals.

RAPID DECLINE In the U.K., the lesser spotted woodpecker's population has fallen by almost 80 percent in the last 30 years, probably due to a shortage of rotten wood for feeding.

SPECIALIZED BILLS

Hornbills are mostly big, strongly built birds, and use their large, downcurved bills to feed on a wide variety of fruits and nuts, as well as insects and small vertebrate prey. In several species, the upper mandible is drawn out into a curved, horny structure called a casque. Hornbill casques are surprisingly light as they contain plenty of air space.

Woodpeckers vary greatly in size, but the bill shape is consistent between all species: the elongated, sharply pointed design is suited to chiseling grubs and other invertebrates out of wood or bark, and excavating nest holes. Some species also use their bills to drum rapidly on trees – a form of territorial song. To cushion the impact of repeated blows and protect the brain, the skull is extra thick and incorporates a "suspension" system of special softening tissues.

WHERE IN THE WORLD

Most of the world's mainland wooded areas are home to woodpeckers, from vast taiga forests in the far north and coniferous forests at the southern tip of Chile to humid tropical rainforests. By contrast, hornbills are exclusive to the Old World tropics, including sub-Saharan Africa, the Indian subcontinent

and Southeast Asia, with a particular diversity of species in the Indonesian and Philippine islands.

Today, nine species of hornbills are endangered to some degree, while half of the remainder are regarded as near-threatened, and this reflects the scale of forest destruction in Southeast Asia. For example, at one time 94 percent of the Philippines was cloaked with lush rainforest, but during the 20th century indiscriminate logging by multinational corporations and uncontrolled forest-clearance for agriculture and open-pit mining removed more than two-thirds of the forest in just 50 years. As a result, the Philippines' Palawan, Sulu, Mindoro tarictic, Visayan tarictic and Visayan wrinkled hornbills are all at risk.

As a group, the woodpeckers appear to be in less trouble than the hornbills, with a total of 11 globally threatened species. However, two similar species died out during the last century – or are close to extinction – the imperial woodpecker of Mexico (last seen in 1956) and the ivory-billed woodpecker of the United States (*see* panel, right). In both cases, commercial logging of old-growth forests was the main problem.

ANCIENT FORESTS

Worldwide, it is old-growth, or primary, forests that are the most important for birds and people alike. They typically have a wider variety of tree species, and thus provide more types of lumber for loggers and more feeding opportunities for hornbills, woodpeckers and other birds. Towering, decades-old trees are most valuable to loggers, but they also are needed by many woodpeckers and hornbills for their nest holes.

It follows that these groups of birds offer a good indication of the health of forest environments. The lesser spotted woodpecker is a good example. Found across temperate Eurasia, its numbers are falling despite there being plenty of forest in its range. Experts blame the removal of the dead, rotting wood it prefers by "tidy" forestry management.

EXTINCT?

Ornithologists debate whether the huge ivory-billed woodpecker still exists. It was fairly common in old-growth forests in the southeastern U.S. until the 1930s, after which its numbers were decimated by logging and hunting. Last seen in 1962, the species was declared extinct, but claimed again in 2005. Some now doubt the reliability of the new record, which stunned the global scientific community.

MOUNTING PRESSURE Native to Philippine islands, the Visayan tarictic hornbill has lost virtually all of its lowland forest, and it is also heavily hunted for its flesh and horny bill.

Songbirds Passeriformes

Two-thirds of all living bird species are songbirds, or perching birds, and they occur in every habitat on Earth's land surface. The catalog of different threats faced by songbirds reads like an inventory of our harmful impact on the biosphere.

SPECIES DIVERSITY

There are more than 5,700 species of songbirds, or passerines (members of the order Passeriformes). This total is actually increasing as studies of avian DNA enable ornithologists to elevate forms previously regarded merely as races, or subspecies, into full species.

Songbirds are therefore arguably the world's most successful group of birds. They range in size from tiny South American flycatchers weighing just a fraction of an ounce to ravens that can reach over 4 pounds (2 kg), while their plumages and bill shapes are equally diverse. Among the many lifestyles in this group there are aquatic songbirds (dippers), highly aerobatic songbirds (swallows and martins), predatory songbirds (shrikes) and parasitic songbirds (some finches and weavers), as well as species that eat almost every kind of seed, fruit and insect.

A PRICE ON ITS HEAD The Bali starling's stunning plumage has been its downfall, with illegally caught birds changing hands for up to US$2,000 during the 1990s. Years of poaching mean that it is virtually extinct in the wild.

RARE AND ABUNDANT

The order Passeriformes includes many of the common species with which we are familiar as garden birds in Europe and North America, such as members of the sparrow, chickadee, thrush, robin, starling and wren families. But it also comprises some of the most threatened species on the planet, including the critically endangered Bachman's warbler of the southern United States, which, having not been

EXTINCT

New Zealand's huia became extinct in 1907, just 12 years after this illustration was published. The species was unusual for the extraordinary difference between the short-billed males (below) and long-billed females. Even before the arrival of European settlers in the 1800s, the huia was rare due to predation by rats and dogs, introduced to New Zealand by Maoris. Hunting to supply exhibits for the Europeans' stuffed bird collections sealed its fate.

FRAGMENTED FOREST
The seven-coloured tanager lives in Brazil's Atlantic forest, 98 percent of which has been cleared. It clings to survival in the small, isolated patches of forest that remain.

sighted since 1988, is probably extinct. The Bali starling has a wild population estimated at just 12 individuals, the Banggai crow of Indonesia and the São Tomé grosbeak both have fewer than 50 individuals, and the Amami thrush of the Japanese Amami archipelago has a global population of about 60. In all, 72 songbird species are considered to be critically endangered – that is, they have a 50:50 chance of becoming extinct within the next 10 years.

BREEDING FAILURE

Many threatened songbirds have small geographic ranges, such as islands or isolated mountains, valleys and forests, for example. However, the demise of a continental species like Bachman's warbler indicates that even formerly widespread songbirds can be driven to extinction by human activities.

Songbirds are essentially short-lived, fast-breeding species (although those found nearer the equator tend to have smaller broods and live longer than those in temperate regions). This life history strategy means that a series of poor breeding seasons, perhaps because of a sudden increase in predation or a depleted food supply caused by habitat degradation, is sometimes capable of reducing plentiful, wide-ranging species to dangerously low numbers.

THE CAGED BIRD TRADE

One in 10 of all the world's globally threatened birds owe their plight to trapping for the bird trade. This figure includes dozens of parrots (*see* pp. 126–127) and many songbird species, such as the Java sparrow and the Bali starling, both from Indonesia, and the red siskin, from Venezuela and Colombia. The problem is worst in Asia, where there are huge markets selling wild-caught birds. At a single market in Java, between 500,000 and 1.5 million wild birds are sold each year.

MANY DANGERS

Songbirds display such diversity that it was possibly inevitable that they should between them end up facing all of the same threats as other bird groups.

Numerous songbirds suffer from the loss of habitat – especially deforestation, the conversion of natural grassland to agriculture, the drainage of wetlands and redevelopment of coastlines. The myriad other dangers facing songbirds include: capture for the pet trade (*see* panel, above); introduced mammalian or reptilian pests; competition

from exotic (introduced) bird species; persecution for food, plumes or sport; excessive pesticide use; and climate change. Often it is a combination of several threats that pushes a species to the brink. Or a single, local hazard may be enough. For instance, the Sidamo lark is vulnerable to military exercises in its native Ethiopia.

DOWNLISTED The Seychelles magpie-robin is one of only a few birds to be "downlisted" from "critical" thanks to direct conservation action. It was rescued by restoring coastal forest and by predator eradication.

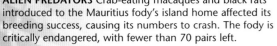

ALIEN PREDATORS Crab-eating macaques and black rats introduced to the Mauritius fody's island home affected its breeding success, causing its numbers to crash. The fody is critically endangered, with fewer than 70 pairs left.

Tortoises Chelonia

Tortoises are distinguished from freshwater turtles and terrapins by their thick, elephantine feet and short, webless toes. They range from tiny 3-inch (8 cm) African speckled padlopers to the 3½-foot (1.1 m) Galapagos giant tortoises. Most tortoise species are under threat and several species have recently gone extinct.

LUMBERING GIANTS

Giant tortoises are among the most vulnerable of all animals. Slow-moving and confined to a few isolated islands, they were easy prey to seafarers desperate for fresh meat. Their ability to survive long periods of inactivity and starvation made them ideal for storage, and ships loaded as many tortoises as they could carry. Even Darwin dined on giant tortoise aboard the *Beagle*. Not surprisingly, many of the island races, subspecies and even species went extinct during the "golden age of exploration" in the 18th and 19th centuries. Tortoise populations were even threatened by the scientists who went to study them, as collecting museum specimens was the primary aim. The need for conservation does not seem to have been recognized as important. Recently, 39 Galapagos giant tortoises were butchered by sea squirt fishermen, in what appeared to be a dispute with environmentalists.

FERTILITY PROBLEM The highly endangered Egyptian tortoise, *Testudo kleinmanni*, is used in Egypt for dubious fertility drugs.

ROADKILL

Tortoises are common road casualties, particularly leopard tortoises and angulate tortoises in southern Africa, dopher tortoises and desert tortoises in the U.S., and Indian starred tortoises in India and Sri Lanka. In many black spots, conservation groups erect warning signs, but the death rates are still far too high.

POPULAR PETS

Tortoises have been popular pets for centuries. Captain Cook is said to have presented the King of Tonga with a pet giant tortoise, and many similar large specimens were kept in the embassies and consuls of European powers. The 18th-century naturalist Gilbert White kept a tortoise called Timothy at Selbourne, in the United Kingdom. However, modern commercial exploitation is a major threat to populations. Shipments of European spur-thighed tortoises, Hermann's tortoises and even the severely threatened Egyptian tortoise are regularly seized by the authorities. Recently, a large number of plowshare tortoises, or angonoka, one of the rarest tortoises in the world, were stolen from a reserve in Madagascar, only to turn up in the exotic pet trade in Europe. The tiny padlopers, *Homopus*, eroded hingeback tortoises, *Kinixys*, and the flat-shelled, crevice-dwelling pancake tortoise of Africa are highly

SLOW PROGRESS Large numbers of desert tortoises, *Gopherus agassizii*, are killed on the roads of California and Arizona.

STOLEN FROM THE WILD The Namaqua speckled padloper, *Homopus signatus*, is one of the world's smallest tortoises. It is increasingly threatened by the illegal pet trade.

prized by unscruplous collectors. The authorities do not always act in the best interests of the endangered species. In 1996, for example, the Swedish Ministry of Agriculture ordered the destruction, by freezing, of 1,000 endangered Horsfield's tortoises that were illegally imported from Tajikstan. The "euthanization" went ahead despite international protests.

HABITAT DESTRUCTION

Deforestation removes the food sources for tortoises and exposes them to high temperatures and the attentions of predators and humans. Fire is a very serious threat since tortoises cannot flee or take cover quickly. Tortoises inside sugarcane fields and crops that undergo an annual burn are regularly killed in the process. Agricultural development in East Africa has led to a loss of habitat for the pancake tortoise, and many other species are suffering a similar fate.

FOOD FOR THOUGHT

Many species are sought for meat or inclusion in Chinese medicine. An unscrupulous poacher using a tortoise-sniffing dog can clear out a population in a very short time if he has a market in which to sell the animals. In Asia, the Burmese starred tortoise, the Asian giant tortoise and the elongate tortoise are just three of the species that are regularly collected for their meat and shells, which are used in Chinese tonics of dubious efficacy.

LOST GIANTS
Of the 15 races of Galapagos tortoises, four are extinct. One race, that from Pinta Island, is represented by a sole surviving male, aptly named Lonesome George.

Freshwater Turtles Chelonia

The plight of sea turtles and giant tortoises is well publicized, but many freshwater turtles and terrapins are even more endangered by the actions of humans. The situation is especially desperate in Asia, home to 15 of the 19 species listed as critically endangered by the World Conservation Union (IUCN). So serious is the issue that it is referred to by conservationists as the "Asian Turtle Crisis."

PIG SNOUT The Fly River turtle, *Carettochelys insculpta*, has a pig-like, long-proboscis snout and flippers like a sea turtle. It is hunted for its flesh by the indigenous people of Australia and New Guinea and is vulnerable to extinction.

TURTLE OR TERRAPIN?

The 11 families of freshwater turtles are divided into "side-necked turtles," which withdraw their long necks in an "S-shape" sideways across the front of the carapace, and the "hidden-neck turtles," which withdraw their heads and short necks straight back into the carapace. Nine freshwater turtles, sea turtles and tortoises belong to this latter group. Freshwater turtles range from terrestrial or semiaquatic forest-dwelling box turtles to the classic hard-shelled, semiaquatic "terrapin" and fully aquatic softshell turtles. Most freshwater turtles can be distinguished from sea turtles by the presence of clawed and webbed forefeet rather than elongated flippers.

ASIAN TURTLE CRISIS

Of the 10 Asian box turtles, *Cuora*, six are critically endangered, including the Vietnamese flowerback box turtle and the yellow-headed box turtle. The Yunnan box turtle is already extinct.

The main threat is collection for food using trained "turtle-sniffing" dogs. For defense, box turtles rely on closing up the front and back of the hinged plastron to form a protective box in which to wait out the threat. Sadly, this is no defense against collection and, each year, thousands of the turtles are transported to markets to supply the demand for turtle flesh.

RIVER TURTLES

The great rivers of South America and Southeast Asia are inhabited by large hard-shelled river turtles that use riverine sandy beaches for their egg laying. Local people harvest the eggs, and the turtles themselves, for meat. Large species like the 30-inch (80 cm) South American river turtle and the 24-inch (60 cm) painted river turtle – and 22-inch (56 cm) mangrove terrapin from Southeast Asia – are heavily exploited. And as the larger species are depleted, hunters target smaller species, which are increasingly threatened.

ISLAND SPECIALITIES

Many smaller turtles are popular in the pet trade, and overcollecting from small populations causes extinction. Island populations are particularly at risk. The Roti Island snake-neck

SNIFFED OUT BY DOGS The Vietnamese flowerback turtle, *Cuora galbinifrons*, is one of the 10 Asian box turtles that have been driven to the brink of extinction by the ever-increasing demand for turtle meat in China.

turtle from Indonesia is now deemed to be "commercially extinct," while the secretive Sulawesi forest turtle is threatened by a triple whammy: collection for meat, for the pet trade and for traditional Chinese medicine.

EATEN INTO EXTINCTION

The alligator snapping turtle of the southeastern U.S. is the largest American freshwater turtle with a maximum carapace length of 30 inches (80 cm) and a weight of 242 pounds (110 kg). Almost totally aquatic, it feeds on fish and crayfish, but it has itself been the target of excessive collection for its meat, which is prized in Cajun cuisine and featured on menus in New Orleans restaurants. Long-lived, slow-growing and easy to

catch in nets and traps, this vulnerable giant is in real danger of extinction and was placed on CITES Appendix III in June 2006. Sadly, controls against collection will not prevent another major threat – the development of lakeside properties and the destruction of turtle nesting beaches.

RAREST TURTLE

The rarest freshwater turtle is the Shanghai softshell turtle. Believed extinct in its native eastern China, there are six specimens in Chinese zoos and an adult male in a polluted lake in Hanoi, Vietnam. Myth tells that a 15th-century Vietnamese "King Arthur" called Le Loi defeated an invading Chinese army. After the battle

MEGA-MOUTH The huge alligator snapping turtle, *Macrochelys temmincki*, is hunted for its meat, which is considered a delicacy in Cajun cuisine. The hard surfacing of lake edges for recreation has removed many nesting sites.

he visited Lake Luc Thuy, where a turtle asked him to return his magical sword to the water. The king threw the sword into the lake, where the turtle caught it in its mouth and took it to the bottom. The lake is now known as Ho Hoan Kiem, "Lake of the Returned Sword", and it is this lake that is home to the last surviving semiwild Shanghai softshell turtle.

GENTLE GIANT
The South American river turtle, *Podocnemis expansa*, was hunted for its eggs and meat by the people who live along all the major Amazonian tributaries.

Sea Turtles Chelonia

Having survived on Earth for over 220 million years, these magnificent and mysterious ocean wanderers are being exploited or disturbed by humans almost everywhere that they are found. All but one of the seven species of sea turtle is endangered through a combination of marine pollution, overharvesting, accidental drowning and damage to nesting beaches.

MAJESTIC REPTILES

During the so-called "Age of Discovery" (*see* pp. 38–39), sailors relied on fresh turtle meat to supplement their meager rations. Sadly, today we continue to exploit or interfere with these majestic reptiles, and drastic action is urgently needed to save some species.

Sea turtles are superbly adapted for a marine lifestyle, with flipper-like limbs, a streamlined shell and an ability to navigate across vast stretches of open ocean. They nest on land, returning to beaches to lay large clutches of white eggs that hatch 6–8 weeks later. There are seven species of sea turtles: the six hard-shelled members of the family Cheloniidae, plus the primeval-looking leatherback turtle, which belongs to its own family, the Dermochelyidae.

DRIVEN TO THE BRINK

Most of the sea turtles have a global distribution. As recently as the 19th century, their populations reached well into the millions, but in the last 100 years or so, humans have overwhelmed their ability to maintain their numbers. Sea turtles are captured for their meat, skin and shells, and accidentally drown in fishing nets or after swallowing the baits on longlines intended for tuna. Their foraging grounds are polluted or destroyed, their eggs collected and their age-old nesting sites turned into tourist resorts where egg-laying females become confused by the bright neon lights and wander inland to die, trapped in the flotsam and jetsam above the beach.

CAUGHT BY MISTAKE
The powerful loggerhead turtle, *Caretta caretta*, is one of the few sea turtles to fight back if molested. Every year thousands of this species die in fishing nets, but special trapdoors are being fitted to nets to let the turtles escape.

Very few sea turtle populations are unaffected by modern-day fishing techniques or by poaching. As a result, six of the species are in serious trouble: only the flatback turtle is not currently regarded as endangered. However, it too may be vulnerable because it has a relatively restricted migratory range off northern and northeastern Australia.

GIANT OF THE GROUP

The largest, most distinctive sea turtle is the leatherback, which has a ridged, shield-shaped shell covered with thick, leathery skin. Some specimens used to grow to almost 6½ feet (2 m) and weighed over 1,545 pounds (700 kg), but leviathans like these are no longer seen – evidence of a long-term population decline.

Leatherbacks can dive as deep as some whales, but usually inhabit the surface waters. Their main prey is open-ocean jellyfish, which has been their downfall because many leatherbacks have made the fatal mistake of trying to catch and eat floating plastic bags. The bags block their gut, causing death by starvation.

CHIEF TARGETS

The hawksbill turtle, which uses its narrow, beak-like mouth to forage for sponges and shellfish, has long been

COMMUNAL NESTING
Olive ridley turtles, *Lepidochelys olivacea*, are vulnerable to overharvesting because they breed at so few sites. Important sites are found in Mexico, Costa Rica and India.

famous for its beautifully marked shell. For this reason it has borne the brunt of hunting to supply "tortoiseshell," which is carved, treated and polished to make ornaments and utensils, from combs to necklaces. Plastics have greatly reduced the demand for tortoiseshell, but it is still used in illicit luxury items.

The green turtle is the most vegetarian of the group, munching seagrass and the leaves of mangroves and other coastal vegetation. It is also the most exploited, as its flesh is used for turtle soup and its eggs are eaten as a delicacy, both by local peoples and in gourmet restaurants around the world. Other turtles suffer

HOMING INSTINCT All sea turtles, including this female leatherback, tend to return to the same beaches to nest. If their favored stretch of coastline is redeveloped or disturbed, their chances of breeding are effectively ruined.

from this trade to varying degrees, but the meat of the loggerhead turtle is considered unpalatable.

Smallest of all the sea turtles are the olive ridley and Kemp's ridley turtles. More than any others, these species often congregate to nest; some mass nestings of olive ridleys involve up to 150,000 females. The gatherings, called arribadas, have become popular tourist attractions. Such ecotourism is a mixed blessing – it raises awareness about the conservation of sea turtles, but human disturbance can disorient the turtles.

INTERNATIONAL PROTECTION

All sea turtles are now legally protected by national and local regulations, and also under international law, including CITES restrictions in the trade of the turtles and their parts and products. However, a thriving illegal trade is still a significant threat and an evident lack of international coordination hampers even the most determined conservation efforts. Sea turtles are blatantly hunted and slaughtered in many parts of the world, and their future is uncertain.

TURTLE RESEARCH

Although marine turtles spend almost all their time at sea, most conservation programs focus on nesting beach activities such as beach patrols or taking eggs to artificial incubators (to boost hatchling survival rates). This emphasis has inadvertently left big gaps in our knowledge about these reptiles: conservation of eggs and hatchlings, without conservation of the adult turtles, might not be enough to save these species. In this photo, scientists tag a female hawksbill turtle on Cousine Island, Seychelles, to learn more about its life history and population trends.

Nonvenomous Snakes
Serpentes

Nonvenomous snakes are threatened by deforestation, habitat loss, collection for the pet trade and hunting for their meat and skins. Also, they suffer from active persecution despite the fact that most nonvenomous species are harmless to humans.

ROUND ISLAND EROSION

Round Island is a small volcanic island situated 13 miles (22 km) northeast of Mauritius in the Indian Ocean. It was home to a startling array of unique animals and plants found nowhere else on the planet. Humans introduced goats and rabbits in the 19th century, and these animals grazed the plant cover, leading to the almost total degradation of the endemic hardwood forest and palm forest and the loss, through erosion, of the island's soil down to the volcanic bedrock. With the soil went the burrowing animals and into extinction passed the unique Round Island burrowing boa, one of only two species in the primitive family Bolyeridae. Being more arboreal, the Round Island boa was more fortunate and was saved from extinction by conservationists.

BOAS OF THE CARIBBEAN

The Caribbean is home to a wide variety of boas including most of the representatives of the genus *Epicrates* that range in size from Cuban boas over 13 feet (4 m) long to the diminutive Bahaman boa and Ford's boa, which hardly reach 3 feet (1 m) in length. Many of these island boas are threatened by deforestation, habitat loss to mining or agriculture and active persecution. This is despite the fact none of these islands possess dangerous

ROUND ISLAND RETURNING The Round Island boa, *Casarea dussumieri*, is now being captive-bred by the Jersey Wildlife Preservation Trust. In the meantime, the goats and rabbits have been eradicated from the Island and vegetation cover is being reestablished.

DEADLY INTRODUCTION
The Jamaican boa has been hunted to near extinction by the Indian mongoose, which was introduced in 1872, and which has caused problems on islands all over the world.

venomous snakes with which the boas could be confused. The Jamaican boa and Puerto Rican boa were being killed so as not to deter visits by tourists, the lifeblood of these islands, and at one time the "no-snakes" message formed part of the tourism campaign. Despite captive breeding programs and the most intensive international protection available for any species, both are still threatened. Puerto Rican boas are also killed for their fat, which some islanders believe has medicinal properties, while the Jamaican boa suffered following the introduction of a voracious mongoose. The Mona Island boa and the Virgin Islands boa from west and east of Puerto Rico respectively are also in dire straits. Both are small subspecies that fall easy prey to feral cats, pigs and rats. The habitat is also under serious threat from commercial development.

Another Caribbean boa under terrible threat, largely through collection for the pet trade, is the Hog's Island boa, a small, pastel-colored population of the Central American boa. It may already be beyond salvation even though measures are now being taken to protect both the boa and its habitat.

RACER IS NOT FAST ENOUGH

Not just boas are endangered in the Caribbean, many of the colubrid snakes, five Antillean racers of the genus *Alsophis* and the St. Vincent blacksnake are in trouble. The Antiguan racer is sometimes referred to as the rarest snake in the world. It was extirpated from Antigua itself by accidentally introduced rats, deliberately introduced mongooses and active persecution by humans. The snake is now the subject of a reintroduction program from its sole surviving natural population on the neighboring Great Bird Island. This collaborative project began in 1995, when only 60 racers remained on Great Bird Island; even today there are only approximately 150 Antiguan racers in existence. Education has played a vital role, developing a national

SNAKESKIN TRADE

Many snakes are collected for their skins. Bags of cobras, ratsnakes and pythons are drowned to kill them without damaging their skins. Snakeskin is a much desired fashion accessory and sometimes snakes are skinned alive to obtain it. It may be small-scale or industrial in its organization. In the Philippines, sea kraits are collected by the handful and taken to factories, while in Indonesia entire slaughterhouses are devoted to processing reticulated and short-tailed pythons – almost one million pythons being slaughtered in Borneo and Sumatra alone each year. The skin trade is a huge threat to the survival of some species.

pride in the species and spreading the message that it is harmless.

RARE SNAKES REDISCOVERED

One of the rarest of all boas is Cropan's boa, which is known from two preserved specimens, which were collected near Sao Paulo, in the heavily deforested Brazilian Atlantic coastal forests, in the 1930s. Occurring so close to one of the most overcrowded cities on the planet, Cropan's boa was long thought extinct. A recent report of a road-killed specimen raises the hope that this strange, ground-dwelling species may yet be found alive. A similar story exists for the Indian egg-eating snake – an extremely rare rear-fanged snake known only from northeastern India and not seen for decades. A live specimen was reported from the rainforests of the Western Ghats of southwest India, which may indicate a much wider range than was formerly known.

YELLOW CRAZY ANTS

Christmas Island is a remote Indian Ocean island under Australia. It is home to a diverse and endemic fauna including shrews, bats, rats and land crabs, geckos and skinks, and even an endemic snake, the pink Christmas Island blindsnake. Blindsnakes are tiny, primitive burrowing snakes with their

eyes reduced to small, pigmented areas under semitranslucent scales. They feed on termites and ant eggs and are rarely seen above the surface, except after heavy rain, and then only at night. Christmas Island fauna has co-existed in isolation until the arrival of humans, and the even more damaging arrival of the yellow crazy ant (so-named because of its erratic

GRASS SNAKE The Cypriot grass snake, *Natrix natrix cypriaca*, is a harmless species that feeds on frogs and the occasional fish, yet it has been persecuted out of ignorance and is now endangered in its Mediterranean home.

movements). Super-colonies of these ants have established themselves, and although they do not bite or sting they spray formic acid as a defense. The high formic acid levels, on the ground and on the other organisms, has caused a crash in the populations of most endemic small animals. Even the blindsnake, normally a predator of ant eggs, may be in decline.

Venomous Snakes Serpentes

Snakes are threatened by habitat destruction or alteration; collection for skin, meat, medicines and the pet trade; the introduction of predators or toxic prey; and death on busy roads. Perhaps most significantly, snakes are victims of active persecution because they are feared and because in some world religions they symbolize "evil."

A LESSER EVIL

Venomous snakes might seem unlikely subjects for concern, and many view declining serpent populations as a good thing. However, the venomous snakes in the two main families, Elapidae (cobras and their relatives) and Viperidae (true vipers and pitvipers) comprise an important part of many ecosystems, especially in the tropics. Although venomous snakes kill over 40,000 humans annually, they indirectly save many more by reducing the numbers of disease-carrying, crop-depleting rodents. Disease and starvation are far greater causes of human mortality than snakebites. Besides, most of the 500 or so front-fanged venomous snakes do not pose a snakebite risk to humans.

ISOLATED VIPERS

Currently, the most endangered snake in Europe is the Milos viper, which occurs on just four small Greek islands. This is a protected species but despite the best efforts of the authorities, and the regular arrest of smugglers, it is estimated that 10 percent of the population are either stolen to supply collectors or killed on the busy roads every year.

The Kenyan mountain viper is a tiny snake found at 9,000–12,500 feet (2,700–3,800 m) in the Mount Kenya and Aberdare National Parks. The viper shelters in grass tussocks, emerging only occasionally to bask, when it becomes vulnerable to birds of prey. Occasional persecution, and increasing habitat fragmentation where small populations become isolated, further endanger this snake's survival.

The 5½–foot (1.7 m) Mangshan pitviper is reputed to be the only snake, other than the spitting cobras, with the ability to spit venom. Endemic to the Nan Ling Mountains in China,

ROCK-DWELLER The broadheaded snake, *Hoplocephalus bungaroides*, is Australia's most threatened venomous snake. It is threatened by "bush rock" collectors disturbing its habitat.

its habitat is being destroyed by the massively increasing human population, and this curious snake may soon be extinct in the wild.

AUSTRALIA'S RAREST

Australia's most endangered snake is the broadheaded snake, a member of the cobra family Elapidae, which inhabits the Hawkesbury sandstone ridges around Sydney. Although much prized by snake collectors, it is probably more threatened by collectors of a different kind who denude its environment. The broadheaded snake lives under flat slabs of sandstone in cliff-edge situations – always between two rocks, never between a rock and earth. It is these slabs that are favored by rock collectors and although the illegality of "bush rock" collecting is signposted on roads in the region it is certain that it continues.

DON'T TREAD ON ME!

Probably the first venomous snake encountered by America's founding fathers, and a symbol of defiance ever since, the timber rattlesnake has been persecuted throughout much of its range in the U.S. Despite protection, many populations are still threatened

CARS AND COLLECTORS
Europe's most endangered snake is the Milos viper, *Macrovipera schweizeri*. Snake collectors and automobiles account for 10 percent of the population reduction each year.

and local conservationists and ecologists are very secretive about the locations of rattlesnake dens. One of the major threats to rattlesnakes in the U.S. is the annual "rattlesnake round-ups," orgies of slaughter and torture of rattlers that began as a means of protecting valued cattle stock from snakebites but which evolved into huge, multimillion-dollar tourist attractions. The practice is especially rife in Texas and Oklahoma, where rattlers may be brought over state boundaries to supply demand. This is something akin to the introduction of the fox to New Zealand, just so the "pest" could be removed again!

Another critically endangered species is the Aruba Island rattlesnake – a small, pastel-colored snake from the interior of Aruba Island, off the coast of Venezuela. This species has been the subject of a coordinated zoo captive-breeding and reintroduction program in recent years. Probably the rarest of all rattlesnakes is the Autlan rattlesnake, which is known from a single western Mexican road-killed specimen.

RARE RAINFOREST DENIZEN
The bushmasters are the largest venomous snakes in the Americas, and the only egg-laying New World vipers. They dislike interference, either with themselves or their habitat. Rainforest snakes, they are among the first species to disappear when the rainforest is felled or radically altered. Since 90 percent of the Brazilian Atlantic forests have been deforested during the 20th century, it is not surprising that the Atlantic coastal bushmaster should be the most threatened of all the bushmasters.

LAKE TANGANYIKA'S RARITY
Lake Tanganyika is the only place where storm's water cobra may be found, if one is lucky! The snake shelters along short areas of shoreline comprised of huge boulders, emerging to enter the lake to catch fish. Local fishermen use gill nets, set in exactly

NATIONAL ICON Once a symbol of America's defiance, the timber rattlesnake, *Crotalus horridus*, has been persecuted so efficiently that it is extinct in Canada and is now endangered in parts of U.S.

the same areas. Unfortunately, any cobra encountering a gill net will become entangled and drown, and most fishermen confess to regularly removing dead cobras from their nets. Water cobras were once common at the southern end of the lake but today their survival is in serious doubt.

INVISIBLE BURROWERS
The bandy-bandys are black and white banded members of the Elapidae that prey on blindsnakes and are considered harmless to humans. They are primarily burrowers and are severely threatened by intensive farming methods in Western Australia. Plowing huge areas of bush into agricultural land unearths and kills bandy-bandys and disturbs their environment. The Fiji burrowing snake is a small relative of the bandy-bandys. It lives in topsoil and also feeds on blindsnakes. Small-scale turning of the earth uncovers them but a more serious threat comes from the keeping of pigs that

MOST VENOMOUS
The most venomous snake of the Americas is the golden lancehead, *Bothrops insularis*, from an island off Brazil. Its unusual biology is the cause of fascination for scientists. Its island is a field-research station.

dig up the small snakes and devour them. The Fiji snake lives thousands of miles from any other terrestrial elapids and is truly unique, yet it is in danger of extinction. The conservation status of snakes is often hard to gauge since they are usually secretive animals, but determining the population density and distribution of burrowing species is even more difficult. There is a danger they will reach critical levels or become extinct before we are aware that they are even under threat.

SPIRALING TOWARD EXTINCTION
The golden lancehead has venom that is three to five times more toxic than that possessed by any other venomous snake of the Americas. It is confined to the rodent-free island of Ilha Queimada Grande off the coast of Brazil, where it survives by ambushing birds. The reproductive biology of the golden lancehead is curious: there are three sexes: males, females and intersex females, which are females with some male genitalia. True females are very rare and some biologists suggest that the estimated 5,000 lanceheads on Queimada Grande, which has been isolated from the mainland for over 100,000 years, may well be spiraling to its own "natural" extinction. This is a protected species, visitors to the uninhabited island are controlled, so if extinction does occur, for once at least, it will probably not be by human hand.

Lizards Lacertilia

Many lizard populations are confined to islands, and extinction can occur quite rapidly. Habitat loss, tourist development, alien introductions and collection can all have drastic effects because island species have "nowhere to run and nowhere to hide."

OUT ON A LIMB The beautiful Fijian banded iguana, *Brachylophus fasciatus*, is threatened by collection for food, habitat destruction and predation by animals introduced by humans.

DRAGONS AT RISK

Even the world's largest living lizard, the Komodo dragon, may be at risk. The dragons can reach a length of 10 feet (3 m) and ambush deer and water buffalo, inflicting a lethal bacteria-loaded bite. About 3,000 dragons remain in the wild, in the Komodo archipelago and on western Flores. Although protected, and a major tourist attraction, they are still threatened by the actions of humans and nature, notably on Flores outside the Komodo National Park. The dragon inhabits one of the smallest ranges of any large predator and if the 2004 tsunami had occurred farther to the southeast we might be talking about wild dragons in the past tense!

ANCIENT SPECIES The tuatara, *Sphenodon punctatus*, and Brothers Island tuatara, *S. guntheri*, look like drab gray iguanas, but they are actually the last survivors of a suborder that vanished 60 million years ago.

RELICTS FROM THE PAST

Tuataras are unique in that they are the last survivors of an ancient suborder. Confined to small, rocky islets off the coast of New Zealand, tuataras existed in isolation from other vertebrates, except seabirds and small lizards. Today, they are threatened by introduced rats and cats, and possibly even the tourists who come to visit the islands. Tuataras can withstand very cold conditions, for a reptile. They have slow metabolic rates and are extremely slow-growing, reaching maturity only after 15–20 years. They lay eggs that may take 16 months to hatch, and they live for over 70 years. They feed on invertebrates and the eggs and chicks of seabirds. Although there are more than 50,000 tuataras, the adult population of the Brother Island tuatara is estimated to be around 400 and is extremely vulnerable.

HERE BE DRAGONS The Komodo dragon, *Varanus komodoensis*, is the world's largest lizard, but its small population is vulnerable. An even larger, 18-foot (6 m) monitor lizard, *Megalania prisca*, disappeared from Australia shortly after man arrived in the Pleistocene.

IGUANAS ON THE BRINK

The Caribbean ground iguanas (genus *Cyclura*) are also threatened. The IUCN today lists three species as vulnerable, one as endangered, five as critically endangered and one as extinct – the Navassa Island iguana disappeared when phosphate miners arrived in the 19th century. The most endangered species today is the Grand Cayman blue iguana, which has suffered from illegal collection and killing, habitat loss for grazing, predation by dogs and cats, rats taking eggs and road kill. The Blue Iguana Recovery Program was initiated in the 1990s, involving protection and the study of the wild population, captive breeding and the establishment of free-ranging populations in controlled semiwild conditions. Although the free-ranging populations thrived, the wild population was down to 25 adults in 2002, and is thought to have suffered further during 2004's Hurricane Ivan. A set of stamps was issued by the Cayman Islands in 2005 to promote blue iguana conservation.

In the Sea of Cortez, spiny-tailed iguanas, *Ctenosaura*, are also threatened by collection and habitat loss.

JEWELS OF THE PACIFIC

The Caribbean Islands do not have a monopoly on endangered iguanas. In the Pacific live the Fijian banded iguana and Fijian crested iguana. The banded iguana, which occurs on Fiji and Tonga and has been introduced to Vanuatu, is endangered, and the larger crested iguana, only described in 1981 and confined to Fiji, is considered to be critically endangered. Both of these species suffer from habitat destruction and human persecution, but the crested iguana is especially at risk because it has a small range on a few dry islands that are threatened by introduced goats. The clearance of the feral goats, the establishment of a sanctuary, a captive breeding program and education all form parts of the recovery initiative for the iguanas.

GIANT SKINKS
The largest skink of modern times was the 24-inch (60 cm) Cape Verde giant skink but, not seen since the late-19th century, it is believed extinct, possibly falling prey to hungry fishermen. The largest living skink is the Solomons monkey-tail skink, an arboreal species with a prehensile tail. It is also eaten

by islanders, but a far more serious threat to these lizards comes from deforestation of its rainforest habitat by the timber industry. A further serious issue is overcollection for the pet trade, for which they are very highly prized in the U.S. and Europe.

GIANT GECKOS
The largest gecko known exists only as a stuffed specimen in the Marseilles Museum in France. *Hoplodactylus delcourti* is believed to have originated from New Zealand, but no further specimens have been found. Today, the largest living geckos are from another South Pacific country, New Caledonia. The largest of all is Leach's giant gecko, which can reach lengths of 13 inches (32 cm), comprising a stout body and short,

VULNERABLE POPULATION The rough-snouted giant gecko, *Rhacodactylus trachyrhynchus* (which may actually be two species), is a live bearer. This reproductive mode makes it especially vulnerable if gravid adult females are removed from the population.

stumpy tail. Deforestation on the mainland and illegal collection on the offshore islands are the main threats. Five of the six species are considered vulnerable, and one, the crested giant gecko, was even believed to be extinct but was rediscovered in the 1990s.

DESERT ISLAND IGUANA The island-dwelling San Esteban iguana, *Ctenosaura hemilopha conspiquosa*, is increasingly threatened by overcollection, smuggling and harvesting for food.

Crocodiles & Alligators
Crocodilia

The crocodiles and alligators are an ancient group of reptiles, more akin to extinct dinosaurs and living birds than to today's snakes or lizards. Formidable predators, they have long been persecuted through fear and for their meat and skin. Worse still is the wholesale destruction of their swamp and river habitats.

ASIAN SUCCESS STORY The Ganges gharial, *Gavialis gangeticus*, a fish-eating crocodile with a long, narrow snout, has come back from the brink thanks to a major captive breeding and habitat restoration program.

PREHISTORIC SURVIVORS

Although on the outside they might look primeval, today's crocodiles and alligators are actually quite advanced animals. For example, they possess a four-chambered heart (like a mammal and in contrast to the three chambers of a lizard or snake) and strange, pore-like sense organs in the skin of their head and body, which may enable them to locate prey or to detect pressure or salinity changes in their environment.

Altogether, there are 23 species in the order Crocodilia: 13 crocodiles, two alligators, six caimans, one gharial and one false gharial. They are referred to collectively as crocodilians. Some of these species, such as the New Guinea and American crocodiles, may actually be species complexes containing more than one species, and there are reports of unknown crocodiles from Borneo and from Palau and New Britain in the Pacific, so the true count could in fact be as high as 30 species.

THE CAUSE OR THE CURE?

Many crocodilians are rare and several teeter on the brink of extinction, with vulnerable, fragmented populations. Four species are listed as critically endangered, and three more as

SPECIES IN PERIL Smaller and more threatened than its American cousin, the Chinese alligator, *Alligator sinensis*, has lost most of its wetland habitat to agriculture. Its relict wild population is persecuted by local people.

endangered. Historically, one of the main threats has been persecution by humans – most crocodilians are large, dangerous predators that therefore may be considered a threat to people and livestock. But crocodilians also possess something that humans covet: a leathery skin useful for making shoes, handbags and fashion accessories. The trade in crocodile skin products almost wiped out several species during the 19th and early 20th century.

Ironically, the desire to profit from crocodile skin without pushing these reptiles to extinction was probably the reason why entrepreneurs shifted from hunting crocodilians to farming them in the early 1900s. Even today, it is the big crocodile farms and the leather industry that are the largest financial contributors to crocodile conservation.

ALLIGATOR ON THE EDGE

There are only two true alligators – the familiar American alligator and the smaller, critically endangered Chinese alligator, from the lower reaches of the Yangtze River. Once distributed more widely, it is now confined to isolated areas within the provinces of Anhui and Zhejiang, where it is threatened by pressure from the increasing human population and the drive to drain wetlands, dam rivers and implement irrigation systems. Several reserves have been set aside for this alligator, but its wild population is probably fewer than 1,000 individuals.

SKIN FOR SALE

Uncontrolled trade in skins has endangered many crocodile species. Seventeen crocodilian species have been listed in Appendix 1 of CITES (the Convention on International Trade in Endangered Species), which effectively means that commercial trade in these reptiles is banned. But several other, more abundant species are still plentiful enough to provide a sustainable source of extra income for local people. This villager from the Pantanal wetlands in Brazil is shown with a spectacled caiman, *Caiman crocodilus*. The trade provides an extra incentive to protect shrinking wetlands.

CARIBBEAN CROCODILES

Four species of crocodile occur in the Americas: the secretive swamp crocodile of Mexico and Central America; the highly threatened Orinoco crocodile of northern South America; the Cuban crocodile of the Zapata and Lanier swamps on Cuba and Isla de la Juventud; and the American crocodile, which is found throughout the Caribbean, north into southern Florida, where it is considered extremely endangered. Humans have forced the latter's Cuban population from some of its original haunts and driven it into the swamps inhabited by the much rarer Cuban crocodile, the possible results being competition or hybridization. However, the American crocodile is not the only threat to the Cuban crocodile. The population in the Lanier swamp may have been extirpated, possibly by introduced spectacled caimans, a relative of the alligator from South America.

MOST ENDANGERED

Candidates for the dubious honor of being the world's most endangered crocodilian include the dwarf crocodile from West Africa and the false gharial, a slender-snouted fish specialist from Borneo and Sumatra. However, the title probably goes to the Siamese crocodile, believed extinct in the wild in 1992.

Formerly distributed across mainland Southeast Asia and on Borneo and Java, this species is now known to exist in small numbers in Vietnam, Cambodia,

SAVING ITS SKIN Exceptionally rare in the wild, the Siamese crocodile, *Crocodylus siamensis*, was hybridized and farmed for its skin.

Laos and Thailand. There are numerous "Siamese" crocodiles in farms, but many of them are unsuitable for restocking in the wild since they are the offspring of hybridization projects with saltwater crocodiles, intended to grow animals to optimum slaughter size quickly.

SOLD FOR FOOD The dwarf crocodile, *Osteolaemus tetraspis*, is at risk from habitat loss and hunting. Thousands are sold in West Africa's markets each year.

Amphibians Anura, Urodela & Gymnophiona

Extremely susceptible to pollution, habitat modification and climate change, amphibians are dying off at an unprecedented rate in many parts of the world. If the trend is not reversed, the fate of amphibians may serve as an early warning as to what may later happen to this planet's other terrestrial organisms – including humans.

EARTH, WATER AND AIR

Amphibians live either in fresh water or on land (including some burrowers). Most terrestrial species return to some form of water to reproduce, while their offspring spend a significant proportion of their early lives in fresh water. Thus amphibians live in close contact with water, solid substrates and, of course, air.

At least 5,600 species of amphibians have been described – almost one-third of these since 1985. They are grouped into three orders. The Anura (tailless frogs and toads) contains 88 percent of all living amphibians; 9 percent belong in the Urodela (tailed salamanders and newts); and the remaining 3 percent in the Gymnophiona (legless caecilians). However, new species are identified and named every year.

BIOLOGICAL INDICATORS

Amphibians are considered excellent biological indicators. This is because, more than any other type of tetrapod (terrestrial vertebrate), they depend on the surrounding conditions.

An amphibian's highly permeable skin permits the transfer of water, salts and gases between its body and the outside world. So it is not surprising that amphibians are badly affected by climate change and respond rapidly to the effects of pollution, habitat change and the introduction of pathogens such as

fungi, viruses or bacteria. Any decline in the health of amphibian populations might serve as an early warning about the worsening health of food chains and ecosystems as a whole.

SHOCKING STATISTICS

Since the 1980s, a great many species of amphibians have become threatened or have gone extinct. Omitting the five caecilian families (which are classed as "data deficient" by the IUCN), 32 out of 43 amphibian families contain species listed as

NARROW ESCAPE
The rare green and gold frog, *Litoria raniformis*, was further threatened by plans to build an Olympic stadium on its breeding site in Australia, but the work was relocated.

critically endangered or endangered. In 12 of these families, 30 percent or more of their species are endangered or are already extinct – and for some of the smaller families, this percentage may increase to 50 percent or even higher. One small family is listed as 100 percent extinct. These figures are among the worst of any major group of animals.

GLOBAL DECLINE

The accelerated die-off of amphibians around the world was first highlighted in 1989, and this phenomenon has since been called "Global Amphibian Decline." The worst-affected areas are the Americas, Australia and (to a lesser degree) Europe. However, the species affected are not always those threatened by drought, habitat loss or degradation, overcollection or the introduction of nonnative predators to an area. Many of the most inexplicable disappearances have occurred in pristine mountainous rainforest habitats in protected areas.

HABITAT AND CLIMATE

Habitat modification poses a severe threat to amphibian populations. This includes the draining of their breeding pools or swamps for building or diverting water supplies for agricultural crops. Species threatened in this way include the great crested newt in the U.K. (*see* panel, right) and the green and golden bell frog in New

HUGE AMPHIBIAN The largest salamander in the world, the Chinese giant salamander, *Andrias davidianus*, grows up to 6 feet (1.8 m) long. It is hunted for its flesh but is also threatened by damming and excessive siltation.

South Wales, Australia. The bell frog's numbers have crashed, possibly as a result of the introduction of mosquito fish from North America in the 1920s to control malaria; these alien fish preyed on bell frog eggs and tadpoles.

Amphibians are not just affected by adverse changes to freshwater habitats. For example, low vegetation controls the temperature and humidity of the microclimate at ground level, especially in hot countries, where plants provide vital humidity, shade and security for amphibians and their invertebrate prey. Removal of this vegetative cover can therefore have a serious impact.

Many salamanders are localized in their distribution and need cool, humid, shady conditions; deforestation in the Appalachian Mountains triggered population collapses in species such as Jordan's lungless salamander. Heavy machinery causes impaction of the soil, making burrowing impossible, while reduced vegetation cover boosts levels of UVB radiation, resulting in growth deformities and poor hatch rates in species less adapted to direct sun. Raised UVB levels may harm an amphibian's immune system, making it vulnerable to attack by pathogens (*see* pp. 152–153).

The Great Crested Newt

With its bright orange belly and jagged crest, *Triturus cristatus* is one of Europe's most impressive amphibians. It is widespread throughout northern and central areas, from Britain to the Ural Mountains of Russia. However, its populations are declining in many areas, particularly in Britain, where it is now fully protected. Over the last 50 years it has suffered heavily from the draining and filling of its breeding ponds to make way for industry, houses and roads. Thousands more ponds on agricultural land have become very weedy and overgrown (and therefore unsuitable for the newt) due to decades of neglect. Other threats include pesticide runoff from farmland and the stocking of ponds with fish such as carp, which eat the newt's eggs and larvae.

BRITISH STRONGHOLD
The great crested newt's sharp fall in numbers in the U.K. is of great concern as traditionally this country was a major stronghold. The species has a preference for so-called "brownfield" sites – the type usually considered to be wasteland and thus of little value. These areas have often been prioritized for urban redevelopment ahead of more scenic "greenfield" sites.

CONSERVATION MEASURES
Action plans to conserve the great crested newt include surveys to assess its populations. If a breeding site is threatened by redevelopment or pollution, its newt colony may be relocated to a different pond. Ponds can be fenced off with plastic mesh (pictured above) to prevent disturbance by animals and people.

TOXINS AND ACIDIFICATION

We have seen that amphibians are highly vulnerable to atmospheric and water pollution, because any stress on their metabolism can lower resistance to disease or reduce their reproductive capabilities. Pollutants come in many forms, such as airborne emissions from industry, vehicle exhausts and forest fires, or runoff containing fertilizers, pesticides and other toxic compounds.

Airborne pollutants enter the Earth's atmosphere and are deposited globally as acid rain. This means that even the most pristine, remote areas, including protected reserves, are not immune to this threat. In the U.K., for example, the rare natterjack toad has been adversely affected by acidification of its breeding ponds in sand dunes and heaths. It has also suffered from increased levels of nitrates in the water (eutrophication), caused by changes in land use.

DISAPPEARING ACT

In the last two decades there have been several well-documented instances in which amphibian species have vanished from a particular area. The most famous of these disappearances occurred in the late 1980s in Monteverde Cloudforest Preserve, Costa Rica. Every year more than 1,500 golden toads would gather to breed in temporary ponds in this cloudforest. In 1989, they failed to appear and have not been seen since; they are now listed as extinct by the IUCN. Many other restricted-range amphibians unique to this area were

HARVESTING FROGS

In many parts of the world people eat frogs as part of their daily diets. In New Guinea, Africa and South America, big river frogs are seen as staple food items, and this has endangered species such as the West African goliath frog, *Conraua goliath*, (below). Indian bullfrogs supply the culinary delicacy of frog's legs, but overcollection has resulted in plagues of insect pests, which multiplied in the absence of these predators.

affected, too, including the Monteverde salamander, a species of harlequin frog (which, despite its name, is actually a toad) and the green-eyed frog. In all, it was estimated that as many as 20 out of the 50 amphibian species resident at Monteverde died out. But what could have caused this catastrophe?

One theory is that these amphibian population collapses might have been due to the El Niño effect that took place two years earlier. According to this theory, the unusually hot,

MATING EMBRACE Golden toads, *Bufo periglenes*, have not been seen at their Costa Rican breeding site since 1989. They are the most famous casualties of global amphibian decline.

dry weather brought by this climatic phenomenon dried out breeding pools, killing all of the amphibian eggs and larvae, while stressed surviving adults became vulnerable to disease.

These population declines were not confined to Costa Rica. For example, many species of harlequin frogs (genus *Atelopus*), found across the tropical Americas, were very badly affected. Of the 77 species in this group, four are regarded as endangered, 62 as critically endangered, and three, from Ecuador and Venezuela, as extinct.

GASTRIC-BROODING FROGS

Amphibians have been dying out in many other parts of the world as well. In the space of just a few years, two fascinating species of aquatic gastric-brooding frogs declined to the point of extinction, reached in 2001. Found in rainforests along Australia's east coast, these frogs were considered so unusual that they deserved their own family, called the Rheobatrachidae.

The frogs were named for a strange quirk of their life history – no other amphibians were known to brood their young offspring inside the stomach. The females must have achieved this by swallowing either the externally fertilized eggs or the tadpoles, although as neither was observed we will never be sure. Chemical compounds within the swallowed eggs or tadpoles would have "switched off" the production of gastric acids in the fasting female, so that the stomach turned into a brood chamber until the froglets were "born" through the mouth. The frog's stomach then returned to its normal digestive purpose. The ability to stop-start gastric acid production could well have had useful medical applications for treating ulcers, but this opportunity has been lost along with the frogs.

Like the golden toads of Costa Rica and numerous other species, the cause of the gastric-brooding frogs' decline is mysterious. Other casualties of "Global Amphibian Decline" include six species of day frogs (genus *Taudactylus*) from New South Wales and Queensland, Australia. These small frogs live in and around rainforest creeks. Four of the species have been classed as critically endangered, while the Mount Glorious torrent frog is thought to be extinct.

FROG-KILLING FUNGUS

Possibly the most important cause of amphibian decline is believed to be chytrid (pronounced "kit-trid") fungus. This deadly pathogen, whose full name is *Batrachochytrium dendrobatidis*, causes a disease known as chytridiomycosis.

In 1993, chytrid fungus was blamed for causing frog deaths in Queensland, but its presence in Australia could be traced back a further 15 years to an outbreak in the dainty green treefrog. Earlier outbreaks include one among Canadian green frogs in 1961, and even earlier, in 1938, the disease was reported from South Africa in African clawed frogs (confusingly also known as African clawed toads).

African clawed frogs do not die from chytridiomycosis, or even demonstrate symptoms of the disease, and therefore they may have acted as "carriers." These frogs were taken worldwide as an early form of pregnancy test (injecting them with a pregnant woman's urine causes them to ovulate), so they could be the link to infected amphibian populations in the rest of the world.

Today, chytridiomycosis is found in many species around the world, having been reported in frog populations from New Zealand, the Pacific, the Americas, Africa and Europe. Recently, it triggered a

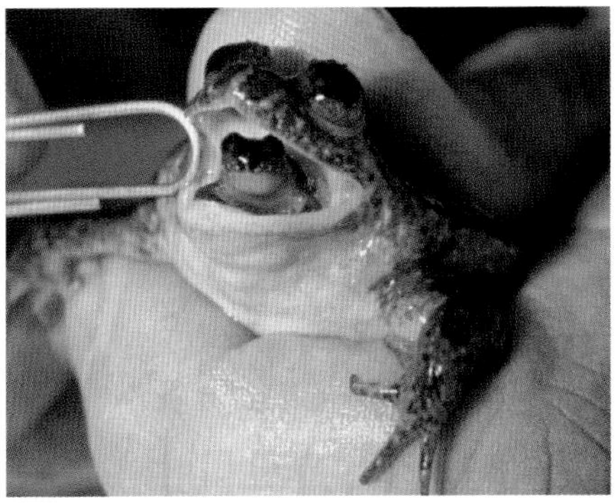

EXTINCT Gastric-brooding frogs could switch off their stomach acid production to brood their offspring during the larval stage. Both species of these amazing frogs (*Rheobatrachus silus* is shown above) became extinct in 2001.

drastic decline in Spanish populations of the European midwife toad, which are heading toward oblivion.

Amphibian chytrid fungus is found in fresh water and infection is believed to be by absorption through a frog's or toad's skin, but how such a pathogenic and fatal disease has managed to reach remote areas such as the Monteverde cloudforest is difficult to determine. It is possible that the fungus is always present at sublethal levels and is able to attack amphibians already subjected to stress through pollution or excessive exposure to UVB radiation.

SECOND CHANCE
The harlequin frog, *Atelopus varius*, was thought extinct when it disappeared from the Monteverde Reserve in Costa Rica, but it survives elsewhere and is critically endangered rather than extinct.

Sharks Elasmobranchii

Sharks have been swimming in the world's seas and oceans for over 430 million years. These powerful hunters use their superbly acute senses for finding prey and navigation, and have few natural predators, except for other sharks. The largest species inspire both fear and admiration in equal measure, but now many shark populations are in danger of collapse due to overfishing and the growing demand for shark products.

TOP PREDATORS

There are around 330 species of sharks, found everywhere from shallow coastal waters to the deep, blue ocean, and from the tropics to icy waters beneath the northern ice cap. Anatomically, sharks differ from most other fish: they have cartilaginous (not bony) skeletons and a rough skin scattered with tiny teeth-like denticles rather than scales. Their teeth, which vary widely in shape according to diet, are replaced throughout their life. Unlike other fish, sharks lack a swim bladder full of air to keep them buoyant; instead, they have an oil-rich liver to stop them from sinking (oil being less dense than water).

HISTORY OF EXPLOITATION

For centuries, humans have benefited from shark-based products. Their skin was at one time used to make sandpaper and leather, and their oil was used in lamps and to waterproof boats. Shark teeth have long been sold as curios or

CRUISE CONTROL Sharks, such as this tiger shark, are often accompanied by remoras that hitch a ride to eat the leftovers and parasites of the bigger fish. Tiger sharks are feared as man-eaters, and so are heavily persecuted.

CLOSE ENCOUNTERS

Swimming with sharks has become one of the "must do" activities for many keen divers. The tourists are lowered into the water in metal cages, or in some cases, snorkel or dive out in the open with the sharks. In the picture below, a diver is watching a blue shark off the coast of New Zealand. Shark watching is usually promoted as harmless ecotourism; it can raise funds for, and public awareness of, shark conservation. However, there is mounting evidence that it may cause behavioral changes in sharks unless managed properly. Whale and basking sharks are easily stressed by human contact, while great whites used to catching baits towed by shark-watching boats might associate people with food, leading to a rise in fatal shark attacks.

AWESOME POWER With a torpedo-shaped body and jaws packed full of vicious teeth, the great white is for many the ultimate shark. But sport fishing, and possibly also disturbance caused by shark watching, threaten its future.

made into jewelry. Their cartilage and oil is used in the treatment of arthritis, and the fact that they appear to be immune to several human diseases, including cancer, now also makes them of great interest for medical research.

TRADE IN FINS

However, the worst threat is overfishing of sharks for their meat and fins. Blue shark flesh in particular is highly prized in Japan, while rock salmon (dogfish) is being caught for the traditional British meal of fish and chips. In recent years, mako and thresher shark steaks have also become popular. But it is the demand for fins to produce shark fin soup that is the main reason sharks are declining. Each year up to 100 million sharks are caught

just to make this soup. The practice of finning involves the removal of the dorsal and pectoral fins of any shark that is caught, and often the sharks are thrown back into the water still alive, where unable to swim they sink to the seabed and drown. Shark finning is now banned in the northeast Atlantic waters, but continues elsewhere.

SLOW TO BREED

Sharks are slow to mature and have a low reproductive rate. The whale shark, for example, may not become sexually mature until it is 30 years old. Great white shark females mature earlier, at about 10–12 years, but they may only reproduce five times during their lifetime. The eight or nine young, called pups, are born alive and fully developed after a long gestation period.

We know little about what happens to great white pups after they are born. This lack of knowledge of the species' lifecycle – together with those of many other shark species – makes it difficult to protect them. However, as sharks are top predators, there is no doubt that their decline will seriously disrupt marine food webs.

GREAT HAMMERHEAD Like all big sharks of surface and mid-level waters, this species is fished for its fins and flesh. Its wing-like head acts as a stabilizer and can probably detect electromagnetic fields produced by its prey.

Skates & Rays Elasmobranchii

Recognized by their flattened bodies and elegant, wing-like fins, skates and rays are predators closely related to sharks. Some cruise seemingly without effort in open water, but most live on the seabed, making them vulnerable to a type of fishing called bottom trawling.

CARTILAGE SKELETONS

Like sharks, the skates and rays have skeletons made of cartilage, which are used by the health industry for treating joint disorders. Also like sharks, these fish are slow-growing, late to mature and produce few offspring. For species with few natural enemies as adults, this is a successful and sustainable lifestyle. The problem is that ever-fewer skates and rays survive long enough to reach breeding age due to overfishing and accidental capture as "bycatch" in nets intended for other fish.

A good example is the common skate of the east Atlantic and Mediterranean, which is at least 10 years old before it first breeds. So called because it was once caught in big numbers, it is now threatened except in places inaccessible to commercial fishing fleets. Of the 450 species of skates and rays, all apart from the smallest varieties are coming under threat from overexploitation.

FISHING PRESSURE

Skates and rays are in demand for their greatly enlarged pectoral fins, which are fleshy but not too bony and have a distinctive texture and flavor. Game fishers who want to land a big fish that puts up a good fight target them, too; once hooked, rays may perform spectacular leaps from the water.

HALF HIDDEN Rays and skates, such as this blue-spotted stingray, often burrow into the seabed when resting. This defensive strategy may work against harpoon fishers, but offers no resistance to heavy-duty drag nets.

Until a century ago, the sea floor and the animals living there were relatively safe. The advent of bottom trawling, in which boats drag heavy nets across the seabed, sweeping up everything, has changed this. Entire habitats can be destroyed in a matter of minutes.

Since skates and rays are generally adapted for life on the sea floor, they are not strong swimmers. Most species have a narrow habitat range and this makes them even more vulnerable to environmental change, especially bottom trawling, as their populations are not large in the first place.

OCEAN CRUISERS

Some pelagic (open-water) species, such as the manta, eagle and bat rays, are less at risk from trawling. Instead, it is their leisurely style of swimming that puts them at risk. Manta rays are harpooned for food in countries such as the Philippines and Mexico, and are also caught in gill nets. The species is vulnerable because its local populations are small and it has the slowest breeding rate of all rays. A female carries her one or two pups for 9–12 months, and after the birth (about which little is known), she rests for at least a year before mating again.

SHOAL FORMATION Spotted eagle rays gather in spectacular shoals at certain seasons. They are caught, not for food, but to make fishmeal and oil, and are also a trophy fish sought after by fishermen.

SMALLTOOTH SAWFISH This amazing fish uses its "saw" to scrounge up prey in the soft sand and mud of coastal waters and freshwater rivers. It is endangered due to overfishing.

FLYING UNDERWATER
A manta ray measures up to
23 feet (7 m) across its
triangular pectoral fins, which
flap like wings. The gills with
which it filters plankton are
clearly visible in this underside
view.

Half of all fish belong to this enormously varied group, ranging from ocean-going tuna to seahorses and tiny gobies. Many of them – especially the colorful residents of coral reefs – are endangered by harvesting for medicines or the aquarium trade.

POISON TIDE In the Indo-Pacific, cyanide fishers visit pristine reefs like this one to catch aquarium fish. Cyanide fishing may cause a toxic buildup in reef ecosystems, killing coral and poisoning big fish at the top of food chains.

ALL SHAPES AND SIZES

Spiny-rayed fish are named for stiff, bone-like spines in their dorsal fin. They form a group of around 13,500 species in the class Osteichthyes, or bony fish. As might be expected with such a large grouping, they display a bewildering variety of body shapes, sizes and behavior, and they face an equally wide variety of threats, from pollution to habitat destruction.

Three threats, in particular, stand out. Increasing numbers of spiny-rayed fish are endangered through collection for the aquarium trade; some species are harvested for use in Asian medicines; and some are caught for food.

AQUARIUM TRADE

In 2005, the aquarium fish industry was worth US$200 million per year in North America and Europe alone, so it is hardly surprising that fishers will resort to any lengths to secure fish for this lucrative market. Usually the most desirable species are small and brightly colored, such as clownfish, angelfish and butterfly fish, or look very bizarre, such as seahorses and lionfish.

The use of cyanide to stun coral reef fish for easy capture first began in the Philippines in the 1960s. Although this method for collecting live fish is illegal, it is still used throughout the region because of weak law enforcement. To date over 35,000 ounces (1 million g) of cyanide has been poured over the coral reefs of the Philippines, and we have little idea of the long-term effect this will have on the reefs. More seriously, since the desired fish species are now depleted in these areas, the practice is becoming more widespread as fishermen widen their search. Cyanide fishing is carried out from the central Pacific to East Africa, and it is also now used to catch larger fish, such as groupers, for sale to specialty restaurants in Asia.

MEDICINE AND FOOD

Lots of different fish parts are used in Asian medicine, and the worst-hit fish are seahorses. All species are under pressure – so great is the demand that it cannot be met by the supply. This, in combination with harvesting for aquaria and dried curios for tourists, resulted in at least 25 million seahorses being caught in 2001.

CAUGHT ALIVE Every year tens of thousands of exotic reef fish, such as this shortfin lionfish, end up in the fish tanks of enthusiasts. By removing key members of the fish community, this trade impoverishes reefs.

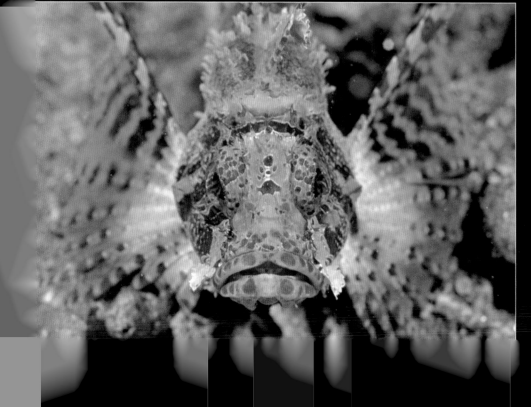

PREGNANT FATHER Due to their small broods and long parental care, seahorses are slow breeders vulnerable to overfishing. The male, such as this rare pygmy seahorse, carries his mate's fertilized eggs in a special brood sac.

The international trade in seahorses is restricted, but all too often an illicit "black market" thrives regardless.

Many legitimate commercial fisheries also exploit spiny-rayed fish, for sale as food. Target species include magnificent open-water predators such as tuna and swordfish, as well as smaller fish such as mackerel, groupers, mullet, snapper and flatfish. Some of these aggregate in the same spot every year to spawn, occasionally in spectacular numbers, and these annual events are exploited by the fishing fleets. More often than not it is the big, reproductively mature fish that are caught, inadvertently causing maximum harm to fish stocks.

TUNA FISHING

Up to four of the nine species of tuna are under threat. They include the bluefin tuna (right), one of the world's fastest bony fish, which has been fished to the brink of extinction. Its flesh was sold as steaks and for canning, and today is highly prized in Japan, where a single fish may sell for $100,000. In the 1960s, 80,000 tons of bluefin tuna a year was taken from the oceans, mainly using purse seine nets and baited longlines. Stocks have since dropped by over 97 percent.

Salmon & Relatives Salmoniformes

Many fish in this large group, including salmon, sea trout and char, are powerful long-distance swimmers that migrate between fresh water and the open ocean. In both of these environments they face growing dangers, especially overfishing, pollution and artificial barriers that block their movements.

DUAL LIVES

There are more than 315 species in the salmon group, Salmoniformes, which is part of the huge class Osteichthyes, or bony fish. Only the species that migrate between salty and fresh water, such as salmon, sea trout, char and smelt, are discussed here. The complex ecology of these fish means that they cannot complete their life cycle if cut off from their spawning grounds in rivers and lakes or from their feeding grounds at sea – they die out. Damage to either aquatic habitat will severely harm their populations. Several other unrelated groups of bony fish, such as sturgeons, lead dual lives like those of salmon and face similar threats.

The life history of migratory salmon and trout starts when an egg hatches in a gravel nest in a quiet stream. The fry (young) travels to a river or lake,

matures into a parr, then continues its journey toward the sea. It turns into a silvery smolt before entering the sea, where it remains for some years, finally returning as an adult to spawn – often in the stream where it was hatched.

CHANGING RIVERS

Throughout history people have settled along river valleys, cutting down the trees and building towns and villages, increasing the amount of sediment and sewage entering river basins. Over the past century this process intensified and new dangers emerged, such as the pollution of water supplies by industry, mining activities, oil exploration and agricultural chemicals washed off the land. All of these changes degrade the aquatic environment for fish. A single gold-dredging operation killed all the salmon in the Yankee River, in the western U.S., in the 1940s.

Increasingly, the natural flow of rivers is disrupted by dams, weirs and various "flood prevention" measures. This spells disaster for salmon and their relatives since they are prevented from reaching their spawning grounds. Huge dams in the Columbia River basin – the fourth largest in the U.S. –

SPAWNING GROUND Each lake in western Canada and Alaska has a distinct breeding population of sockeye salmon, so this species is vulnerable to problems on a local scale.

made many Pacific salmon populations extinct. Despite a billion-dollar salmon restoration effort, numbers have not recovered so far.

Another threat to salmon and char comes from the growing demand for their roe (eggs). Due to its high market value, poaching has become a lucrative trade in Russia and Asia.

ALL AT SEA

Wild salmon in the oceans are at risk everywhere from overexploitation, to the extent that 23 percent of all Pacific salmon stocks are at moderate or high risk. In the Atlantic, salmon numbers are also depleted; stocks are thought to have halved over the last 20 years.

In the future, climate change might be the worst threat to these fish. Rising sea and river temperatures may wreak havoc with their internal "body clocks," by delaying spawning or affecting how young fish mature, for example.

FISH FARMING

Nowadays, most salmon and trout sold in North America and Europe is farmed, either in purpose-built freshwater pools or, as here in Scotland, in floating cages in sea lochs. Farming was thought to be the ideal solution to overfishing, but the farmed fish are kept at high densities, so are prone to parasites and disease, which spread to wild stocks. Escapes from the farms erode the gene pool of wild fish through interbreeding, and feces from the farmed fish pollute water supplies.

STURGEON Although not closely related to salmon, this rare European fish also migrates between rivers and the sea. It is ruthlessly exploited for caviar – the unshed eggs of females – slashing its breeding rate.

FROZEN FISH Arctic char are the most northerly freshwater fish in the world. Some migrate to icy northern seas to mature, but others stay in tundra lakes all their lives. Lake residents have the brightest red bellies.

SPEARING FISH
Modern commercial fishing has endangered the Arctic char in Finland, and caused its populations to decline elsewhere in Scandinavia. Here, an Inuit hunter uses a traditional (and sustainable) method to catch char.

Cod, Herring & Anglerfish
Gadiformes, Clupeiformes & Lophiiformes

These groups of marine fish include probably the most commercially exploited food fish on the planet. In the past, their numbers were thought to be infinite, and for years vast quantities were harvested annually. Now we are paying the price – stocks of several species are so low in some areas that the fisheries have collapsed.

GETTING SMALLER The Atlantic cod's populations are not the only thing to have shrunk due to overexploitation. The fish themselves are smaller, too, as few now survive to reach the giant proportions reported in the past.

FEEDING THE WORLD

Many of the sea fish people buy from supermarkets and restaurants around the world belong to one of these major groups. The order Gadiformes includes the Atlantic cod, haddock, pollock and hake, all predatory fish that can form massive shoals. Members of the order Clupeiformes also gather in impressive concentrations, and include numerous small, streamlined fish such as herring, anchovies, pilchards, sardines and sprats. The anglerfish, or Lophiiformes, are solitary bottom-living predators, of which the monkfish is among the best-known commercial species. All three of these groups are contained in the class of bony fish, Osteichthyes.

COD IN CRISIS

As techniques for catching fish rapidly improved, our understanding of how to harvest the oceans sustainably failed to keep pace, sometimes with terrible consequences. The cod fishery off the Newfoundland coast of Canada used to

TRAWLING THREAT The monkfish used to be mainly a "bycatch" victim in nets set for other species. But as their usual target fish declined, fishing fleets began to harvest this seabed dweller using new bottom-trawling methods.

be one of that country's most valuable natural assets – but it no longer exists. It was ruined by factory fishing vessels and the use of huge drag nets, which cause immense damage to the ocean floor. In the 1980s, the annual catch of Newfoundland cod was still in excess of 250,000 tons, but the subsequent trawling of spawning grounds affected cod reproduction and resulted in high mortality of juvenile cod. The fishing

of these northern Atlantic cod was banned in 1992, but this came much too late; two years later, the biomass of the entire population of northern cod was estimated to be just 1,700 tons.

Now a similar situation has arisen in European waters, where cod numbers have crashed in recent years. Since the late 1990s, scientists have called for a complete moratorium on cod fishing in the North Sea to allow for recovery, but such a move would be politically difficult, so governments in Europe have been unable to agree on a ban.

DISRUPTED FOOD CHAINS

The disappearance of top-tier predators, such as Atlantic cod, forces fisheries to seek alternative catches elsewhere in the food chain. Studies indicate that this is happening in at least 60 percent of marine ecosystems worldwide. The artificial pressure on selected "target" fish species upsets the delicate balance of food chains, in which the numbers of each species are in equilibrium. If a predator is overfished, its prey then may start to increase in numbers, in turn causing the numbers of their prey to fall, and so on.

Formerly an unimportant commercial fish, the monkfish, or angler, is heavily exploited to compensate for declining cod stocks. Public tastes soon adjusted to this "new" addition to menus and fish markets. So today monkfish populations have come under pressure, and their stocks are suffering, too.

CANNERY ROW

There are many other similar examples in fisheries across the globe, and the statistics speak for themselves. A single factory ship can salt 200 tons of herring per day, as well as produce 5 tons of fish oil. No fish can withstand this level of exploitation indefinitely.

Located on the Monterey Peninsula in California, Cannery Row was once home to a huge sardine fishery.

In 1937, 800,000 tons of these sardines, also called California pilchards, were being caught annually – so many that the cannery could not cope and the excess was made into fishmeal for use as fertilizer. Some shoals in the region may have held as many as 10 million individual sardines, leading people to believe that there was no limit to how many could be caught.

Despite being small fish, sardines such as the California pilchard live for up to 15 years and do not start spawning until 3–4 years. With each succeeding year, the age of the sardines caught off the Monterey Peninsula declined until they were being harvested before they had the chance to breed and the fishery suddenly crashed. Northern anchovies took over the ecological niche vacated by the sardines. Today, both species exist in Monterey Bay, which is now a national marine sanctuary.

SUSTAINABLE FISHING

Small, surface-feeding marine fish such as herring, anchovies and sardines are easy to catch and their shoals are large enough to be tracked by satellite. This makes them vulnerable to overfishing, despite their natural abundance. They can be fished sustainably if the numbers and size (or age) of the fish caught are regulated through an agreed quota system, and fishing grounds are closed at certain times of the year.

OCEAN WARMING
Apart from fishing, anchovies are threatened by rising sea temperatures, such as the El Niño phenomenon in the Pacific. This disrupts supplies of their plankton food.

Freshwater Fish Various spp.

Rivers and lakes may seem like fairly placid habitats, but under the surface they often are changing beyond recognition. Human activities modify centuries-old drainage systems, impoverish the water and interfere with naturally balanced fish populations.

LIFE IN FRESH WATER

Freshwater fish do not form a coherent scientific group – thousands of species from many different families occur in fresh water. They exhibit a tremendous range of behaviors, with some spending part of their lives out at sea.

A natural freshwater drainage system is made up of a number of rivers, which may be upland or lowland and have fast- or slow-flowing sections, together with lakes that may be large or small, shallow or deep. Every part of the system, although connected, is a separate habitat, and it often has many endemic (unique to that area) species of fish. Because these fish have adapted over time to their particular aquatic environment, sudden changes in their surroundings may endanger them.

RIVERS OF SILT

All around the world, excessive loads of silt are ruining the water quality of rivers. The dirty water kills aquatic plants and suffocates fish. Various

CLEAN LIVING Although some freshwater fish can thrive in dirty conditions, most prefer clean water. This rare loach, for example, is under threat because it cannot cope with the low oxygen levels associated with pollution.

AUSTRALIAN LUNGFISH Dams threaten the survival of this primitive river fish. The species in its family are thought to be the closest living relatives of the first four-legged animals to emerge on land.

human activities produce the extra silt, including construction work, dredging, farming and, above all, deforestation. As trees are cut down, rainfall washes exposed topsoil off the land and into rivers, staining them red or brown. At least one species of fish, the harelip sucker of the U.S., is known to have become extinct due to river siltation; today, one of the worst affected areas is the Amazon basin in South America.

RESTRICTED FLOWS

Diverting rivers and abstracting water for agriculture or drinking can lower the water table. This is particularly dangerous for cave fish, which tend to be specific to cave networks and thus have small, vulnerable populations. If rivers are made to run at reduced levels – especially in the summer when river flows are already low – many of their fish are potentially at risk.

Dams and weirs are another major type of watercourse modification that affects fish. They alter the usual flow of nutrients and water and stop migratory fish from traveling to their spawning grounds. For example, a series of big dams ensured that the thicktail chub, once among the most common fish in California, had died out by the 1950s. Numerous other species, including the Australian lungfish and Mekong giant

LAKE MENACE The lakes of Africa's Rift Valley are famous for their variety of cichlid fish such as this one. But when Nile perch were released in Lake Victoria, they fed on its cichlids, making more than 300 of the lake's 500 species extinct.

catfish, may yet encounter the same fate. Despite this danger to fish stocks, some of which are commercially useful to local people, massive dam-building projects are planned or underway in rapidly developing countries such as China, India and Brazil.

RIVER BARRIERS Paddlefish are vulnerable due to dams in the Mississippi basin that cut their reproductive rate. Dams destroyed many of their spawning sites and split up surviving populations, creating the risk of inbreeding.

POLLUTED WATERWAYS

Pollution is a widespread problem for freshwater fish. Industrial development is concentrated along river and lake shores, because in the past machinery was powered by steam and water, and because many modern factories and power stations still need access to a plentiful supply of water. All kinds of industrial waste, from toxic chemicals to heavy metals and even hot water, is discharged into local drainage systems. In the worst pollution incidents, mass die-offs of fish have been recorded.

Agricultural fertilizers and pesticides also pollute rivers and lakes, since rain gradually leaches the chemicals from the soil and into the nearest drainage system. In recent years, acid rain has had a drastic impact, too, causing 100 percent mortality in some Canadian lakes. Even if the fish survive, they may fail to breed or produce young that are malformed or sterile.

ALIEN FISH

Some freshwater fish are threatened by the introduction, either intentional or accidental, of nonnative rivals. There are several disastrous instances of fish being released into rivers or lakes for recreational fishing. In 1970, the Nile perch was introduced to Lake Victoria in Africa as a game fish. It fulfilled this role, but destroyed more than half of the 500 cichlid fish species that once inhabited every part of the lake.

MEKONG RIVER CRISIS

The critically endangered Mekong giant catfish has become a flagship species for the plight of its native river. Weighing up to 650 pounds (300 kg), it is the world's largest freshwater fish, so perhaps unsurprisingly it has always been popular with fishermen. But catches declined during the 20th century until, between 2001 and 2003, fewer than a dozen giant catfish per year were being caught. Overfishing is only part of the reason. The Mekong River flows through a densely populated region – millions of people in China, Laos, Thailand, Cambodia and Vietnam rely on it for food, transport and hydroelectric power. These pressures have degraded its water quality to the point where parts of the river are starved of fish, and the giant catfish symbolizes this catastrophe.

Molluscs Mollusca

After fish, molluscs are probably the world's most successful and diverse aquatic organisms. They vary in shape from oysters to snails and squid, and live in both salt and fresh water, as well as on land. Molluscs are threatened by overfishing for their flesh and shells, worsening water pollution and habitat destruction.

MAJOR PHYLUM

Molluscs make up the second-largest invertebrate phylum, after arthropods (*see* pp. 170–175), with around 100,000 species described so far. Roughly 1 percent of these are currently classified as threatened, but this reflects the lack of data for many species and the true figure is likely to be much higher.

Two important groups of molluscs are considered here: the bivalve molluscs, which are named for their two-part, hinged shells and include species such as clams, mussels, oysters and scallops; and the gastropods, such as snails and conchs, which typically have a spiral shell and a sucker-like foot.

SUFFOCATION RISK

Most bivalves are filter feeders and use their gills both to respire and to feed. They do this by drawing a current of water over their gills: oxygen is taken into the circulatory system and food trapped among the many gill filaments is directed toward the mouth. Human activities that increase the amount of sediment in the water therefore present a suffocation danger, as clouds of silt clog the molluscs' delicate gills. Any coastal development has a detrimental effect – building a new marina or tidal barrage, dredging, tunneling across a bay or construction work on shore.

These sensitive marine organisms are also vulnerable to pollution. Pumping raw sewage into the sea harms bivalves by raising bacteria levels in the water and making them more susceptible to disease. There is mounting evidence that pollutants can disrupt their sexual development, too. Hormone-disrupting chemicals such as the human female contraceptive pill malform the sexual organs of clams and other bivalves, so that they cannot reproduce.

JEWELRY TO FOOD

For centuries bivalves and gastropods have been collected for their shells. The glossy shells of cowries, a type of gastropod, were a form of currency in parts of the Indian Ocean and West Africa until as recently as the mid-19th century. Nowadays, attractive shelled molluscs are still in demand for trinkets and jewelry (*see* panel, left).

The other major use of shellfish is as a valuable source of protein all around the world. Most shellfish are sedentary,

QUEEN CONCH This Caribbean gastropod has a handsome shell, tasty flesh and makes good fish bait, so it has been widely overexploited. It can be bred in captivity, but when released seems unable to cope in the wild.

so are easy to harvest, particularly along coasts or in shallow water. As a result, some of the more popular edible species have been collected excessively. The largest of all bivalves, giant clams, were once abundant in the Indo-Pacific region, but their numbers have been decimated by harvesting for their meat, considered a delicacy in Japan.

Even a few deep-water molluscs are at risk, including the endangered white abalone. This sea snail declined rapidly off the U.S. west coast in 1973–78 due to a large commercial and recreational fishery; only 2,500 abalone are left out of a thriving population estimated to have numbered four million individuals.

ACCIDENTAL CARGO

Ships carry encrusting molluscs from one continent to another, sometimes with terrible consequences for native varieties. The local mollusc species may be outcompeted or even eaten by the new arrivals. A similar situation arose when the Suez Canal opened in 1869, enabling sea snails, mussels and clams to spread freely between the Red Sea and eastern Mediterranean. Molluscs have also been deliberately introduced to create new fisheries.

SHELLS FOR SALE

Gathering washed-up seashells – the remains of dead molluscs – may seem a harmless enough pastime. However, in order to find enough to sell, traders have to collect the living animals, too, and this harms populations of the most sought-after molluscs. Desirable species quickly become scarce off populated coastlines, forcing the fishers to go ever further afield. A number of beautiful, large-shelled molluscs are now at risk, and their international sale is restricted by trade agreements such as CITES.

The Oyster Family

In the past oysters were a cheap staple food, but overfishing depleted their populations in Europe, North America and parts of Asia to such an extent that they became a luxury item. There are more than 100 species of oyster. Many are edible, but the Pacific, or Japanese, oyster is eaten most widely today. This adaptable, fast-growing species is ideal for cultivation, so it has been taken all around the world. Unfortunately, it is a carrier of virulent diseases that are fatal to local molluscs. Stocks of the "native," or common, European oyster and of the eastern oyster of the U.S.'s Atlantic coast have suffered in this way.

CULTIVATING OYSTERS

Oyster aquaculture depends on clean water – even small traces of pollutants are absorbed by the molluscs and become concentrated in their tissues, making the flesh unfit for consumption. Marine biologists often use bivalve molluscs to monitor pollution levels in coastal waters.

PEARL PRODUCTION

All oysters – and many other bivalves – produce pearls, but only those of pearl oysters (Pteriidae) are considered valuable. To reduce the pressure on stocks of wild pearl oysters, artificial pearls can be cultivated by inserting a piece of grit or a small chip of pearl into farmed oysters.

GIANT CLAMS

These huge bivalves are vulnerable due to overfishing in the Pacific, and have disappeared from countries such as Fiji. Clam-farming may offer a chance of restocking affected areas.

Corals Cnidaria

Spectacular coral reefs teeming with life are a sign of a healthy marine environment, but today corals face myriad threats, from overheating seas to pollution, coastal development and dynamite fishing. All over the world, reefs are dying.

RICH ECOSYSTEMS

Just 0.2 percent of the Earth's ocean environment is made up of coral reefs, but they support by far the richest marine ecosystems, so are of immense global importance. For example, a coral reef in the Indo-Pacific may comprise more than 700 coral species and give shelter and food to more than 2,000 types of fish. Worldwide, but especially in the tropics, reefs are at risk from human activities, threatening not only the corals but also a staggering diversity of other marine organisms.

CORAL REEF TOURISM

Snorkeling or diving over coral reefs is a thrilling experience enjoyed by millions of people a year, but the pastime puts a huge strain on this fragile habitat. Boat anchors drag across reefs, novice divers knock against corals or stand on them while trying to control their buoyancy or take photographs, and people break off chunks of coral as souvenirs. In many places, the sheer number of visitors is disturbing shy species of fish and turtles. Large resorts do the most damage, but there is now a growing trend of smaller hotels with their own protected reef.

"Coral" is a common name for up to 3,000 species in the phylum Cnidaria, a major group of invertebrate animals. Most corals have a stony skeleton made of calcium carbonate, which provides a substratum to support the tiny living animal, or polyp. It is the accumulated skeletons of hard, reef-building corals that forms the structure of coral reefs.

DAMAGED REEFS

In warm, shallow, tropical waters the polyps of reef-building corals have evolved symbiotic (mutually beneficial) relationships with tiny algae, called zooxanthellae, that live inside their tissues and provide them with essential nutrients. However, these relationships are delicate – when stressed the coral polyps and algae separate, the coral dies and what is known as "bleaching" of the reef occurs.

Corals are stressed by various factors, including disease and excessively high water temperatures. The latter scenario is already thought to be a reality: it is being caused by global warming and by depletion of the ozone layer, which increases the amount of UV radiation reaching the Earth's surface. Because reef corals are already living near to their upper tolerance limit, even small changes in water temperature can be critical to their survival.

Another major cause of stress is urban expansion. The development of coastal land greatly increases surface runoff in the form of silt, and this affects water clarity and smothers corals. Sewage and other waste discharged into the sea provides superabundant nutrients (a process called eutrophication), which upsets the ecological balance of the reefs; for example, it allows numbers of animals such as sponges to explode at the expense of corals.

BLEACHED CORAL Coral bleaching events have been increasing in frequency worldwide since the 1970s. The worst epidemics, such as at Australia's Great Barrier Reef in 1998 and 2002, can kill coral over thousands of miles.

HARMFUL TRADES

Over 90 percent of all coral reefs have been affected by human interference of one kind or another. Dynamite fishing is a particularly destructive activity that is widely used, especially in the Philippines, to collect coral for sale as souvenirs. The stores buy their supplies from commercial collectors, who harvest only large, healthy coral colonies as these are the most profitable.

Coral harvesting is not new – it has been used as a gemstone and carving material for millennia. It was also widely believed that coral could stop wounds from bleeding, cure madness, quell storms

EATEN ALIVE During periodic outbreaks, crown of thorns starfish congregate on reefs, forming huge armies that devour all the coral in their path. It is possible that these "plagues" are triggered by human interference.

and offer protection against magical spells. What has changed is the scale of the trade in coral. For instance, pink and red corals, highly valued for use in jewelry and homeopathic medicines, lost two-thirds of their population in the Mediterranean alone in 1990–2005.

STARFISH PLAGUES

Crown of thorns starfish are natural predators of hard corals and one of the few animals that can eat living coral tissue. Normally, they do not harm reefs, but large numbers of starfish eating away at a coral reef causes enormous damage. Recently, there have been several population explosions of these starfish in the Pacific. They may be a natural phenomenon, but it is also possible that eutrophic algal blooms caused by pollution provide so much food for the starfish larvae that an outbreak occurs. Another theory is that we have inadvertently reduced the numbers of the starfish's enemies, such as trumpet shellfish.

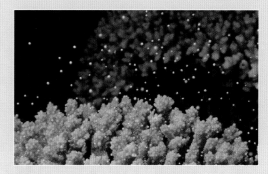

SYNCHRONIZED SPAWNING Most corals spawn together, and a reef often releases vast quantities of floating eggs and sperm at once. This means that surface-borne pollutants such as oil and other toxins can affect coral reproduction over a large area.

DELICATE BALANCE
Coral reefs depend on very specific growing conditions. A rise in water temperature of just 1.8–3.6°F (1–2°C) for 5–10 weeks may be enough to suffocate a tropical reef.

Arthropods Arthropoda

Two-thirds of all the described living species on Earth belong to a single group of animals – the arthropods. These creatures first appeared in oceans during the Cambrian Period, and diversified to colonise virtually every habitat on land and in the air.

AMAZING DIVERSITY

The success of the arthropods in terms of both species richness and biomass (weight of numbers) is unparalleled in the animal kingdom. They make up a huge grouping, or phylum, called Arthropoda, which is subdivided into four large groups. The hexapods, which include insects, are discussed on the following four pages, while crustaceans, myriapods and arachnids are covered on pages 174–175.

Arthropods are bilaterally symmetrical and all have a segmented body with an outer protective cuticle (skin-like layer) that acts as a rigid exoskeleton. They have pairs of jointed legs that arise from body segments, which may be fused into separate functional units such as a head, thorax and abdomen.

HEXAPODS

The hexapods are the most successful of all the arthropods, with one million described species. By far the most abundant and diverse hexapods belong to the class Insecta: these alone make up 56.3 percent of all living species.

Our knowledge of Earth's biodiversity, or rather lack of it, has always been shaped by our fundamental ignorance of several key groups – bacteria, algae, fungi, roundworms and especially the insects. Estimates suggest there may be 5–10 million species of insects that remain unknown to science. Although found everywhere on the surface of the planet, insects are very much more common in tropical and subtropical regions, particularly in humid tropical forests. For example, 43 species of ants can be found on a single tree in the Peruvian Amazon, which is equal to the entire ant fauna of the U.K.

LOSS OF SPECIES

Despite their abundance, many insects are threatened with extinction, and although we may not have names for them all yet, we know that loss and fragmentation of habitats will result in a loss of species richness. In some parts of the world, for instance Madagascar and coastal regions of South America, 90 percent of the forest has been lost in the past 150 years – it is safe to say that half of all the insect species found there have already vanished.

The insects that are most threatened are generally large species of butterflies, moths and beetles. Big insects such as these tend to have longer lifecycles, reproduce more slowly, and, as a result, they are much more affected by factors such as habitat loss than small species. Beautiful, showy insects also attract the attention of collectors. Butterfly and beetle collecting developed in the 19th century, when the

PRIZE SPECIMEN The birdwing butterflies of Southeast Asia, such as this endangered Queen Alexandra birdwing, are highly sought after by collectors. Sadly, this and other protected insects are still widely sold, often on the Internet.

BUTTERFLY FARMS

Many butterflies can be "farmed" and in the last few decades of the 20th century butterfly houses developed into popular tourist attractions. Butterfly farms have sprung up all around the world; in the picture below, chrysalises are awaiting pupation at a farm in Ecuador. These farms sell dead specimens to collectors and as ornaments, providing a good source of income to local communities. By rearing rare species, they also reduce the collecting pressure on wild butterfly populations, although it can be difficult to be sure that specimens for sale have come from a sustainable reared source.

COLLECTOR'S ITEM Although it is a protected species, this South African colophon stag beetle is still frequently captured for sale to unscrupulous collectors.

naturalists and explorers of European empires such as Alexander von Humboldt, Margaret Fontaine, Alfred Wallace, Ernst Haeckel and Charles Darwin brought back exotic species to stock Europe's museums. Today, the global trade in butterflies alone is probably worth around US$200 million per year, with the rarest species fetching astronomical prices.

CHANGING CLIMATE

Some factors threaten many groups of insects, whether bold in appearance or small and insignificant. Chief among these threats are habitat loss and use of pesticides (see pp. 172–173), but climate change could yet be added to this list. As the world gets warmer, many insects might benefit, but others may struggle, especially those adapted to cooler climates.

For example, the Apollo butterfly's caterpillars feed only on a stonecrop that grows in mountains in Europe and Central Asia. In parts of the Apollo's range, such as Scandinavia, there is evidence that rising temperatures are changing the distribution of this cold-loving alpine plant, forcing the insect to abandon its former haunts.

The Apollo butterfly's predicament is only just becoming clear, but little is known about the status of most insects. Around 20 percent of mammal species and 12 percent of birds are classed as vulnerable, endangered or critically endangered, but the same is true for just 0.06 percent of insects. This does not mean insects are safer – it reflects how little we know about them. In any tropical location there will be hundreds of new insects waiting to be discovered, about which we know nothing.

LATE DEVELOPER Many of the world's rarest beetles, such as this longhorn beetle, *Rosalia alpina*, feed on rotten wood as larvae and take a long time to develop into adults. This makes them vulnerable to changes in their habitat.

CLIMATE DEPENDENCY
The Apollo butterfly's decline in Europe may be caused by global warming. Like many herbivorous insects, it is tied to specific food plants, the distribution of which is linked to a region's climate.

DANGER IN PARADISE

The beautiful Lord Howe Island, which lies 375 miles (600 km) east of Australia, is the only home of an impressive stick insect, *Dryococelus australis*, colloquially known as the land or tree "lobster" as it grows up to 6 inches (15 cm) long. This giant insect provides a good case study of the threats facing island-dwelling arthropods. Since European settlers discovered Lord Howe Island in 1788, its fragile flora has been damaged by feral pigs and goats, and the stick insects were also killed by escaped black rats. They were believed extinct, but in 2001 a single colony of stick insects was found, and they are now being bred at Melbourne Zoo.

FARMING REVOLUTION

It is likely that about 10 percent of the world's known insects – roughly 100,000 species – are threatened, and without doubt one of the main culprits is the intensification of agriculture. Farming is taking over more and more land and this, together with drainage of marshes, bogs, floodplains and other wetlands, has greatly reduced suitable habitat for insects. Since 1700, the world's irrigated cropland has expanded 24 times. In ecological terms such a uniform landscape is relatively sterile, because the vegetation is dominated by the particular crops being grown. There are not enough feeding opportunities to support a wide range of insects and other animals (*see* pp. 40–41).

CHEMICAL WARFARE

One of the problems with monoculture is that certain insect species find this artificial habitat ideal, and therefore can reach plague proportions. Since World War II, the solution increasingly has been to turn to a new and deadly range of pesticides, such as DDT. These powerful chemicals are indiscriminate, affecting non-target beneficial species such as bees as well as the pests they are intended to remove. Another class of agricultural chemicals, herbicides, kill off noncrop plants such as herbs and wildflowers, further reducing food availability for insects.

ISLAND PERILS

Although conservationists have tended to concentrate on saving larger species, insects with restricted island ranges are just as susceptible to the harmful effects of invasive rats, pigs and other animals (*see* panel, left).

St. Helena, a remote and mountainous island in the South Atlantic, has a large number of unique insect species. Some of them are almost certainly extinct, including the St. Helena dragonfly and the giant St. Helena earwig, which grew up to 3 inches (8 cm) long. Their demise was caused by the introduction of alien species, as well as habitat loss.

Introduced predators have also been a severe problem for wetas, which are native to New Zealand. There are 20 known species of these large, flightless, nocturnally active relatives of crickets, several of which are very vulnerable to predation by rats, cats, weasels, stoats and other "alien" mammals.

INTRODUCED INSECTS

Sometimes it is the arrival of another insect that causes havoc with an area's established insect populations. Ants are major insect predators in almost any land habitat, and so have a particularly big impact on other invertebrates. One of the world's worst invasive species is the imported red fire ant, a native of South America that has the potential to spread worldwide – it has already invaded Australia, North America and some oceanic islands. This species is very aggressive, breeds rapidly and can

EATEN BY RATS Introduced rats have already exterminated the Poor Knights giant weta on mainland New Zealand. The species is named after its sole remaining haven – Poor Knights Island, which is free of rodents.

BURYING BEETLE
Nicrophorus americanus is endangered in North America, for reasons that are still unclear. This master scavenger survives in scattered localities in one-tenth of its former range and is the subject of several conservation projects.

survive in a wide range of habitats. It eats other insects and has a powerful sting, enabling it to consume or drive away a range of vertebrates, too. In the southern U.S. it has reduced numbers of birds, reptiles and small mammals, and has locally reduced the indigenous arthropod numbers by 30 percent.

MYSTERIOUS DECLINE

In some cases, it is difficult to be sure exactly what is causing the decline of an insect. The largest North American burying beetle, *Nicrophorus americanus*, which locates the carcasses of small mammals on which to lay its eggs, has become increasingly rare during the last 100 years. Many potential factors have been put forward, from habitat loss and pesticides to artificial nighttime lighting and growing competition for carcasses from skunks, raccoons and other mammals.

DISAPPEARING POLLINATORS

Since the 1960s, there has been an accelerating decline in numbers of bees in many developed countries, and the same trend is now noticeable in other parts of the world where farming is becoming industrialized. Since 20–25 percent of all the food we eat relies on insect pollination, a reduction in pollinators could have a serious impact on global food security. Mobile trailers loaded with bee hives can be used to ensure good crops, but the best long-term solution is to improve the natural environment for bees.

VALUABLE LAND
Workman's jumping spider
lives only in a certain type of
scrub found in Florida. Much
of this wilderness area has
been lost due to the intense
pressure to develop the land.

CRUSTACEANS

The group Crustacea comprises 34,000 species, which are very diverse in appearance, ranging from water fleas that are barely visible to the unaided eye to barnacles, shrimps, crabs and lobsters. Crustaceans are primarily aquatic and they occur in fresh water and oceans throughout the world, although woodlice and some crabs live on land. Around 400 species are categorized as threatened, of which 60 are critically endangered.

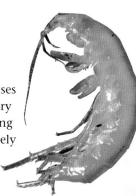

CAVE AMPHIPOD Underground springs and streams support lots of rare, specialized crustaceans, such as this shrimp-like species from the U.S.'s Ozark Plateau.

Many threatened crustaceans inhabit freshwater or cave ecosystems. They include 16 species of burrowing crayfish from Tasmania and numerous cave-dwelling shrimps and amphipods. These species have tended to evolve for a long period in isolation and often are found at a tiny number of localities, or even a single location, making them highly vulnerable to changes in groundwater availability and other types of habitat disturbance. Several air-breathing, tree-climbing crabs that live in leaf axils and tree holes are also at risk, usually from deforestation in the tropics.

CRAYFISH PLAGUE The white-clawed crayfish has undergone a severe decline across most of its European range. Its populations have been devastated by crayfish plague, a disease carried by introduced American signal crayfish.

MYRIAPODS

There are 13,700 described species of myriapods, terrestrial arthropods with an elongated body typified by the carnivorous centipedes and herbivorous millipedes. In common with most arthropods, little is known about their conservation status. Species that have been identified as threatened tend to live on islands or have a very restricted distribution, such as the bird-eating Serpent Island centipede, found on two islands in Mauritius.

ARACHNIDS

The group Arachnida contains 76,000 species, of which the commonest are ticks and mites but the most familiar are spiders and scorpions. All arachnids have two main body segments and

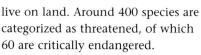

LEGAL PROTECTION This *Spelungula* cave spider from New Zealand is a rare example of an arachnid that has been awarded legal protection. However, arachnids often benefit from conservation targeted at other species.

four pairs of legs. Most species live on land, although one in 10 mites occur in fresh water, as does the water spider, which is native to Europe and Asia.

Like other arthropod groups, many arachnids have localized distributions or very specific habitat requirements. They are thus vulnerable to disturbance at quite a local level, in addition to pesticide use and other more general, wide-ranging threats. For example, the raft (fishing) spider of northwestern Europe requires clean lowland marshes with plenty of lush vegetation, and is at risk from wetland drainage and the lowering of the water table. Another rare species, the large and colorful Workman's jumping spider, is confined to scrubland in Florida. Much of the scrub in this densely populated state has been plowed for citrus orchards or housing developments.

"*For global conservation, only one-thousandth of the current annual world domestic product, or US$30 billion out of approximately US$30 trillion, would accomplish most of the task. One key element, the protection and management of the world's existing natural reserves, could be financed by a one-cent-per-cup tax on coffee.*"

– Edward O. Wilson, *The Future of Life*, 2002

STEMMING THE TIDE

The desert bandicoot, the golden toad, the passenger pigeon, the harelip sucker fish and a host of other species became extinct within the last 100 years and we can do nothing for them now. But we can do something for the species we have not yet lost. Some may have been reduced to such low numbers that we will not be able to pull them back from the brink – they are already on borrowed time, so are effectively the "living dead." However, for many other species it is not yet too late. Awareness of our negative impact on the planet has been growing steadily, as has the will to do something about it, but much remains to be done.

We should be striving now for a world where there are far fewer humans, where there is more equality and certainly less waste. It is not a wholly impossible dream, but we may be incapable of achieving it, partly because of our evolutionary inheritance. Historically, we have always taken the short-term view and protected our own immediate interests. This approach has stood us in very good stead – until now. Recent studies show that we are running an overdraft with the ecosystems that sustain us and all other species. Common sense alone tells us that this situation cannot be maintained indefinitely.

Preserving Nature *in situ*

Efforts to save wildlife often focus on large, charismatic species that top the endangered list – an understandable response in a world driven by hard-hitting images and media appeal. But even these efforts will come to nothing if there is nowhere left for the animals to live. It is essential that we preserve large swathes of habitat and their complex ecosystems.

EARTH AS AN ASSET

In 1997, a team of scientists calculated the value in dollars of the ecological services that sustain life on Earth. That is the amount of money we would theoretically have to spend to do the jobs, such as climate regulation, food production and soil formation, that are presently carried out by the species that make up the Earth's ecosystems. The amount, a conservative US$33 trillion per annum, is more than the total world gross economic product! There is no question that biodiversity must be preserved, but how can it best be done?

THE AMAZON

When resources are limited and time is short, efforts to preserve nature might be best concentrated in areas where biodiversity is at its richest.

Rainforests cover less than 5 percent of Earth's land-surface area and contain more than half of all species and must therefore be a priority. The World Wildlife Fund (WWF) has been working for over 40 years to save the Amazon rainforest. By helping to establish protected areas across the Amazon, such as the Alto Purús National Park in Brazil (an area that is nearly the size of Massachusetts), the WWF and its partners are making a big difference. Alto Purús is home to many endangered species such as the black spider monkey and the jaguar. The WWF and similar conservation groups raise awareness of the dangers of deforestation, and build partnerships with governments, businesses and local

NEW SPECIES This remarkable poison dart frog, *Epipedobates* sp., was recently discovered in the Amazonian rainforest's Yavari Valley, in Peru. Many similar species are critically endangered.

ECOLOGICAL DIVERSITY The Yavari Valley, in Peru's Amazonian rainforest, has one of the highest recorded primate diversities in the world. Other endangered species found there include tapirs, macaws and giant otters. The WWF and a host of other conservation bodies are currently battling to achieve protected status for this area of astonishing biodiversity.

populations to preserve the rainforest. However, in Brazil alone in the last 15 years we have lost 190,000 square miles (500,000 sq km) of rainforest – a rate of 380 football fields every hour. There is still much to do. Obstacles include development pressures from commercial agriculture, particularly soybean crops, cattle ranching, illegal logging and infrastructure building, all of which destroy or fragment the vulnerable ecosystem.

HIDDEN TREASURES

More than 70 percent of the Earth's surface is covered by oceans and it is here that most of the variety of life exists. Despite the fact that 80 percent of all the major groups of organisms are marine, 95 percent of this biome remains unknown. To an extent there is a problem of the habitat being "out of sight and out of mind." Whereas damage to the Amazon rainforests is clearly visible from aerial photography, the devastation caused by bottom-trawling the seafloor can only be imagined. In fact, many marine habitats, such as the immensely rich coral reefs, are in dire need of protection, without which they may disappear in the next 50 years.

The International Coral Reef Initiative (ICRI), a partnership of nations and organizations originally initiated by the governments of Australia, France, Japan, Jamaica, the Philippines, Sweden, the U.K. and the U.S., is helping to raise

NATURE RESERVES Protected areas of all kinds around the world, from small local nature reserves to enormous national parks covering millions of acres, constitute only around 6 percent of the total land-surface area.

awareness of the value of coral reefs and the threats they face. In an effort to "protect and sustainably use fragile coral reef resources worldwide," 1997 was designated the International Year of the Coral Reef (IYOR).

CONSERVATION HOT SPOTS

Another approach to conservation is to target areas where there are very high levels of endemic species – species that are found nowhere else on Earth. Based on plants and vertebrate species a total of 25 of these biodiversity hot spots have been identified. They include the Mediterranean basin; the forests of West Africa; the coastal forests of Tanzania and Kenya; Madagascar; the Atlantic forests and dry forests (cerrado) of Brazil; Central America; much of Southeast Asia; and the oceanic islands of the Pacific. Originally covering nearly 12 percent of the total land-surface area, they have now fallen to just under 1.5 percent but still harbor more than 60 percent of the planet's diversity. Although some of these areas already have a degree of protection, more than one billion humans live in them and more than half of all the major nature reserves around the world are already farmed, some heavily. Today, strenuous efforts are being made to encourage wildlife-friendly farming practices, but it is hard to see

SECRETS OF THE SEA Coral reefs are very rich, yet incredibly fragile and little understood. It is estimated that at least 30 percent of reef ecosystems should be completely protected, but less than 5 percent is currently safeguarded.

how the environment can be protected and an increasing human population fed at the same time. Ultimately, both human and environmental welfare issues must be addressed simultaneously as they are dependent on each other. Protected areas that are of no benefit to local communities will be ineffective in the long run.

ECOTOURISM

A growing appreciation of nature and the value of biodiversity has led to an increased desire to see it firsthand. There is some legitimate concern that ecotourists may ultimately disturb and damage the very species and habitats they have come to see. But tourism of this kind, if properly managed, can bring wealth and prosperity to local communities and can emphasize the value of preserving wildlife.

Preserving Nature *ex situ*

Zoological parks (and aquaria) have come a long way since they originated as live displays of exotic species, primarily for commercial gain and public entertainment. In the last 50 years mounting concern over species decline around the world has led to a large number of zoos becoming very active in research, education and maintaining populations of threatened species.

NEW ZOOS

While great efforts are being made by some zoos to improve the conditions in which animals are kept, detractors still question whether it is necessary to keep large species such as elephants, which can suffer behavioral and other problems in captivity. Some people also question whether nonendangered wild species should be confined at all, especially in conditions that may be climatically and environmentally different from their original habitat.

However, there is no doubt that zoos have an educational value and have inspired an appreciation of wildlife in many people who would never otherwise see such animals firsthand. This is more true today than ever before as zoos and aquaria have found a new purpose and direction by supporting captive breeding programs that have developed into an important conservation tool.

RAISING THE DEAD

It is generally agreed that the chances of bringing species such as the thylacine (*see* p. 53) "back from the dead" are exceedingly small, mainly because of the damaged condition of the DNA and the near impossibility of obtaining a complete genome. It has been suggested that sections of DNA taken from the remains of extinct species, such as the thylacine skull pictured below, could be spliced into the genome of closely related species to recreate animals with characteristics of the extinct animal. But it is not clear what the benefits of this might be. It would be much better to put more resources into conserving species in their natural habitat in the first place.

RELUCTANT SURVIVORS Although captive breeding programs have a high success rate, some species are difficult to breed in captivity. The giant panda is notoriously difficult, as are cheetahs, elephants and penguins.

breeding and subsequent reintroduction of species that have become extinct in the wild or are critically endangered. Such species may be reintroduced after the problem that led to the extinction has been eradicated. Alternatively, where the problem is too persistent or the habitat no longer exists, captive-bred animals can be introduced into suitable habitats where they did not exist previously.

OVERCOMING DIFFICULTIES

There are, however, many difficulties associated with captive breeding programs. Inbreeding, especially in mammal species, can lead to lower reproductive success stemming from such factors as low sperm counts and lower female fertility, as well as higher mortality rates in offspring. Breeding from a few captive individuals, and thus a very reduced genetic stock, or gene pool, may have damaging effects. For instance, a genetic defect that is rare in large populations may become common if it was present in one of a small number of "founder" individuals. For example, several of the Mauritius

CAPTIVE BREEDING

Ex-situ conservation – zoos, aquaria, gene banks and all forms of species

maintenance outside the natural habitat – has made major progress in the last few decades and some very important research and education programs are now underway.

Through caring for and rearing captive species, much can be learned about the details of their biology that can be directly applied to their conservation in the wild. One of the most important roles of zoos recently has been in the captive

REINTRODUCED The Arabian oryx was declared extinct in the wild in 1972 but has since been reintroduced successfully into reserves in Oman, Jordan, Israel and Saudi Arabia.

pink pigeons bred in captivity from a small number of birds caught in the wild suffered from congenital foot problems and brain abnormalities.

WHEN BIGGER IS BETTER

Greater genetic variety gives wild populations other advantages, including a good chance of surviving disease, and a better ability to cope with challenges such as climate change. To mimic this in captivity, genetic data is kept in an international studbook. With critically endangered species such as the Sumatran tiger, black rhino and gorillas, zoo staff can "mix and match" breeding pairs to ensure a wide exchange of genes, improving the population's reproductive health.

Another problem is knowing how big specific populations need to be to be viable in the long term. Some species require large numbers to be successful and, below a threshold population size, will not breed well. Smaller populations can also be much more readily wiped out by chance events such as storms or droughts, and there has been much debate about how well captive-bred animals will fare once they are released into the wild and have to fend for themselves.

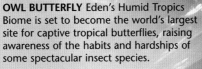

OWL BUTTERFLY Eden's Humid Tropics Biome is set to become the world's largest site for captive tropical butterflies, raising awareness of the habits and hardships of some spectacular insect species.

Ultimately, the process is expensive and possibly only suited to preserving a few high-profile species. And for the many species that do not respond well to captive breeding, zoos may turn out to be the last stop before they vanish from the Earth. However, despite all these difficulties, captive breeding has been a great success for the Arabian oryx, black-footed ferret, Przewalski's horse, Pere David's deer and the California condor. All these species, and many others, were extinct in the wild and were pulled back from the brink by captive breeding. It is by no means a viable alternative to conserving species in their natural habitat, but it does provide a safety net when other protective methods have failed.

PARADISE REGAINED Zoos, aquaria and gardens, which help to conserve and study nature, have come a long way in the past few decades. The Eden Project in the U.K. is at the cutting edge of *ex-situ* conservation.

International Rescue

Many of the world's biggest problems have a political solution, and it is world governments, elected democratically or otherwise, that must act on our behalf to tackle them. Advice to governments comes from a variety of sources: national and international specialists, non-governmental organizations, pressure groups of various types and public opinion.

CHANGING ATTITUDES

In recent surveys across 60 countries, 66 percent of people questioned thought that their governments were not doing enough to protect the environment. In similar surveys across 24 countries, over 80 percent of people said they thought that species loss was serious or very serious, but only 60 percent said they would prefer to see environmental protection take precedence over growth of their economies. It might seem like we want to have our cake and eat it too, but the good news is that the message that our well-being depends entirely on the survival of healthy ecosystems is finally starting to get through to the people, the politicians and the policy makers.

INTERNATIONAL LAW

Most countries now have local and national laws relating to the protection of wildlife and natural resources, and in the last 40 years numerous declarations, treaties and a host of other international agreements have been put in place to protect the environment. International agreement and action is vital because biodiversity, natural capital and ecosystem processes – for example, migratory fish stocks, fresh water and climate regulation – are not confined by national boundaries.

The World Conservation Union, originally known as the International Union for the Conservation of Nature and Natural Resources

A VITAL ROLL Although we still focus most of our attention on so-called charismatic creatures, there is a growing appreciation for the often vital roles played by insect species in sustaining healthy ecosystems.

·DUNG BEETLES HAVE RIGHT OF WAY·

(IUCN), was set up in 1948 and has its headquarters in Gland, Switzerland. It brings together over 1,000 members including national and international nongovernmental organizations (NGOs) and government agencies. Its mission statement is "to influence, encourage and assist societies throughout the world to conserve the integrity and diversity of nature and to ensure that any use of natural resources is equitable and ecologically sustainable." The IUCN has played a crucial role in formulating and establishing a number of worldwide environmental initiatives and conventions, the most important of which are the Convention on the International Trade in Endangered Species of Wild Flora and Fauna (CITES) and the Convention on Biological Diversity (CBD).

CITES

The aim of CITES, which came into force in 1975, is to protect wild animals and plants by controlling commercial international trade in approximately 5,000 species of animals and 28,000 species of plants listed under one of three appendices. The 169 countries that are currently signatories to the convention have agreed to ban, except in exceptional circumstances, any commercial trade of those species listed under Appendix I, which are most at risk from extinction. Trade in species listed under Appendix II is controlled to prevent them from *becoming* endangered. Species that are protected in at least one country, and where other countries have been asked to help in controlling their trade, are

ORPHANED RHINO In Zimbabwe, Africa, an orphaned black rhino is cared for by a warden. Although the black rhino is still listed as critically endangered on the IUCN "red list" of threatened species, its population is increasing. About 90 percent of the rhino population has been wiped out in the last 60 years, largely because of the value of its horn.

listed under Appendix III. Anyone wishing to import, export or reexport a CITES-listed species to or from a country that is party to the convention must first obtain documentation from the relevant national authorities. Species listed under each appendix can be found on the CITES website. The annual world trade in wildlife and wildlife products is valued in billions of dollars, and as long as there is a demand, people will take the risk of being caught and convicted.

CBD

The Convention on Biological Diversity, which came into force in 1993, was one of the major documents that resulted from the United Nations Conference on Environment and Development, informally known as the Earth Summit, which was hosted by Brazil in 1992. More than 180 nations signed the

convention, a legally binding agreement, which has as its major objectives "the conservation of biological diversity, the sustainable use of its components and the fair and equitable sharing of benefits arising out

PROTECTED U.S. customs officials uncover a shipment of critically endangered Asian box turtles (*see* p. 138). The turtles are packed into boxes and delivered to supply the illegal pet trade. Many do not survive the transportation.

of the utilization of genetic resources." While CBD recognizes that individual countries have control over their own biological resources, each party to the convention agreed to "conserve and sustainably use biological diversity for the benefit of present and future generations."

Despite all the agreements that are in place, extraordinary habitats such as tropical forests are still being cleared and burned for short-term gain. Only a very small percentage of Earth's forests are sustainably managed and most of these are in temperate regions, not the species-rich tropics. Protection of large habitats is extremely difficult, expensive to run and places huge burdens on countries where biodiversity is most threatened. The world's wildlife needs even more powerful safeguards and adequate resources to put them into effect.

Learning the Lessons

The fabric of life has been well and truly frayed by the sheer numbers of humans. We can either carry on doing what we have been doing until something stops us – the "business as usual" approach – or we can try to make some sensible decisions about our future. As a starting point, people in developed countries need to adjust to less wasteful lifestyles.

ACTION GROUPS

Everything that we do affects wildlife locally and globally. Ultimately, we all have to change our lifestyles and our way of thinking. We need to develop new, environmentally friendly habits, cut down our levels of consumption and wage war on waste.

The fact that you are reading this book is a pretty clear indication that you are concerned about the environment and probably want to do something to help. The good news is that you can do a great deal to help. We can't all raise the funds to buy a ship and sail off to "save the whales," but we *can* help the people who are willing and able to do so. Supporting an organization such as the WWF is a great place to start making a positive impact, and their website (and those of countless similar nonprofit organizations) is a great place to keep up to date with environmental issues, so that you can keep yourself informed and spread the word to your friends and family. Such organizations have been in the front line of the battle to protect wildlife for decades – funding research programs, raising awareness through education and supporting many smaller local organizations working toward similar aims.

STARTING AT HOME

The fact is that a lot of little changes *can* make a very big difference.

Switch off the lights when you leave a room and, in the rooms where you spend most of your time, replace the bulbs with low-energy brands. If you are buying a new kitchen appliance, buy the most energy-efficient model (they will pay for themselves through lower energy bills). Insulate your hot-water tank, and the walls, attic and

SAVE ENERGY Wherever possible, buy locally produced food in season to avoid the pollution associated with transporting food products.

floors of your house. Again, you will find you are saving up to 20 percent off your heating bills as a result. Turning your thermostat down by just a degree or two will reduce your heating bill further. Avoid leaving electrical appliances on standby mode. In the U.S. alone, leaving equipment in sleep mode uses enough power to keep 26 average-sized power stations busy for a whole year! Perhaps most importantly, buy your electricity from a creditable green energy supplier. Many renewable energy sources are now available for domestic use. Where you live will affect what is the best option for you. Norway, for example, produces more than 90 percent of its electricity using hydro power; Israel is leading the way in solar power; Germany now has more than 16,000 wind turbines; and Iceland has led the way in geothermal systems, which use thermal energy from the

earth. Biomass heating is a popular option in Canada. Although it may seem that burning wood is not an eco-friendly option, with proper management the biomass resource base can be sustained indefinitely and is considered to be CO_2 neutral.

REDUCE, REUSE, RECYCLE

Recycle everything you can – paper, glass, plastic, clothes, metal and motor oil. If your local authority does not provide recycling facilities then write to them and demand they be made available. Try to avoid buying products or packaging that cannot be recycled.

In the bathroom, take shorter showers or install a water-saving shower head, and don't leave taps running needlessly.

In the laundry, wash clothes at a low temperature whenever possible and only wash when you have a full load. Don't put hazardous substances down the drain or in the garbage. Again, where practical, use a microwave rather than a conventional oven for cooking. When you use the stove, cook with a pan that is the same size as the burner. Compost any vegetable matter from your kitchen and use it in your garden or take it to a recycling facility.

In the yard, avoid the use of pesticides and pull out weeds rather than using herbicides. Use organic fertilizer, and use mulch to save water. Use a hand mower to mow the lawn rather than an electric or gas mower. Remember, grass absorbs far less carbon than trees and bushes and needs over 50 percent more water, so use some of that lawn space to plant a tree and some bushes to help reduce carbon emissions and provide a home for birds at the same time. You might like to put out bird baths, nesting boxes, bat roosts and similar products to encourage local wildlife. Let the birds and wasps deal with your caterpillar problem and the ladybugs help with the aphids. But keep your cat indoors, especially at dusk and dawn, when birds are most vulnerable. Or, at the very least, attach a bell to the cat's collar to give the local birds a chance. In the U.S. alone, cats kill hundreds of millions of birds each year. In many developed countries the unnatural numbers of these very efficient feline predators is a huge environmental problem.

ON THE ROAD

Drive an energy-efficient car and use it as little as possible. Walk or bike to work if you can and get fit while you help save the planet. Keeping your tires inflated and removing the roof rack when not in use will significantly increase the energy efficiency of your vehicle. Avoid flying as much as possible as airplanes release huge quantities of pollutants.

ECO-FRIENDLY SHOPPING

Avoid buying food with unnecessary packaging and remember to reuse your shopping bags. Buy locally grown produce wherever possible, because transporting food from long distances is a major contributing factor to pollution. A hundred years ago practically all of our food came from within 20 miles (32 km) of our homes. Today, food is transported for hundreds of miles, which is bad news for the roads, the environment and our health. Buy organic produce, which avoids the use of pesticides and is generally better for wildlife and the environment.

There is a lot more that we in the

developed world can do, and the websites of organizations such as the WWF, Sierra Club, OneWorld, Friends of the Earth and Greenpeace are packed with information and conservation tips. Of course, as individuals, our ability to make a major impact on global issues is limited. We cannot invest millions of dollars into new technology or force the pace of international agreements, but we can and should demand action from our elected representatives. In any case, it is becoming increasingly clear that carrying on with "business as usual" is no longer a viable option.

ENERGY EFFICIENCY
It might be hard to imagine how switching off a light can help to make a difference, but by looking at the Chicago skyline it is easy to see how many people doing a small thing can make a big difference. The U.S. uses more than one-quarter of the world's energy resources. While the amount of renewable energy in the U.S. is increasing it still accounts for less than 10 percent of total energy consumption.

CARBON CAPTURE Norway's Sleipner field in the North Sea uses the latest carbon capture and storage (CCS) technology to remove harmful carbon dioxide from natural gas. The technology to reduce carbon emissions massively is already available, but it is expensive, and global market forces generally encourage cheaper, "dirtier" production.

Knowing what the problems are and being able to do something about them are two entirely different things. Awareness of conservation and environmental issues has grown considerably in the last 50 years and is now moving toward center stage in local, national and international politics. But can we work together, or will we just fight over diminishing resources?

SUSTAINABLE GROWTH?

It is population growth and increasing consumption that drives every aspect of environmental degradation. The need for more and more agricultural and urban land leads to the loss of biodiversity and the overexploitation of natural resources. The idea that growth can be sustainable is nonsense. When resources are finite, any growth, however small, will ultimately become unsustainable. Environmental problems such as salination through excessive irrigation, desertification and over-consumption has caused the collapse of numerous civilizations in the past. In some cases, emigration from the despoiled area to a new land flowing with "milk and honey" was possible; in others, humans degenerated into internecine war and perished.

The number of humans is predicted to rise to around nine billion by the year 2050. Without widespread changes to policy and patterns of consumption, living standards across the world will decline, and for some they will deteriorate disastrously. The difference in human lives around the planet is already very marked. Some live long and productive lives relatively free of disease, while others suffer hunger and disease and have a life expectancy of as little as 40 years.

ECOLOGICAL FOOTPRINT

We need to reduce what has become known as our ecological footprint – the total area of productive land required to support each and every one of us sustainably. It has been calculated that the amount of available productive land per person is around 4.2 acres (1.7 ha), but the world average footprint is 6.9 acres (2.8 ha), meaning there is already a demand that exceeds

that which can be replenished. For humans living in the most developed countries the footprint is many times larger than that of people living in the least developed countries. If the whole of the world's population were to attain the highest levels of consumption (that of the average U.S. citizen), it is estimated that we would need three more Earths.

PRECIOUS COMMODITIES

Imagine setting up a colony on another planet similar to Earth. What ecosystem would we need to bring along to ensure our survival? We would need a range of animals and plants. But which ones would be essential and which ones might we do without? We would need food plants and animals and whatever they need to grow and reproduce. We would need fibers, oils and fuels. We would need water. And what about soil? A single gram of garden soil contains around 30,000 protozoans, 50,000 algal cells, 400,000 fungal cells and billions of bacteria. The interactions of large numbers of species are needed to produce stable ecosystems. But how do you put a value on their "work"?

The two most precious commodities, on which all terrestrial life depends, are soil and water. Every year many billions of tons of soil are being lost and, in years to come, well over half of the world's agricultural land may be degraded. For a natural resource that provides anchorage and nutrients for all plant life, ameliorates the effects of pollutants, purifies groundwaters and recycles nutrients, we seem to pay it scant attention.

Around 97 percent of all Earth's water is salty. Of the remaining 3 percent that is fresh water, most is

locked up in the polar ice caps, deep in underground aquifers, wetlands or permafrost, in the atmosphere or already contained in the tissues of all living organisms. The amount of fresh water in rivers and lakes that you could actually drink is less than half a percent of all the fresh water that exists. Seven times more drinking water is needed now than 100 years ago and in some parts of the world so much water is taken for agriculture that even large rivers can run completely dry before they reach the sea. As the population increases, the hunger and starvation already suffered by large numbers of the world's humans will become more widespread, with appalling consequences for the world's wildlife.

POLITICAL ACTION

Many nations in the developed world have set ambitious targets for air quality, water pollution and vehicle pollution, but it is a sad truth that environmental aspirations rarely translate into positive results. At the turn of the millennium, the European Environmental Agency examined the progress made across Europe since 1991 on 12 key environmental problems. Positive development in the state of the environment was found with respect to just one of the 12 problems – the ability to address technological and natural hazards. In seven of the 12 areas – including degradation of soil, loss of biodiversity and climate change – matters had deteriorated.

BLUE PLANET Around 97 percent of all the planet's water is salty. Fresh water is a precious commodity that is already scarce. As the population grows, the demand for water will be unsustainable.

The sad truth is that environmental protection has always been a poor cousin to economic growth.

TIPPING THE BALANCE

Although we have not even completed the task of cataloging the Earth's wonderful biodiversity, it is now certain that because of the sheer scale of our own success and activities, we will face the future with far fewer species. What is not certain is what effect this loss will have on the functioning of planetary ecosystems. The Earth has, after all, recovered from several mass-extinction events and gone on to produce a myriad of species. The truth is we simply do not know how many species can be safely lost. It is just as if we are all aboard a plane that is flying blind, and losing species can be compared to taking rivets from the plane at random. Many are redundant, and, so far, the plane has managed to stay in the air. But it is a situation that cannot continue forever. The challenge today is to stem the tide of species loss, before we become endangered ourselves.

Index

Page numbers in *italics* indicate illustrations.

Acknowledgments

The author would like to thank Damien Moore, Amanda Lunn and the rest of the first-rate team at Cactus. Thanks also to Andy Gosler, Steve Parker, Mark O'Shea and Kim Bryan for their expertise and enthusiasm. Special thanks to David Burnie. Finally, thanks to my wife, Lois, for her support throughout the project.
Studio Cactus would like to thank Rob Walker for picture research, Claire Moore for illustrations, Phil Carre for DTP, and Louise Secker for the index. We would also like to thank the following for their invaluable help with picture research on this project: David Johnson of the Global Owl Project (www.globalowlproject.com), Heli Hottinen and Aila Järvenpää from Otava Publishing, Carmen Swanepoel of Images of Africa, and Tatja Livonen from Luonnonkuva archive. Special thanks to Tim Harris and the fabulous team at NHPA. Many thanks also to Joanne Wilson, Auberon Hedgecoe and Iain MacGregor from Cassell Illustrated.

The publisher would like to thank the following for their kind permissions to reproduce their photographs:

Key: a = above; b = below/bottom; c = center; l = left, r = right; t = top.

Abbreviations: Al = Alamy; GI = Getty Images; SS = Shutterstock; NH = Natural History Picture Library (NHPA)

JACKET CREDITS: Front NH/Martin Harvey; Spine Photos.com; Back top row (left to right) 1. NH/Jordi Bas Casas; 2. NH/Michael Patrick O'Neill; 3. NH/James Warwick; 4. NH/John Shaw; 5. NH/John Shaw; second row 1. NH/Mark Bowler; 2. NH/Martin Harvey; 3. NH/Daryl Balfour; 4. NH/Dave Watts; 5. NH/A.N.T. Photo Library; third row 1. NH/Jordi Bas Casas; 2. Photos.com; 3. NH/Martin Harvey; 4. NH/Paal Hermansen; 5. NH/Martin Harvey; fourth row 1. NH/Martin Harvey; 2. NH/Andy Rouse; 3. NH/Jordi Bas Casas; 4. NH/David Middleton; 5. NH/Martin Harvey; Back flap tl Tim Fogg.

INTERIOR CREDITS: 1 NH/B & C Alexander; 3 NH/Andy Rouse; 4-5 NH/Martin Harvey; 6-7 NH/B & C Alexander; 8-9 NH/Jordi Bas Casas; 9tc Derek Hall; 9tr Andy Gosler; 9cr Roger Finnigan; 9bc Alan Jones; 9br C K Bryan; 10fcra SS/Panyovin Ivan Sergeevich; 10cra GI/Peter Scoones; 10cla SS/Nikolajs Strigins; 10fcla NH/Daniel Heuclin; 11ca Photos.com; 12b NH/Andy Rouse; 13cr NH/George Bernard; 13tc NH/Kevin Schafer; 13bl NH/Nick Garbutt; 14ca NH/Daniel Heuclin; 14crb NH/Kevin Schafer; 15cr Derek Siveter; 15b NH/Bill Coster; 16clb NH/Robert Thompson; 16-17 GI/Peter Scoones; 17tc NH/Tom Ang; 17crb NH/Gerald Cubitt; 18bl NH/Kevin Schafer; 19cra SS/Carolina K. Smith M.D.; 19br NH/Daryl Balfour; 19c SS/Mike Tolstoy/photobank.kiev.ua; 19r NH/Kevin Schafer; 20bl NH/Kevin Schafer; 21l NH/Patrick Fagot; 22tc SS/Alejandra McKenna; 23l Al/Barrie Rokeach; 23br NH/T Kitchin & V Hurst; 24-25 NH/B & C Alexander; 26b Al/View Stock; 27br Al/ACE STOCK LIMITED; 27tl NH/John Shaw; 28fcra NH/N A Callow; 28cra NH/Alan Williams; 28cla Photos.com; 28fcla Photos.com; 29tc Photos.com; 30bl NH/Christophe Ratier; 31tl NH/Stephen Krasemann; 31cr NH/Daniel Heuclin; 31b NH/John Shaw; 32b NH/John Shaw; 33cra NASA/Leroy Chiao; 33bc NH/K Kitchin & V Hurst; 34 NH/Anthony Bannister; 35bc NH/Stephen Krasemann; 35bl NH/Anthony Bannister; 35fbl NH/Daniel Heuclin; 35tl NH/Daniel Heuclin; 35tr NH/Anthony Bannister; 36bl NH/Laurie Campbell; 37b NH/Martin Harvey; 37cr NH/Kevin Schafer; 38b NH/Stephen Dalton; 39bl NH/George Bernard; 39br NH/A.N.T. Photo Library 39tl NH/Laurie Campbell; 39tr NH/David Middleton; 40cr NH/Tom Ang; 40bl NH/Mark Bowler; 41bl GI/Inge Spence; 41br NH/John Shaw; 42cra Mary Evans Picture Library/Engraving in La Nature, 1895 vol 1, page 125 ; 42b NH/Paal Hermansen; 43tr NH/Martin Harvey; 43bl SS/Wizdata, inc.; 44bl NH/Laurie Campbell; 45tr NH/Martin Harvey; 45br NH/B & C Alexander; 45tl NH/B & C Alexander; 46clb NH/Andy Rouse; 46cra NH/Pete Atkinson; 46bl NH/Anthony Bannister; 47l NH/Martin Wendler; 48ca NH/Anthony Bannister; 48b NH/Anthony Bannister; 49br NH/Joe Blossom; 49tc NH/Mike Lane; 49bl NH/Manfred Danegger; 50fcra SS/Darlene Tompkins; 50cra NH/B Jones & M Shimlock; 50cla NH/Adrian Hepworth; 50fcla Photos.com; 51tc NH/Kevin Schafer; 52bl NH/A.N.T. Photo Library; 52tr NH/Daniel Heuclin; 52br NH/Dave Watts; 52c NH/Dave Watts; 53tr NH/Dave Watts; 53b NH/Dave Watts; 54b NH (US)/Photo Researchers; 54cra NH/K Kitchin & V Hurst; 55br NH/Martin Harvey; 55tr NH/Stephen Dalton; 55tl NH/Daniel Heuclin 56bl NH/A.N.T. Photo Library; 56br NH/Alan Williams; 57tl NH/A.N.T. Photo Library; 57tr NH/Alan Williams; 57cl NH/Nick Garbutt; 57br NH/Stephen Dalton; 58 NH/Nigel J Dennis; 59blNH/Daniel Heuclin; 59tlNH/Kevin Schafer; 59trNH/Andy Rouse; 59brNH/Gerald Cubitt; 60 NH/Martin Harvey; 61bl NH/Martin Harvey; 61br NH/Kevin Schafer; 62bl NH/Mark Bowler; 62br NH/Martin Harvey; 62tl NH/Gerald Cubitt; 63cla NH/Morten Strange; 63r NH/Martin Harvey; 64tr NH/Mark Bowler; 64cl NH/Ernie Janes; 64b NH/Martin Harvey; 65tl NH/Steve Robinson; 65r NH/Mark Bowler; 66bl NH/Jany Sauvanet; 66tl NH/Haroldo Palo Jr; 67tr NH/Jany Sauvanet; 67br NH/Kevin Schafer; 66-67 NH/Jany Sauvanet; 68 Images of Africa/Tony Camacho; 69tr Al/Steven J. Kazlowski; 69br NH/Laurie Campbell; 70bl NH/Susanne Danegger; 70tr NH/Michael Leach; 70br NH/A.N.T. Photo Library; 71r NH/Stephen Dalton; 71tl NH/Guy Edwardes; 72b NH/Alan Williams; 73bc NH/Daniel Heuclin; 73tl NH/Gerard Lacz; 73tc NH/K Kitchin & V Hurst; 73br NH/Roger Tidman; 73cr NH/Darek Karp; 74b NH/Kevin Schafer; 75br NH/Rich Kirchner; 75bc NH/Mark Carwardine; 75tr NH/Pete Atkinson; 76cra NH/A.N.T. Photo Library; 76bl NH/Dr. Eckart Pott; 77b NH/Foto Natura; 77cra NH/B & C Alexander; 77tc NH/Mark Carwardine; 78clb NH/Stephen Krasemann; 78tr NH/Andy Rouse; 78b NH/Martin Harvey; 79br NH/K Kitchin & V Hurst; 79tr NH/Stephen Krasemann; 80tr NH/James Warwick; 80bl NH/Dave Watts; 81b NH/Andy Rouse; 81tr NH/Martin Harvey; 82 NH/Kevin Schafer; 83ca NH/Eero Murtomaki; 83bl NH/Martin Wendler; 83br NH/James Warwick; 84tr SS/Alvaro Pantoja; 84bl Photos.com; 85b NH/Andy Rouse; 85tr NH/Eric Soder; 86tr Luonnonkuva Arkisto/Jouko Kuosmanen; 86b NH/Kevin Schafer; 87tl NH/Linda Pitkin; 87bl NH/Haroldo Palo Jr; 87br NH/B & C Alexander; 87cr NH/B & C Alexander; 88cl NH/Pete Atkinson; 88cra NH/Henry Ausloos; 88bl NH/Michael Patrick O'Neill; 89 NH/Tom & Therisa Stack; 90b NH/Andy Rouse; 91b NH/Jany Sauvanet; 91tl NH/Christophe Ratier; 91cra NH/Jany Sauvanet; 92tr NH/Martin Harvey; 92bl NH/Daniel Heuclin; 92br NH/Martin Harvey; 93cra NH/Martin Harvey; 94tr NH/Martin Harvey; 94br NH/Martin Harvey; 95bc NH/Adrian Hepworth; 95cr NH/Ann & Steve Toon; 95br NH/Nick Garbutt; 95cla NH/Martin Harvey; 96bl NH/Martin Harvey; 97bl NH/Daniel Heuclin; 97cr NH/Steve Robinson; 97tr NH/Mirko Stelzner; 98tr NH/Kevin Schafer; 98bl NH/George Bernard; 99b NH/Yves Lanceau; 99tr NH/Laurie Campbell; 100cl NH/Jany Sauvanet; 100tr NH/Joe Blossom; 100bl NH/James Warwick; 101tl Luonnonkuva Arkisto/Hannu Huttu; 101b NH/Mike Lane; 102bl NH/Martin Harvey; 102tr NH/Anthony Bannister; 103cra NH/Robert Erwin; 102-103 NH/Andy Rouse; 104br NH/A.N.T. Photo Library; 104bl NH/Ann & Steve Toon; 104tr NH/Haroldo Palo Jr; 105br NH/Gerald Cubitt; 105cra NH/A.N.T. Photo Library; 105bl NH/Daniel Heuclin; 106 NH/Haroldo Palo Jr; 107tl NH/Kevin Schafer; 107br NH/John Shaw; 107tr NH/Andy Rouse; 108cl NH/Kevin Schafer; 108tr NH/Rod Planck; 108br NH/Martin Harvey; 108bl NH/John Shaw; 109b NH/Kevin Schafer; 110tr NH/Dave Watts; 110b NH/Jari Peltomaki; 111bl NH/Michael Leach; 111br NH/Alan Williams; 111tc NH/Martin Harvey; 112tr NH/Roger Tidman; 112bl NH/Bill Coster; 113b NH/Ernie Janes; 113tr NH/Roger Tidman; 114bl NH/Mike Lane; 115bc NH/Martin Harvey; 115t NH/Martin Harvey; 115br NH/Mark Bowler; 116b NH/Tom Ang; 116cl NH/Nick Garbutt; 116tr NH/Jordi Bas Casas; 117b NH/John Shaw; 117tr NH/Jany Sauvanet; 118l NH/Nick Garbutt; 119t NH/Stephen Dalton; 119br NH/George Bernard; 119bc NH/Joe Blossom; 120br NH/Kevin Schafer; 120tr NH/Daniel Heuclin; 120l NH/Martin Harvey; 121tr NH/Bill Coster; 121b NH/Andy Rouse; 122bc NH/Laurie Campbell; 122br NH/William Paton; 122ca NH/Bill Coster; 123tr NH/John Shaw; 123br NH/George Bernard; 123bl NH/A.N.T. Photo Library; 124ca NH/Nick Garbutt; 124cra NH/George Bernard; 124b NH/Mirko Stelzner; 125 NH/Mark Bowler; 126b NH/Thomas Arndt; 127tr NH/George Bernard; 127tl NH/Daniel Heuclin; 127br NH/Martin Wendler; 127bc NH/Dave Watts; 128 Paul Bannick; 129tl NH/Kevin Schafer; 129cr BNHS-India/Girish Jathar; 129br NH/Nigel J Dennis; 130bl Luis Mazariegas; 130br NH/Martin Harvey; 131l Luis Mazariegas; 131bc NH/Bill Coster; 131br Vince Murphy; 131cr Vince Murphy; 132b NH/Gerald Cubitt; 133cra NH/George Bernard; 133tl NH/Mike Lane; 133br NH/Daniel Heuclin; 134tr NH/Mirko Stelzner; 134bl NH/George Bernard; 134b NH/Haroldo Palo Jr.; 135bl NH/Nick Garbutt; 135br NH/Martin Harvey; 135tr NH/Roger Tidman; 136tr Mark Namaqua; 136bl NH/Daniel Heuclin; 136cla NH/A F Papazian; 137 NH/Kevin Schafer; 138bl Asian Turtle Network/Douglas Hendrie; 138tr Mark O'Shea; 139b Mark O'Shea; 139tr Mark O'Shea; 140b NH/Michael Patrick O'Neill; 141bc NH/Martin Harvey; 141cra NH/Jany Sauvanet; 141tr NH/Martin Wendler; 142cra NH/Nick Garbutt; 142b NH/Karl Switak; 143cr Tell Hicks; 143tr NH/Martin Wendler; 144cra Mark O'Shea; 144bl NH/Daniel Heuclin; 145tc Mark O'Shea; 145br Mark O'Shea; 146tr Mark O'Shea; 146cla NH/John Shaw; 146bl NH/Martin Harvey; 147tr Mark O'Shea; 147b Mark O'Shea; 148bc NH/Martin Wendler; 148tr NH/Daniel Heuclin; 148cl NH/Joe Blossom; 149b NH/Martin Harvey; 149tr Mark O'Shea; 150b NH/Ken Griffiths; 151cr NH/Simon Booth; 151br NH/Simon Booth; 151tl NH/Daniel Heuclin; 152ca NH/Daniel Heuclin; 152bl NH/Bill Coster; 153b NH/Jordi Bas Casas; 153tr NH/A.N.T. Photo Library; 154br NH/Michael Patrick O'Neill; 154t NH/A.N.T. Photo Library; 155b NH/Michael Patrick O'Neill; 155cl NH/Pete Atkinson; 155tr NH/Michael Patrick O'Neill; 156br NH/Yves Lanceau; 156bl NH/Taketomo Shiratori; 156ca NH/Trevor McDonald; 157 NH/Taketomo Shiratori; 158bl NH/B Jones & M Shimlock; 158tr NH/Taketomo Shiratori; 159b NH/B Jones & M Shimlock; 159tr NH/Norbert Wu; 160br NH/Hellio & Van Ingen; 160bl NH/Laurie Campbell; 160tr NH/K Kitchin & V Hurst; 161cla Al/blickwinkel; 161 NH/B & C Alexander; 162cb NH/Photo Researchers; 162ca NH/Roy Waller; 163cra NH/B & C Alexander; 163b NH/Norbert Wu; 164tr NH/Roger Tidman; 164b NH/A.N.T. Photo Library; 165ca NH/Anthony Bannister; 165bc NH/Gerald Cubitt; 165tr NH/Kevin Schafer; 166tr NH/George Bernard; 166bl NH/Martin Harvey; 167cr NH/B Jones & M Shimlock; 167br NH/Daniel Heuclin; 167l NH/Trevor McDonald; 168tr NH/Trevor McDonald; 168br NH/Trevor McDonald; 168bl NH/Pete Atkinson; 168b SS/Ian Scott; 169tr NH/Pete Atkinson; 170crb NH/Nick Garbutt; 170tr NH/Daniel Heuclin; 170bl NH/Martin Harvey; 171tr NH/Daniel Heuclin; 171b NH/Helmut Moik; 172cl NH/Kevin Schafer; 172bl NH/Gerald Cubitt; 173br NH/Martin Harvey; 173tl NH/Photo Researchers; 173bc NH/N A Callow; 174 NH/Jordi Bas Casas; 175tc NH/Photo Researchers; 175bl NH/David Woodfall; 175tr NH/Gerald Cubitt; 176cla Photos.com; 176cla NH/Dave Watts; 176cra NH/Andy Rouse; 176fcra SS/Yang Xiaofeng; 177tr NH/Jordi Bas Casas; 178b NH/Jordi Bas Casas; 178cra NH/Mark Bowler; 179bl NH/Kevin Schafer; 179tr NH/B Jones & M Shimlock; 179br NH/B & C Alexander; 180bl NH/Lady Phillipa Scott; 180c NH/Dave Watts; 180cra NH/Andy Rouse; 181c NH/Lee Dalton; 181r NH/Alberto Nadi; 182bl NH/Ann & Steve Toon; 182cr NH/Pete Atkinson; 183b NH/Martin Harvey; 183ca American Fish and Wildlife Service/John & Karen Hollingsworth; 184ca SS/Steven Pepple; 185cra NH/George Bernard; 185br Statoil; 187b NASA.